# The Production of Alternative Urban Spaces

Alternative urban spaces across civic, private, and public spheres emerge in response to the great challenges that urban actors are currently confronted with. Labour markets are changing rapidly, the availability of affordable housing is under intensifying pressure, and public spaces have become battlegrounds of urban politics.

This edited collection brings together contributors in order to spark an international dialogue about the production of alternative urban spaces through a threefold exploration of alternative spaces of work, dwelling, and public life. Seeking out and examining existing alternative urban spaces, the authors identify the elements that provide opportunities to create radically different futures for the world's urban spaces. This volume is the culmination of an international search for alternative practices to dominant modes of capitalist urbanisation, bringing together interdisciplinary, empirically grounded chapters from hot spots in disparate cities around the world.

Offering a multidisciplinary perspective, *The Production of Alternative Urban Spaces* will be of great interest to academics working across the fields of urban sociology, human geography, anthropology, political science, and urban planning. It will also be indispensable to any postgraduate students engaged in urban and regional studies.

**Jens Kaae Fisker** is a postdoctoral researcher in the Danish Centre for Rural Research at the University of Southern Denmark. Working at the intersection of rural and urban studies, his research is rooted in political geography with a particular emphasis on the spatial dimensions of contentious politics and the material and political pursuit of post-capitalist futures.

**Letizia Chiappini** is a PhD candidate in urban studies at the University of Milano-Bicocca and in the Geographies of Globalization group at the University of Amsterdam. Her research interests revolve around urban transformations and the generation of societal change under late capitalism. In particular, she attends to the relations between urban policy making and hyped phenomena such as the sharing economy and the maker movement.

**Lee Pugalis** is chair of urban studies at the Institute for Public Policy and Governance, University of Technology Sydney, and a visiting professor at Leeds Beckett University. He is an international urban scholar, whose research traverses local and regional economic development, urban regeneration, and strategic planning. He has a particular interest in metropolitan governance and urban entrepreneurship.

**Antonella Bruzzese** is associate professor at the Politecnico di Milano in the Department of Architecture and Urban Studies. She teaches urban planning and her research interests cover urban design and transformation strategies. She is particularly interested in the relationships between urban policies and practices 'on the other side', including participatory processes, communication strategies, and temporary artistic interventions.

Regional Studies Association

THE GLOBAL FORUM FOR CITY AND REGIONAL RESEARCH, DEVELOPMENT AND POLICY

Routledge
Taylor & Francis Group

## Regions and Cities



In today's globalised, knowledge-driven, and networked world, regions and cities have assumed heightened significance as the interconnected nodes of economic, social, and cultural production, and as sites of new modes of economic and territorial governance and policy experimentation. This book series brings together incisive and critically engaged international and interdisciplinary research on this resurgence of regions and cities, and should be of interest to geographers, economists, sociologists, political scientists, and cultural scholars, as well as to policy-makers involved in regional and urban development.

For more information on the Regional Studies Association visit www.regionalstudies.org.

There is a **30% discount** available to RSA members on books in the ***Regions and Cities*** series, and other subject-related Taylor and Francis books and e-books including Routledge titles. To order just e-mail Joanna Swieczkowska, Joanna.Swieczkowska@tandf.co.uk, or phone on +44 (0)20 3377 3369 and declare your RSA membership. You can also visit the series page at www.routledge.com/Regions-and-Cities/book-series/RSA and use the discount code: **RSA0901.**

**129. Fragile Governance and Local Economic Development**
Theory and Evidence from Peripheral Regions in Latin America
*Edited by Sergio Montero and Karen Chapple*

**130. The Production of Alternative Urban Spaces**
An International Dialogue
*Edited by Jens Kaae Fisker, Letizia Chiappini, Lee Pugalis, and Antonella Bruzzese*

**131. Creating Smart Cities**
*Edited by Claudio Coletta, Leighton Evans, Liam Heaphy, and Rob Kitchin*

**132. China in the Local and Global Economy**
History, Geography, Politics and Sustainability
*Steven Brakman, Charles van Marrewijk, Peter Morgan, and Nimesh Salike*

For more information about this series, please visit:
www.routledge.com/Regions-and-Cities/book-series/RSA

# The Production of Alternative Urban Spaces

## An International Dialogue

**Edited by Jens Kaae Fisker, Letizia Chiappini, Lee Pugalis and Antonella Bruzzese**

Routledge
Taylor & Francis Group
LONDON AND NEW YORK

First published 2019
by Routledge
2 Park Square, Milton Park, Abingdon, Oxon OX14 4RN

and by Routledge
52 Vanderbilt Avenue, New York, NY 10017, USA

First issued in paperback 2020

*Routledge is an imprint of the Taylor & Francis Group, an informa business*



*British Library Cataloguing-in-Publication Data*
A catalogue record for this book is available from the British Library

*Library of Congress Cataloging-in-Publication Data*
A catalog record has been requested for this book

ISBN 13: 978-0-367-66481-7 (pbk)
ISBN 13: 978-1-138-09978-4 (hbk)

Typeset in Bembo
by Integra Software Services Pvt. Ltd.

# Contents

# Figures

# Tables

# Maps

# Contributors

**Antonella Bruzzese**, PhD, is associate professor at the Politecnico di Milano, where she teaches and carries out research and consultancy activities. She works in the field of urban design and urban transformation strategies with the aim of investigating the processes of place making.

**Cristina Cerulli**, PhD, is a senior lecturer in architecture at Sheffield Hallam University. Her current research focus is on community-led housing development models, shared models of living, and 'alternative' and creative forms of management and procurement.

**Letizia Chiappini** is a PhD candidate in urban studies (UrbEur Doctorate) at the University of Milano-Bicocca and in the Geographies of Globalisation research group at the University of Amsterdam (joint doctorate). Her research interests revolve around urban transformations and the generation of societal change under late capitalism.

**Esther Yeboah Danso-Wiredu**, PhD, is lecturer in geography at the University of Education, Winneba-Ghana. She completed her PhD at the Social Geography Unit of the Department of Earth and Environmental Sciences, Katholieke Universiteit, Leuven.

**Vítor Peiteado Fernández** is a PhD student at Roskilde University (Denmark) and Malmö University (Sweden). He holds master's degrees in political science and urban studies. His research interests include the study of antagonism, the construction of alternative models of housing, and the development of the right to the city.

**Jens Kaae Fisker**, PhD, is a post-doctoral fellow with the Danish Centre for Rural Research at the University of Southern Denmark. He is a critical geographer working at the intersection of urban and rural studies with a point of departure in political geography.

**Silvia Gullino**, PhD, is senior lecturer in spatial planning at the School of Engineering and the Built Environment, Birmingham City University. With an interdisciplinary background in spatial planning, architecture, and urban policies, her research addresses debates about people's different experiences of, and engagement with, the urban environment.

**Hannibal Hoff** is a PhD fellow at The Danish Centre for Rural Research at the University of Southern Denmark. In his dissertation he explores the social practices related to urban non-supermarket food provisioning initiatives, and the desires dominating these practices.

**Pia Heike Johansen**, PhD, is associate professor in The Danish Centre for Rural Research at the University of Southern Denmark. She has carried out empirical studies on the dynamic relationship between rural and urban settings in Denmark, including both qualitative and quantitative data. Theoretically, Pia is inspired in particular by Gabriel Tarde's work on monads and imitation, Michel Foucault's work on power, Lefebvre's rhythmanalysis, and Deleuze and Guattari's work on territory.

**Christine Mady**, PhD, is assistant professor in urban planning, urban design, and architecture in the Faculty of Architecture, Art and Design at the Notre Dame University, Louaize, Lebanon. Her research interests include public space and property rights, temporary urban uses, and a focus on public space planning in post-conflict situations, particularly in relation to mitigating social divides.

**Carolina Pacchi**, PhD, is associate professor at Politecnico di Milano, where she teaches planning theory and practice, and urban conflict analysis. She has a planning and urban studies background and is currently involved in research on the dynamics of urban governance patterns, social mobilisation and activism at the local level, and forms of stakeholder involvement in public policies in urban contexts.

**Lee Pugalis** is chair of urban studies at the Intsitute for Public Policy and Governance, University of Technology Sydney, and a visiting professor at Leeds Beckett University. He is an international urban scholar, whose research traverses local and regional economic development, urban regeneration, and strategic planning. He has a particular interest in metropolitan governance and urban entrepreneurship.

**Fausto Di Quarto**, MA, is a PhD candidate in the URBEUR-QUASI PhD programme (University of Milano-Bicocca) in urban and regional studies, where he conducts research on urban political ecology, environmental politics, and participatory governance. He holds an MA in human geography from the University of Bologna (2009), with a thesis on urban segregation and public space conflict in the city of Belo Horizonte (Brazil).

**Heidi Seetzen**, PhD, is a freelance social researcher, director of research at EnMaaS.tech (a start-up focusing on enabling inclusive transport), and a sculptor at Thames-side Studios. Her research interests include urban sociology, the construction and negotiation of community and identity, cultural and creative practices, ethnography, and visual research methods.

**Samir Shalabi** holds a master's degree in Middle Eastern studies and works as a research associate in an urban development and research organisation in Egypt. His research interests include urban transport, housing, informality, the everyday, and the urban sensorium. He is currently involved in comparative research at Lund University on Syrian refugees in Lebanon, Egypt, and Sweden.

**Preetika Sharma**, MSc, is senior research fellow (University Grants Commission) at the Indian Institute of Science Education and Research Mohali. Her research focuses on understanding the relationship between sexuality and urban spaces, focusing primarily on experiences of queer populations in the planned city of Chandigarh, India.

**Basak Tanulku**, PhD, is an independent researcher from Istanbul, Turkey. She works on urban studies, spatial theory, space making and identity, socio-spatial fragmentation across various categories of identity (class, ethnicity, religion, and gender), gated communities, urban transformation, urban social activism, protests and alternative urban spaces, urban commons and greens (gardens), urban voids and ruins, and urban and rural heritage.

**Petter Törnberg**, PhD, is a postdoctoral researcher in political sociology at the University of Amsterdam. His background is interdisciplinary, including degrees in computer science (BSc), physics/complex adaptive systems (MSc), and complex systems (PhD). His current research lies on the boundary between social science and complex systems, with a focus on polarisation and conflicts through the lens of digital trace data, combining computational methods with qualitative approaches to contribute to sociological theory.

# 1 Conceptualising the production of alternative urban spaces

*Jens Kaae Fisker, Letizia Chiappini, Lee Pugalis, and Antonella Bruzzese*

## Introduction

In October 2016 a broad range of representatives and stakeholders convened in Quito for the United Nations' Habitat III conference to create and adopt a New Urban Agenda, signalling their collective commitment to the initiation of no less than an urban paradigm shift. Full of sweeping declarations, the New Urban Agenda promises people-centred efforts that empower 'all individuals and communities while enabling their full and meaningful participation' while also 'promoting equally the shared opportunities and benefits that urbanization can offer and that enable all inhabitants, whether living in formal or informal settlements, to lead decent, dignified and rewarding lives and to achieve their full human potential' (United Nations, 2017: 7). Crucially, the declaration also acknowledges that current urban development trajectories do not generally point in this direction, hence the perceived need for a paradigm shift.

For us, the New Urban Agenda embodies at the same time a moment of hope and concern. On the hopeful side, it reaffirms the urgent need for a radical change of direction and amplifies this message by giving it a global and multi-facetted voice. The participation of an unprecedented breadth of urban stakeholders, including representatives of the least privileged of urban inhabitants, has made its mark on a declaration text that does not shy away from the affirmation that what ultimately matters most is the lived lives of urban dwellers and the future of the planet as our shared space of habitation. The text makes it clear that no other priority should be allowed to trump this, and even endorses the enshrinement in urban policy and legislation of the right to the city:

> We share a vision of cities for all, referring to the equal use and enjoyment of cities and human settlements, seeking to promote inclusivity and ensure that all inhabitants, of present and future generations, without discrimination of any kind, are able to inhabit and produce just, safe, healthy, accessible, affordable, resilient and sustainable cities and human settlements to foster prosperity and quality of life for all. We note the efforts of some

> national and local governments to enshrine this vision, referred to as 'the right to the city', in their legislation, political declarations and charters.
> (United Nations, 2017: 3)

We take heart from the recognition that things will need to change radically and from the endorsement of the right to the city as an indispensable ingredient in urban development going forward. But we also sense a worrying discord between the contents of the declaration and the actual urban realities we observe around us, both in our own everyday urban lives and as reflected in urban scholarship from around the world. This reminds us of the fact that lofty declarations are relatively easy to make compared to the immense difficulties of implementing them. We also note that, while the New Urban Agenda reinforces the view that cities are for people, it sidesteps the arguable corollary that they cannot simultaneously be for profit (Brenner et al., 2009). Instead it seemingly harbours the old belief that cities can function as human habitats and capitalist growth machines at the same time without detrimental implications for the former.

In this book we have sought to harness these mixed feelings of hope and concern in the pursuit of constructive and evidence-based scholarly visions of other ways forward in our collective production of urban space. Our concern equips us with a sense of urgency and reminds us continually that change does not happen by itself. Our hope reminds us that no effort is futile, even if it seems diminutive and inconsequential in the present moment. By focusing on the production of alternative urban spaces we have specifically sought out 'spaces of hope' (Harvey, 2000), but in every case we have been careful to address both sides of the proverbial coin by attending critically to the ways in which hope can so easily be turned to despair (and, hopefully, back again). In *Spaces of Hope*, David Harvey suggested usefully that:

> The task is . . . to define an alternative, not in terms of some static spatial form or even of some perfected emancipatory process. The task is to pull together a spatiotemporal utopianism – a dialectical utopianism – that is rooted in our present possibilities at the same time as it points towards different trajectories for human uneven geographical developments.
> (Harvey, 2000: 196)

By seeking out already existing alternative urban spaces, however imperfect and ambiguous they may be, our efforts in this book fall decidedly on the side of the present possibilities, identifying at least some of the seeds of change which potentially can be nurtured into broader trajectories towards radically different urban futures. This does not imply a rejection on our part of that other, utopian, side of the coin. We simply direct our efforts towards the teasing out of present possibilities from current realities, asking always if a wider transformative potential is present instead of simply praising the alternative for being alternative. Assessing that potential requires some utopian sense of what alternative urban futures might look like, but it is not our primary purpose here to develop those ideas. Instead we focus on the present-day urban realities from which they too will have to be realised.

This introductory chapter sets out key conceptual markers which are useful to keep in mind when reading the eleven empirically grounded chapters that follow. We seek to provide a shared point of departure in the form of an opening statement from which a cross-disciplinary and international dialogue can proceed and to which it can return. Three simple questions that all pertain to the title of the book provide our impetus: what do we mean by 'alternative'? What do we mean by 'urban'? And what do we mean by the production of spaces that are simultaneously alternative and urban? The answers loosely frame the subsequent chapters, but they are deliberately non-restrictive, necessarily partial, and ultimately open to discussion and contestation. Our aim is to chart alternative urban becomings in heterogeneous spatio-temporal conjunctures and to stage an open-minded dialogue between them. This is only possible if we eschew the temptation to set prohibitive boundaries. To the extent that the book can be accurately located in the academic landscape, its primary dwelling place is the field of urban studies. But it is hardly a sedentary text; it has many secondary homes and also makes explorative excursions from which it returns to look at its origins with fresh eyes. As such it attempts to embody the cross-disciplinary spirit of urban studies by acknowledging from the outset that its object of study cannot be adequately grasped from within the confines of any one academic discipline or, indeed, from any one point of view.

The current chapter follows a simple two-part structure. First, we consider the three questions posed above in a section that aims to clarify what we mean by the production of alternative urban spaces. Second, we use the conceptual markers thus arrived at to outline a set of guiding principles that serve to sharpen the focus of our empirical gaze. In this second part of the chapter we also introduce each of the three thematic parts that organise the book: (1) spaces of work, exchange, and consumption; (2) spaces of dwelling; and (3) spaces of public life. Individual chapters are briefly introduced along with an attempt at positioning each part vis-à-vis existing urban literature. Chapter findings, however, are not considered here but are thoroughly covered in Chapter 13, which both revisits each of the three themes and highlights how the chapters have also broken various other ground.

## What is an alternative urban space and how is it produced?

We begin quite simply by attending in turn to each element of this composite term: alternatives, the urban, and the production of space. Guided by a principle of openness, the conceptions outlined below are deployed to engender elaboration, reinterpretation, and critique. As such they comprise what Bob Jessop (2008) has called abstract-simple entry points from which concrete-complex accounts and analyses can proceed. While the book as a whole cannot claim to be a fully fledged instance of the 'strategic-relational approach', we do find its epistemological principles useful for framing the kind of translocal dialogue that we seek: 'Rather than seeking to resolve concrete-complex issues of practical action in specific conjunctures through abstract epistemological or methodological fiat, the "strategic-relational approach" leaves these issues under-determined on an abstract-simple level and permits their resolution through appropriately detailed conjunctural analysis' (Jessop, 1996: 127).

The following reflections and the conceptual markers they engender are all located at the abstract-simple level, but it is only through the conjunctural analyses conducted in the empirical chapters that concrete-complex accounts can be completed. The empirical exercise, to be sure, is not one of making findings 'fit' within rigid abstract frameworks, but can better be described as a movement beyond, acknowledging that to move anywhere it is necessary to start from somewhere. Our conceptual markers simply locate that somewhere and sketch possible directions of travel. The travelling itself takes place in subsequent chapters.

### *Alternatives: difference, possibility, and otherness*

To articulate something as 'alternative' necessarily involves an assertion of difference in relation to something else. It also typically implies some kind of dissatisfaction with the present situation and an impetus to explore and demonstrate other ways forward. Assuredly, our mission in this book is not to somehow figure out what *the* alternative is. On the contrary, we seek, first, to identify and elucidate some of the various openings towards alternative urban futures that appear in current conjunctures, and second, to document and analyse the efforts undertaken to generate and utilise such openings. As to the exact nature of alternatives, we retain an agnostic and open-ended perspective which is nevertheless grounded in existing work on difference, possibility, and otherness.

The social sciences in general, and urban studies in particular, have produced numerous fields and traditions in which difference, otherness, and alternatives have been explored both theoretically and empirically. While we cannot do justice to the full breadth and depth of such work here, there is merit in outlining the most pertinent insights. Across a number of fields (e.g. subaltern and post-colonial studies, feminist and post-modern geographies) scholars have consistently and convincingly pointed out how academic discourse, even in its most critical guises, has often worked to produce monolithic and totalising world views that leave little if any room for difference and severely limit the space of political possibility within which (new and old) alternatives can emerge and come into view (e.g. Gibson-Graham, 1996). Post-colonial writers in particular have rigorously exposed the invariably partial and geographically situated origins of conceptual frameworks masquerading as universal and all-encompassing. Whereas the ills of eurocentrism, capitalo-centrism, and other 'centrisms' are by now widely acknowledged, their various symptoms have by no means been eliminated. The basic task of rendering difference, otherness, and the possibility of alternatives visible therefore remains an important one.

Crucial as they are for 'messing with the project' (Katz, 2006), such interventions should not be used as excuses for rejecting out of hand any old approach to scholarship that aims ultimately at grasping totalities. As scholars such as Henri Lefebvre and Edward Soja have forcibly demonstrated, it is possible to combine a sophisticated attentiveness and sensibility to difference, plurality, and indeterminacy without losing sight of the various totalities that emerge from the messy jumble of our world(s). One such totality is of course capitalism, and even if one takes an open stance towards the contingent hegemonies in relation to which urban alternatives are posed, it would be highly surprising if capitalism turned out to play no part at all in their (re)production. In the current day and age, we can point more precisely to the geohistorically variegated, evolving, and mutating processes of neoliberalisation as co-constitutive elements of contingent and localised hegemonic formations across the globe. We can, and must, do so without stipulating either that hegemony is always and only neoliberal (and capitalist) or that neoliberalism is somehow more foundational in constituting current hegemonies than other elements such as patriarchy, racism, authoritarianism, and so forth. In this way we can avoid a narrow focus on alternatives posed only in relation to urban neoliberalism (compare Cumbers & Routledge, 2004; Leitner et al., 2007; Purcell, 2008). In the messy realities of urban worlds, alternatives are rarely, if ever, posed solely in relation to neoliberalism and, in any case, neoliberal regimes manifest in vastly different ways across urban contexts (Brenner & Theodore, 2002). A crucial task in enabling translocal dialogue between urban alternatives is therefore to carefully unpack, in every case, the differential relations that warrant the label 'alternative'; i.e. in relation to what exactly is something posed as an alternative?

It should be clear that our aim is not to celebrate difference and otherness per se, but rather to explore instances of significant otherness which generate alternative urban politics. Appropriating Donna Haraway's (2003: 3) words, we can tentatively conceptualise the alternatives we are looking for as embodying 'an ethics and politics committed to the flourishing of significant otherness'. In terms of empirical engagements, and staying with Haraway, this translates into 'vulnerable, on-the-ground work that cobbles together non-harmonious agencies and ways of living that are accountable both to their disparate inherited histories and to their barely possible but absolutely necessary joint futures' (Haraway, 2003: 7). This book is a heterogeneous collection of such engagements converging on the animating scholarly challenge of recognising the moments when urban otherness becomes politically significant. Such moments may involve (1) the opening up, as opposed to the closing down, of possibilities whether reflected through the performativities of language, material practice, or both; (2) the attenuation of difference as a generator of hope for more liveable futures; (3) the recognition of 'other' views, ways, and means even as particular urban futures are pursued through a specific set of ways and means; and (4) the critique, challenge, and circumvention of widely accepted truths, norms, and commonplaces, whether actualised in oppositional and confrontational modes of struggle, through a more agonistic politics based on outreach and cooperation, or perhaps by means of a combination of the two. In short, an alternative disposition to the production of urban space emits a radical potency to recast the status quo and can therefore be understood as interjecting revolutionary potential.

### *The urban: socio-spatial processes with constitutive outsides*

From our diverse disciplinary vantage points we share a broad interest in an urban world that cannot, in our view, be meaningfully constricted to the confines of geographically bounded units of human settlement such as cities, towns, and villages. Instead, we side with the likes of Brenner and Schmid (2015) who hold that urban studies ought to focus on urban processes rather than be preoccupied with settlement types and urban forms. Yet, even if we eschew such methodological cityism (Angelo and Wachsmuth, 2015), we are also not ready to endorse the alternative offered by Brenner and Schmid in their search for a new epistemology of the urban, what Brenner (2014) has also called urban theory without an outside. Rather, we prefer to insist, with Jazeel (2017: 12), that 'urban studies does have an outside' and that 'it is from this outside that a usefully unsettling supplementary historical logic/analysis can emerge'. It is, in other words, only by retaining constitutive outsides of the urban that we can hope to 'stretch our understandings of the socio-spatial processes at work in the production of cities in a world of difference' (Jazeel, 2017: 12); and that is precisely what we aim to do in this book.

Our abstract-simple entry point, then, is to conceive of the urban as a set of socio-spatial processes with constitutive outsides. But what does this mean for our study of alternative urban spaces and their production? To answer this, we need to dwell for a moment on the notion of a constitutive outside, imported and appropriated for urban studies by Ananya Roy (2011, 2015) through her reading of Chantal Mouffe (2000), but originating in Henry Staten's (1984) earlier interpretation of Jacques Derrida. According to Staten (1984: 16), Derrida 'takes the outside to be *necessary* to the constitution of a phenomenon in its as-such, a condition of the possibility of the inside'. Staten thus boiled down Derrida's thinking on constitutive outsides to the following schema:

> X is constituted by non-X. X here means essence or self-identity as conceived by philosophy, and non-X is that which functions as the 'outside', or limit, to the positive assertion of this self-identity, that which keeps ideality from complete closure, yet in *limiting* it remains the *positive* condition of the possibility of the positive assertion of essence.
>
> (Staten, 1984: 17)

This is not meant to suggest that 'identity is drowned in otherness, but that it is *necessarily* open to it, contaminated by it' (Staten, 1984: 18). What this means for our current purposes is that, if constitutive outsides are not retained and kept alive in urban scholarship, then the result is an artificial decontamination, a false purity, through which the important workings of multiple constitutive outsides are hidden from view, kept out of analytical sight. This serves only to impoverish and degenerate urban studies as a field of scholarship that could otherwise be capable of pointing out pathways towards alternative urban futures, especially given that constitutive outsides arguably contain some of the seeds that can be nurtured into radical change. Roy (2015: 4) has taken a particular interest in the rural outside but is also quick to caution that 'by no means is the rural the only or even a privileged constitutive outside'. It is also important to note that 'outside' in this sense is not a question of geographical location; the rural outside that permits the positive assertion of an urban inside may reside anywhere, including the geographical inside of cities however defined.

Our insistence on keeping urban outsides squarely within our field of vision, then, speaks both to the field of urban studies in general and to the particular project at hand. It is our way of approaching the challenge posed by Jennifer Robinson (2002: 539) when she argued that 'urban studies ought to be able to contribute its resources more effectively to the creative imagining of possible city futures around the world'. Working creatively with constitutive outsides and keeping a tight focus on urban process rather than urban form is our preferred way of enacting such creative imaginings from the present possibilities of our shared urban worlds. But Robinson's critique of urban studies was also directed at the peculiar relations between empirical sites and urban theory that the field has engendered over the years: the problematic fact that urban theory tends to be based on fieldwork conducted within a relatively small and homogeneous number of urban places. This is a problem that urban studies has inherited from its early beginnings with the Chicago School of urban sociology, whose stated mission was to generate universal urban theory (Wirth, 1938), but whose empirical work was almost entirely carried out in its own Chicago backyard. While the field has seen substantial changes since then – not least with the emergence and ascendency of critical urban studies in the 1970s (e.g. Harvey, 1973; Castells, 1977 [1972]) – the tendency to ignore large swaths of urban reality in favour of a small number of world or global cities (cf. Friedmann, 1986; Sassen, 1991) has only recently been seriously challenged. Robinson (2002) has thus been joined by Bell and Jayne (2009), Waitt and Gibson (2009), and Lorentzen and Van Heur (2012) among others in calling for research and theory on ordinary and small cities, while Bishop et al. (2003), Roy and Ong (2011), and many others have called for urban research that takes seriously the heterogeneous urban realities beyond Europe and North America.

### *Space: relational, real-and-imagined, and multiple*

The sections above already indicate the kind of spatial imaginaries that we seek to invoke, explore, and explicate. We are obviously in need of a spatial imagination that goes well beyond the containerised sterility associated with purely Cartesian conceptions of space. Rather we proceed from an understanding that conceives of space as simultaneously active, multiple, situational, and relational: active in the sense of space being co-constitutive with the social, multiple in the sense that socio-spatial relations are multidimensional, situational in the sense that spatial becomings are both historically and geographically contingent, and relational in the sense that space does not pre-exist the relations that define it but is continually produced through them, entailing also that space is processual. Our conception, then, is broadly aligned with that of Doreen Massey (2005) whose three propositions about space can be usefully highlighted as conceptual signposts. She suggests:

> *First*, that we recognise space as the product of interrelations; as constituted through interactions, from the immensity of the global to the intimately tiny. . . . *Second*, that we understand space as the sphere of the possibility of the existence of multiplicity in the sense of contemporaneous plurality; as the sphere in which distinct trajectories coexist; as the sphere therefore of coexisting heterogeneity. . . . *Third*, that we recognise space as always under construction. Precisely because space on this reading is a product of relations-between, relations which are necessarily embedded material practices which have to be carried out, it is always in the process of being made.
>
> (Massey, 2005: 9)

While holding on to these propositions, we also find it necessary to move beyond any simplistic distinction between discursive/mental and material/physical spaces as though they were somehow separate realms. Instead we follow Edward Soja's (1996) insistence that space is always both 'real-and-imagined' and consequently needs to be treated as such. For Soja, this composite term was shorthand for the Lefebvrian spatial trialectics of perceived (real), conceived (imagined), and lived space (Lefebvre, 1991 [1974]), where the latter serves to add the 'and' and the hyphens, not as a simple Hegelian synthesis but as an 'other' term that allows analysis to proceed heuristically, practising what Soja calls 'thirdspace epistemology' or, quite simply, 'thirding'.

Among geographers of a critical, Marxist bent, the Lefebvrian triad has often been elevated to the status of a holy spatial trinity, an unfortunate side effect of which has been the proliferation of peculiarly forced analyses in which empirical material gets squeezed into three predefined boxes with no apparent purpose, engendering a sterilised exercise of stale categorisation. That was most definitely not Lefebvre's intention and we find it important to stress that what *The Production of Space* provided was a radical Marxian heuristic that introduced an openness and an embrace of indeterminacy that had otherwise been marginalised by dogmatic and orthodox Marxism. It offered an approach to space that recognised it from the outset as deeply political, always in process, and, although path-dependent, ultimately indeterminate. For our current purposes this is important for two key reasons: first, it underlines the necessity of exposing how relations of power and dominance are imbricated in (re) producing space, and second, it keeps open the possibility for imagining and realising alternative modes of spatial production. The spatial triad retains its heuristic capacity by demanding us to imagine alternative spaces that are not free-floating utopias but differential trajectories grounded in the material realities from which they will have to spring forth.

The challenge that thus presents itself is to conjure up images of, and routes towards, alternative futures that are radically different from our present situation while knowing that precisely this situation will have to be their cradle, all ills of injustice, repression, and exploitation included. While the conceptions of space found in the work of Massey, Soja, and Lefebvre are well placed to facilitate such an undertaking, the work of a number of feminist geographers allows us to move somewhat further. Gillian Rose (1993: 155), for instance, usefully surveyed the spatial imaginations of feminist thought and concluded, in line with our sentiment above, that 'the subject of feminism ... depends on a paradoxical geography in order to acknowledge both the power of hegemonic discourses and to insist on the possibility of resistance'. Hence, she called for

> a geography that acknowledges that the grounds of its knowledge are unstable, shifting, uncertain and, above all, contested. Space itself – and landscape and place likewise – far from being firm foundations for disciplinary expertise and power, are insecure, precarious and fluctuating. They are destabilized both by the internal contradictions of the geographical desire to know and by the resistance of the marginalized victims of that desire. And other possibilities, other sorts of geographies, with different compulsions, desires and effects, complement and contest each other.
>
> (Rose, 1993: 160)

It is precisely this kind of spatial imagination that is needed if the production of alternative urban spaces is to be conceived of and explored in meaningful and politically relevant ways. Moreover, it is explicitly sensitive to – indeed it actively invites and demands – heterogeneity of perspective, form, and content, and so is well adept as a basis for instigating a truly open-minded international dialogue where diverse urban experiences actually get to count in their own right.

## A three-act dialogue

The conceptual markers set out above sketch the outlines of a collective effort to tease out of specific urban conjunctures the present possibilities for enacting alternative urban futures. What we look for in this search are differential socio-spatial becomings, understood specifically as multidimensional spatio-temporal processes that point in other directions than those reflected in currently prevailing trajectories of urban development. Avoiding both methodological cityism and totalising views of the urban, we furthermore insist not just on retaining constitutive outsides but also actively seeking out such outsides, based on the proposition that they contain source material from which alternative urban futures can be created. Combined with an insistence on a conjunctural mode of analysis which respects the contingency of urban processes, this approach is intended to ensure that our findings, first, are rooted in contemporary urban realities with all the challenges their dwellers are currently faced with, and second, move beyond mere diagnosis of the urban condition and into a prognostic mode capable of elucidating other possible ways forward. In other words, we take inspiration from the strategic-relational approach to enact a dialectical utopianism by searching for politically significant otherness in messy, indeterminate urban worlds. The alternatives in question, then, are not merely different but capable of mobilising that difference to challenge, subvert, and change their 'other(s)'. They may even be posited explicitly as responses to the deep political, economic, social, and environmental crises that have come to define the early decades of the twenty-first century (cf. Kirwan et al., 2016).

We find it important to underline that political relations between the urban alternatives that we seek and prevailing urban regimes may oscillate between confrontational antagonism and cooperative agonism and need not be stable; indeed, analysis may beneficially proceed precisely by mapping how these relations change (e.g. Daskalaki and Mould, 2013). This also speaks to a wider need to move beyond binaries; an imperative which is particularly important to keep in mind because alternatives ostensibly begin life in binary terms. It is therefore easy to get caught in a dichotomous web which obscures more than it reveals, a trap that can be sidestepped by replacing an 'either/or' with a 'both/and also' frame of mind. This includes the introduction of other terms that depart from the original binary in ways that work to fundamentally redefine it – i.e. Soja's heuristic practice of thirding. Binaries such as contestation/cooperation, reform/revolution, and top-down/bottom-up are particularly relevant here, but others such as urban/rural, production/consumption, and public/private are also brought under critical scrutiny. The structure of the book follows a threefold analytical distinction between (1) spaces of work, exchange, and consumption; (2) spaces of dwelling; and (3) spaces of public life. This distinction is purely thematic and reflects a crude typology of the kinds of alternative urban spaces that preoccupy the empirical work of our authors. At the same time, however, it is designed to cover key aspects of urban life. These are obviously deeply entwined and this is reflected in the fact that the dialogue enacted in Chapter 13 is far from enclosed within each part but permeates thematic boundaries freely.

### *Alternative spaces of work, exchange, and consumption*

The key question addressed by chapters in Part I is how urban actors reinterpret prevailing urban economies and produce alternative spaces of work, exchange, and consumption. The alternatives in question thus can be said to relate in one way or another to the capitalist mode of production. As emphasised for instance by Rogers (2014), however, it is beneficial here to make a distinction between alternatives *to* capitalism and alternative capitalisms. We do so by reiterating Gibson-Graham's (2006) more elaborate typology which distinguishes between capitalist, alter-capitalist, non-capitalist, and anti-capitalist economies. Alternative urban spaces of the sort in focus here thus respond in diverse ways to prevailing urban economies in which the majority of wealth is increasingly concentrated in fewer hands, while many others are left to contend with precarious working conditions, unemployment, and economic exploitation. Precariat classes are burgeoning (Standing, 2011) and it is especially from within their ranks that alternative spaces of work and production, exchange and consumption are being sought.

The prevailing practices they have to contend with include, but are far from limited to, established regimes of wage labour and precarianisation (Castree et al., 2004; Gill & Pratt, 2008; Ross, 2008; Standing, 2011), market-based regimes of commodity exchange (Harvey, 2010), conventional money systems and financialisation (Leyshon and Thrift, 1997; Haiven, 2011; Sotiropoulos et al., 2013; Adkins, 2015), commercialised cultural activities (Throsby, 2001), food systems (Schanbacher, 2010), etc. Responses in the form of alternative urban economies (Lee et al., 2003) are correspondingly diverse and include the rejection of wage labour (Carlsson and Manning, 2010), worker-owned enterprises (Wolff, 2012; Vieta, 2014; Kokkinidis, 2015), non-commercialised cultural production (Shaw, 2013; Buser et al., 2013; Valli, 2015), low-intensity production for local markets (Bialski et al., 2016), informal economies (Davis, 2006; Gibson-Graham, 2006; but see also Samers, 2005), 'prosumption' (Toffler, 1990; Ritzer and Jurgenson, 2010; Bruns, 2012), self-organised work spaces (Cornwell, 2012; Merkel, 2016), etc. Crucially, the ills of prevailing urban economies are not just about exploitative social relations, but often extend into the realm of mere survival and basic necessities such as food, safety, and shelter (Davis, 2006; Lancione, 2013).

Part I consists of two thematic pairs: Chapters 2 and 3 attend to alternative food spaces while Chapters 4 and 5 address alternative work spaces. More specifically, in Chapter 2 Pia Heike Johansen and Hannibal Hoff investigate the arenas of tension generated by the emergence of alternative urban spaces of food provisioning in Copenhagen; while in Chapter 3 Christine Mady uses the case of a Beirut-based food non-governmental organisation (NGO) to show how, in unstable, post-conflict conjunctures, alternative food spaces can be about much more than just food. In Chapter 4, Carolina Pacchi travels between Berlin and Milan to critically evaluate the transformative potential of coworking spaces as sites for the emergence of organised precarian labour struggles. This is complemented by Letizia Chiappini and Petter Törnberg who turn attention, in Chapter 5, to another kind of alternative urban work-space: makerspaces, again based on fieldwork in Milan, where 'makers' have come to play a somewhat surprising role as partial substitutes for church- and state-based welfare provision.

### *Alternative spaces of dwelling*

From homeless people roaming the streets to urban elites residing in the enclosures of gated communities, the sites and practices of dwelling are some of the most visible markers of the often absurd levels of urban inequality today. The global financial crisis that unfurled in the late 2000s has made issues concerning urban dwelling even more pertinent. Thoroughly financialised housing markets were thus at the heart of what caused the crisis and urban dwellers have been among those hit the hardest by its consequences (Harvey, 2012). It follows that provision of, and access to, affordable and adequate housing continues to comprise one of the main battlegrounds of contemporary urban struggles.

Examples of alternative spaces of dwelling include squatting (Montagna, 2006; Pruijt, 2013; Vasudevan, 2015b), slum dwellings and other informal settlements (Davis, 2006; McFarlane, 2009; Roy, 2011), co-living arrangements and radical enclaves (Miles, 2008; Ergas, 2010; Jarvis, 2011), etc. Key roles have been played by broadly constituted housing movements (Bradley, 2012; Beitel, 2013; Romanos, 2014) as well as various forms of self-organisation at the neighbourhood level (Winders, 2014). Social movements in particular have insisted on staking claims concerning basic rights to housing, thereby mounting serious challenges to prevailing urban property regimes under which the urban poor have to contend with ever-lurking threats of eviction and homelessness (Brickell et al., 2017). In addition to the articulation of housing rights there has also been a widespread tendency to invoke various conceptions of housing as an urban common (Pithouse, 2014; Huron, 2015; Chatterton, 2016). Responses from urban governments and authorities have ranged from violent repression of protest (Benson, 2015; Zheng, 2017) to collaborative outreach and state recognition (Morrison, 2017). The production of alternative urban dwelling spaces has thus relied on a diversity of actor constellations which include progressive planners and politicians (Beitel, 2013), social enterprises (Gerrard, 2017), and NGOs (Das and Randeria, 2015), in addition to the aforementioned grassroots and social movements.

Chapters in Part II attend to the heterogeneous ways in which such actor ensembles are created under varying socio-spatial circumstances, and how they result in the production of alternative spaces of dwelling by challenging, disrupting, and reorienting consolidated regimes of housing provision and private property. Because of the key role played by the housing question in recent rounds of social, political, and economic crises, special emphasis has been placed on cases that reflect timely responses to such crises. Furthermore, a particular aim has been to generate translocal dialogue that transgresses perceived divides between the global North and South. We begin in the outskirts of Cairo, where Samir Shalabi and Lee Pugalis (Chapter 6) use urban ethnography to show how Syrian refugees are struggling to turn a neglected area of a desert new town into an urban home of their own. From there we travel to the other end of the Mediterranean Sea, where Vitor Peiteado (Chapter 7) elucidates how the Spanish housing movement PAH has managed to turn the discursive tide by reframing housing issues from matters of private property to questions of the rights of urban dwellers. In Chapter 8 we return to Africa, this time to Accra, where Esther Yeboah Danso-Wiredu, Jens Kaae Fisker, and Lee Pugalis use the Old Fadama slum as an exemplary case to show how solutions to the urban issues related to slums can be found within the slum itself by taking seriously the agency of slum-dwellers. Finally, we shift continents once more, when Preetika Sharma invites us on an ethnographic journey into the urban village of Kajheri in Chandigarh, where the marginalised *kothi* gender minority have turned to the urban interstices in order to enable and sustain their precarious mode of urban dwelling.

### *Alternative spaces of public life*

The latest rounds of capitalist restructuring and transformation of urban space have involved the enrolment of urban public life as a vehicle for sustaining and accelerating capital accumulation (Brenner et al., 2009). The touristification of city centres (Colomb & Novy, 2017), the rise of commercialised and speculative cultural quarters (Shorthouse, 2004; Mould and Comunian, 2015), and more recently the commodification of 'sharing' (Richardson, 2015; Martin, 2016) are just a few examples of this. In the name of inter-urban competition, planners and politicians have been involved in facilitating these and other processes, based to some degree upon influential academic work on creative cities, cultural economies, and related concepts (Peck, 2014). Within all spheres of urban society, however, counter-hegemonic voices and responses are making themselves heard and felt. The most visible and popularised manifestations of this have arguably been associated with a number of widely publicised 'occupations' of central public spaces such as the transnational Occupy movement (Sparke, 2013; Sbicca and Perdue, 2014), the 15M movement in Spain (Lopez and Bernardos, 2015), Gezi Park and Taksim Square in Istanbul (Dursun, 2015), and Tahrir Square in Cairo (Ramadan, 2013; Said, 2015), etc.

The question that animates contributions to Part III of this book is concerned with the ways in which urban actors create, develop, and appropriate heterogeneous urban spaces for alternative ways of staging, performing, and practising public urban life. The sites of protest mentioned above may figure prominently as symbolic spaces for alternative urban becomings (Barnett, 2014; Hurd, 2014), but our interest here goes beyond these particular sites, and the spectacular moments of protest associated with them, to include also the more vernacular aspects of urban life in public spaces. This can involve various forms of occupation and alternative uses of public squares, parks, infrastructures, and private properties (Hölzl, 2015; Vasudevan, 2015a), interim uses of the built environment (Bishop & Williams, 2012; Andres, 2013; Ferreri, 2015), struggles over access to and use of public space (Anwar, 2012; Newman, 2013), etc. The sites and practices in question often evolve into various hybrids of political, cultural, and social space, which are either explicitly or implicitly associated with broader movements for urban change. Chapters in Part III focus on the socio-spatial conditions within which such spaces are produced, the ways in which the differential production of public space actually plays out, and the aftermath that it engenders. The key point is to gaze beyond the moment of spectacular protest into the vernacular becomings that follow in order to elucidate whether and how sustained trajectories of urban change are actually generated.

We begin, in Chapter 10, in the Brazilian city of Belo Horizonte, a planned city based on strict rationalistic principles, where the public life of most urban dwellers has not been a priority of city authorities. Fausto Di Quarto shows how artistic interventions, based primarily on hip-hop culture, in urban interstices have come to play a key role in the struggles of marginalised urban dwellers of the suburbs and the favelas to reappropriate their city. With Basak Tanulku and Jens Kaae Fisker in Chapter 11 we gain important insights into the afterlife of one of the most notable occupations of public squares and parks in recent years: Gezi Park in Istanbul. The protests have had a ripple effect in the form of alternative urban spaces emerging in various neighbourhoods around the city; Tanulku analyses the emergence, development, and decline of a social centre in Yeldegirmeni and a guerrilla garden in Uskudar. Finally, in Chapter 12, Silvia Gullino, Cristina Cerulli, Heidi Seetzen, and Carolina Pacchi take a step back to include in their field of vision alternative mechanisms of funding the production of urban spaces of public life. They engage in a critical evaluation of the transformative potential engendered by civic crowdfunding platforms as a means by which a bottom-up mode of spatial production may be enacted. To this end they investigate four cases in London and Milan where civic crowdfunding has been used to initiate and fund various urban regeneration projects.

## References

Adkins, L. (2015) What Can Money Do? Feminist Theory in Austere Times. *Feminist Review*. 109. 31–48.

Andres, L. (2013) Differential Spaces, Power Hierarchy and Collaborative Planning: A Critique of the Role of Temporary Uses in Shaping and Making Places. *Urban Studies*. 50(4). 759–775.

Angelo, H., Wachsmuth, D. (2015) Urbanizing Urban Political Ecology: A Critique of Methodological Cityism. *International Journal of Urban and Regional Research*. DOI: 10.1111/1468-2427.12105.

Anwar, N.H. (2012) State Power, Civic Participation and the Urban Frontier: The Politics of the Commons in Karachi. *Antipode*. 44(3). 601–620.

Barnett, C. (2014) What Do Cities Have to Do with Democracy? *International Journal of Urban and Regional Research*. 38(5). 1625–1643.

Beitel, K. (2013) *Local Protest, Global Movements: Capital, Community, and State in San Francisco*. Philadelphia, PA: Temple University Press.

Bell, D., Jayne, M. (2009) Small Cities? Towards a Research Agenda. *International Journal of Urban and Regional Research*. 33(3). 683–699.

Benson, K. (2015) A 'Political War of Words and Bullets': Defining and Defying Sides of Struggle for Housing in Crossroads, South Africa. *Journal of South African Studies*. 41(2). 367–387.

Bialski, P., Derwanz, H., Otto, B., Vollmer, H. (2016) 'Saving' the City: Collective Low-Budget Organising and Urban Practice. *Ephemera: Theory and Politics in Organization*. 15(1). 1–19.

Bishop, P., Williams, L. (2012) *The Temporary City*. Abingdon: Routledge.

Bishop, R., Phillips, J., Yeo, W.W. (eds) (2003) *Postcolonial Urbanism: Southeast Asian Cities and Global Processes*. New York: Routledge.

Bradley, Q. (2012) A 'Performative' Social Movement: The Emergence of Collective Contentions within Collaborative Governance. *Space and Polity*. 16(2). 215–232.

Brenner, N. (2014) Urban Theory without an Outside. In: Brenner, N. (ed) *Implosions/Explosions: Towards a Study of Planetary Urbanization*. Berlin: Jovis. 14–35.

Brenner, N., Schmid, C. (2015) Towards a New Epistemology of the Urban? *City: Analysis of Urban Trends, Culture, Theory, Policy, Action*. 19(2–3). 151–182.

Brenner, N., Theodore, N. (2002) Cities and the Geographies of 'Actually Existing Neoliberalism'. In: Brenner, N., Theodore, N. (eds) *Spaces of Neoliberalism: Urban Restructuring in North America and Western Europe*. Malden, MA: Blackwell.

Brenner, N., Marcuse, P., Mayer, M. (2009) Cities for People, Not for Profit: Introduction. *City*. 13(2–3). 176–184.

Brickell, K., Arrigoitia, M.F., Vasudevan, A. (eds) (2017) *Geographies of Forced Eviction. Dispossession, Violence, Resistance*. London: Palgrave Macmillan.

Bruns, A. (2012) Reconciling Community and Commerce? *Information, Communication and Society*. 15(6). 815–835.

Buser, M., Bonura, C., Fannin, M., Boyer, K. (2013) Cultural Activism and the Politics of Place-Making. *City*. 17(5). 606–627.

Carlsson, C., Manning, F. (2010) Nowtopia: Strategic Exodus? *Antipode*. 42(4). 924–953.

Castells, M. (1977 [1972]) *The Urban Question: A Marxist Approach*. Translated by A. Sheridan. London: Edward Arnold.

Castree, N., Coe, N.M., Ward, K., Samers, M. (2004) *Spaces of Work: Global Capitalism and the Geographies of Labour*. London: Sage.

Chatterton, P. (2016) Building Transitions to Post-Capitalist Urban Commons. *Transactions of the Institute of British Geographers*. DOI: 10.1111/tran.12139.

Colomb, C., Novy, J. (eds) (2017) *Protest and Resistance in the Tourist City*. Abingdon: Routledge.

Cornwell, J. (2012) Worker Co-operatives and Spaces of Possibility: An Investigation of Subject Space at Collective Copies. *Antipode*. 44(3). 725–744.

Cumbers, A., Routledge, P. (2004) Alternative Geographical Imaginations. *Antipode*. 36(5). 818–828.

Das, V., Randeria, S. (2015) Politics of the Urban Poor: Aesthetics, Ethics, Volatility, Precarity. *Current Anthropology*. 56(S11). S3–S14.

Daskalaki, M., Mould, O. (2013) Beyond Urban Subcultures: Urban Subversions as Rhizomatic Social Formations. *International Journal of Urban and Regional Research*. 37(1). 1–18.

Davis, M. (2006) *Planet of Slums*. London: Verso.

Dursun, A. (2015) Muslim Groups in the Gezi Park Protests: Identity Politics and Contentious Politics under Authoritarian Neoliberalism. In: Gerges, F.A. (ed) *Contentious Politics in the Middle East: Popular Resistance and Marginalized Activism beyond the Arab Uprisings*. New York: Palgrave Macmillan. 373–390.

Ergas, C. (2010) A Model of Sustainable Living: Collective Identity in an Urban Ecovillage. *Organization & Environment*. 23(1). 32–54.

Ferreri, M. (2015) The Seductions of Temporary Urbanism. *Ephemera*. 15(1). 181–191.

Friedmann, J. (1986) The World City Hypothesis. *Development and Change*. 17. 69–83.

Gerrard, J. (2017) Welfare Rights, Self-Help and Social Enterprise: Unpicking Neoliberalism's Mess. *Journal of Sociology*. 53(1). 47–62.

Gibson-Graham, J.K. (1996) *The End of Capitalism (As We Knew It): A Feminist Critique of Political Economy*. Minneapolis: University of Minnesota Press.

Gibson-Graham, J.K. (2006) *A Post-Capitalist Politics*. Minneapolis: University of Minnesota Press.

Gill, R., Pratt, A. (2008) In the Social Factory? Immaterial Labour, Precariousness and Cultural Work. *Theory, Culture & Society*. 25(7–8). 1–30.

Haiven, M. (2011) Finance as Capital's Imagination? Reimagining Value and Culture in an Age of Fictitious Capital and Crisis. *Social Text*. 29(3). 93–124.

Haraway, D. (2003) *The Companion Species Manifesto: Dogs, People, and Significant Otherness*. Chicago, IL: Prickly Paradigm Press.

Harvey, D. (1973) *Social Justice and the City*. London: Edward Arnold.

Harvey, D. (2000) *Spaces of Hope*. Edinburgh: Edinburgh University Press.

Harvey, D. (2010) *The Enigma of Capital and the Crisis of Capitalism*. Oxford: Oxford University Press.

Harvey, D. (2012) *Rebel Cities: From the Right to the City to the Urban Revolution*. London: Verso.

Hölzl, C. (2015) The Occupation of the Parque Indoamericano in Buenos Aires: Discourse Dynamics and Stakeholder Practices. *Latin American Perspectives*. DOI: 10.1177/0094582X15602661.

Hurd, M. (2014) Social Movements: Ritual, Space and Media. *Culture Unbound: Journal of Current Cultural Research*. 6. 287–303.

Huron, A. (2015) Working with Strangers in Saturated Space: Reclaiming and Maintaining the Urban Commons. *Antipode*. 47(4). 963–979.

Jarvis, H. (2011) Saving Space, Sharing Time: Integrated Infrastructures of Daily Life in Cohousing. *Environment and Planning A*. 43. 560–577.

Jazeel, T. (2017) Urban Theory with an Outside. *Environment and Planning D: Society and Space*. DOI: 10.1177/0263775817707968.

Jessop, B. (1996) Interpretive Sociology and the Dialectic of Structure and Agency: Reflections on Holmwood and Stewart's *Explanation and Social Theory*. *Theory, Culture and Society*. 13(1). 119–128.

Jessop, B. (2008) *State Power: A Strategic-Relational Approach*. Cambridge: Polity Press.

Katz, C. (2006) Messing with 'the Project'. In: Castree, N. and Gregory, D. (eds) *David Harvey: A Critical Reader*. Malden, MA: Blackwell. 234–246.

Kirwan, S., Dawney, L., Brigstocke, J. (eds) (2016) *Space, Power and the Commons: The Struggle for Alternative Futures*. London: Routledge.

Kokkinidis, G. (2015) Spaces of Possibilities: Workers' Self-Management in Greece. *Organization*. 22(6). 847–871.

Lancione, M. (2013) Homeless People and the City of Abstract Machines: Assemblage Thinking and the Performative Approach to Homelessness. *Area*. 45(3). 358–364.

Lee, R., Leyshon, A., Williams, C. (eds) (2003) *Alternative Economic Spaces*. London: Sage.

Lefebvre, H. (1991 [1974]) *The Production of Space*. Translated by D. Nicholson-Smith. Oxford: Blackwell.

Leitner, H., Peck, J., Sheppard, E. (eds) (2007) *Contesting Neoliberalism: Urban Frontiers*. New York: Guilford Press.

Leyshon, A., Thrift, N. (1997) *Money/Space: Geographies of Monetary Transformation*. London: Routledge.

Lopez, M.A.M., Bernardos, A.G. (2015) The Occupation of Squares and the Squatting of Buildings: Lessons from the Convergence of Two Social Movements. *ACME*. 14(1). 157–184.

Lorentzen, A., Van Heur, B. (eds) (2012) *Cultural Political Economy of Small Cities*. Abingdon: Routledge.

Martin, C.J. (2016) The Sharing Economy: A Pathway to Sustainability or a Nightmarish Form of Neoliberal Capitalism? *Ecological Economics*. 121. 149–159.

Massey, D. (2005) *For Space*. London: Sage.

McFarlane, C. (2009) Translocal Assemblages: Space, Power and Social Movements. *Geoforum*. 40. 561–567.

Merkel, J. (2016) Coworking in the City. *Ephemera*. 15(1). 121–139.

Miles, M. (2008) *Urban Utopias: The Built and Social Architectures of Alternative Settlements*. Abingdon: Routledge.

Montagna, N. (2006) The De-commodification of Urban Space and the Occupied Social Centres in Italy. *City*. 10(3). 295–304.

Morrison, N. (2017) Struggling for the Right to be Recognized: The Informal Settlement of Old Fadama, Accra, Ghana. In: Brickell, K., Arrigoitia, M.F., Vasudevan, A. (eds) *Geographies of Forced Eviction: Dispossession, Violence, Resistance*. London: Palgrave Macmillan. 25–45.

Mouffe, C. (2000) *The Democratic Paradox*. London: Verso.

Mould, O., Comunian, R. (2015) Hung, Drawn and Cultural Quartered: Rethinking Cultural Quarter Development Policy in the UK. *European Planning Studies*. 23(12). 2356–2369.

Newman, A. (2013) Gatekeepers of the Urban Commons? Vigilant Citizenship and Neoliberal Space in Multiethnic Paris. *Antipode*. 45(4). 947–964.

Peck, J. (2014) Entrepreneurial Urbanism: Between Uncommon Sense and Dull Compulsion. *Geografiska Annaler B*. 96(4). 396–401.

Pithouse, R. (2014) An Urban Commons? Notes from South Africa. *Community Development Journal*. 49(S1). 31–43.

Pruijt, H. (2013) The Logic of Urban Squatting. *International Journal of Urban and Regional Research*. 37(1). 19–45.

Purcell, M. (2008) *Recapturing Democracy. Neoliberalization and the Struggle for Alternative Urban Futures*. New York: Routledge.

Ramadan, A. (2013) From Tahrir to the World: The Camp as a Political Public Space. *European Urban and Regional Studies*. 20(1). 145–149.

Richardson, L. (2015) Performing the Sharing Economy. *Geoforum*. 67. 121–129.

Ritzer, G., Jurgenson, N. (2010) Production, Consumption, Prosumption: The Nature of Capitalism in the Age of the Digital 'Prosumer'. *Journal of Consumer Culture*. 10(1). 13–36.

Robinson, J. (2002) Global and World Cities: A View from off the Map. *International Journal of Urban and Regional Research*. 26(3). 531–554.

Rogers, C. (2014) *Capitalism and Its Alternatives*. London: Zed Books.

Romanos, E. (2014) Evictions, Petitions and *Escraches*: Contentious Housing in Contemporary Spain. *Social Movement Studies*. 13(2). 296–302.

Rose, G. (1993) *Feminism and Geography: The Limits of Geographical Knowledge*. Cambridge: Polity Press.

Ross, A. (2008) The New Geography of Work: Power to the Precarious? *Theory, Culture & Society*. 25(7–8). 31–49.

Roy, A. (2011) Slumdog Cities: Rethinking Subaltern Urbanism. *International Journal of Urban and Regional Research*. 35(2). 223–238.

Roy, A. (2015) What is Urban about Critical Urban Theory? *Urban Geography*. DOI: 10.1080/02723638.2015.1105485.

Roy, A., Ong, A. (eds) (2011) *Worlding Cities: Asian Experiments and the Art of Being Global*. Malden, MA: Wiley-Blackwell.

Said, A. (2015) We Ought to Be Here: Historicizing Space and Mobilization in Tahrir Square. *International Sociology*. 30(4). 348–366.

Samers, M. (2005) The Myopia of 'Diverse Economies', or a Critique of the 'Informal Economy'. *Antipode*. 37(5). 875–886.

Sassen, S. (1991) *The Global City: New York, London, Tokyo*. Princeton, NJ: Princeton University Press.

Sbicca, J., Perdue, R.T. (2014) Protest through Presence: Spatial Citizenship and Identity Formation in Contestations of Neoliberal Crises. *Social Movement Studies*. 13(3). 309–327.

Schanbacher, W.D. (2010) *The Politics of Food: The Global Conflict between Food Security and Food Sovereignty*. Santa Barbara, CA: Praeger.

Shaw, K. (2013) Independent Creative Subcultures and Why They Matter. *International Journal of Cultural Policy*. 19(3). 333–352.

Shorthouse, J. (2004) The Engineered and the Vernacular in Cultural Quarter Development. *Capital & Class*. 84. 159–178.

Soja, E. (1996) *Thirdspace: Journeys to Los Angeles and Other Real-and-Imagined Places*. Malden, MA: Blackwell.

Sotiropoulos, D.P., Milios, J., Lapatsioras, S. (2013) *A Political Economy of Contemporary Capitalism and Its Crisis: Demystifying Finance*. Abingdon: Routledge.

Sparke, M. (2013) From Global Dispossession to Local Repossession: Towards a Worldly Cultural Geography of Occupy Activism. In: Johnson, N.C., Schein, R.H., Winders, J. (eds) *The Wiley-Blackwell Companion to Cultural Geography*. Malden, MA: Wiley-Blackwell. 387–408.

Standing, G. (2011) *The Precariat: The New Dangerous Class*. London: Bloomsbury.

Staten, H. (1984) *Wittgenstein and Derrida*. Lincoln: University of Nebraska Press.

Throsby, D. (2001) *Economics and Culture*. Cambridge: Cambridge University Press.

Toffler, A. (1990) *Powershift: Knowledge, Wealth, and Violence at the Edge of the 21st Century*. New York: Bantam.

United Nations. (2017) Resolution Adopted by the General Assembly on 23 December 2016. *Resolution 71/256*. New York: United Nations.

Valli, C. (2015) When Cultural Workers Become an Urban Social Movement: Political Subjectification and Alternative Cultural Production in the Macao Movement, Milan. *Environment and Planning A*. 47. 643–659.

Vasudevan, A. (2015a) The Autonomous City: Towards a Critical Geography of Occupation. *Progress in Human Geography*. 39(3). 316–337.

Vasudevan, A. (2015b) The Makeshift City: Towards a Global Geography of Squatting. *Progress in Human Geography*. 39(3). 338–359.

Vieta, M. (2014) The Stream of Self-Determination and *Autogestión*: Prefiguring Alternative Economic Realities. *Ephemera*. 14(4). 781–809.

Waitt, G., Gibson, C. (2009) Creative Small Cities: Rethinking the Creative Economy in Place. *Urban Studies*. 46(5–6). 1223–1246.

Winders, J. (2014) Making Space in the Multicultural City: Immigrant Settlement, Neighbourhoods and Urban Politics. In: Davidson, M., Martin, D. (eds) *Urban Politics. Critical Approaches*. London: Sage. 156–171.
Wirth, L. (1938) Urbanism as a Way of Life. *The American Journal of Sociology*. 44(1). 1–24.
Wolff, R. (2012) *Democracy at Work: A Cure for Capitalism*. Chicago, IL: Haymarket Books.
Zheng, Y. (2017) 'It Felt Like You Were at War': State of Exception and Wounded Life in the Shanghai Expo-Induced Domicide. In: Brickell, K., Arrigoitia, M.F., Vasudevan, A. (eds) *Geographies of Forced Eviction: Dispossession, Violence, Resistance*. London: Palgrave Macmillan.

## Part 1

# Alternative urban spaces of work, exchange, and consumption

# 2 The production of *rurbal* space

## Alternative food provisioning in Denmark

*Pia Heike Johansen and Hannibal Hoff*

### Introduction

Over the last twenty years new spaces of food provision have emerged in yet more urban settings. In this chapter we explore these spaces as alternative urban food spaces to find out: (1) in what ways they can be said to be alternative; (2) how they are produced; and (3) why alternative food spaces are designated specifically as urban. The chapter suggests that alternative urban food spaces involve practices that usually relate to rural life. When performed in urban settings these practices merge and entangle the urban and rural in new ways, ways that are nevertheless known from past rural-urban relationships. With this as well as recent debates about rural-urban dynamics in mind, in particular the idea of the rural as the 'constitutive outside' (Roy, 2016), we suggest framing the new food provisioning spaces as *rurbal*. Thus, in addition to investigating the production of an alternative urban space, the chapter contributes to the debate about the rural-urban continuum. This debate has been a point of philosophical interest for more than a century, as exemplified for instance by Tarde (1903) on differences in imitation, Simmel (2002 [1903]) on differences in ways of knowing, Durkheim (1984 [1893]) on differences in the pivotal point of community, Tönnies (2001 [1887]) on differences in the formality of relations, and Lefebvre (2004 [1992]) on differences in rhythms.

The chapter starts from the premise that the production of an alternative food space in an urban setting is a re-territorialisation that is performed by sedentary inhabitants and/or migrants in a territory of food provisioning performances that is already there (Deleuze and Guattari, 1987: 380–385). The performances affectively create tensions in specific arenas of performance within the territory of food provisioning. In conceptualising 'tensions', the chapter draws upon the seminal work of Michel Foucault (1982). Foucault disclaims the idea that power may be given, exchanged, and recovered; the question of power is a matter of practising rather than possessing. When applying Foucault's conceptualisation of power it is the forms of resistance and attempts to dissociate such relations which become the focus of investigation (Johansen and Chandler, 2015). Thus the findings suggest not only how alternative urban food spaces are produced but also in what ways they can be said to be alternative.

The contribution of this chapter to the literature on alternative urbanism is two-fold. First, by introducing the notion of 'arena' the chapter enriches the debate about the everyday production of alternative urban spaces. The affective everyday production of space often has been debated as one of the more difficult fields for investigation, since it centres on the immaterial (Halfacree, 2006). Lefebvre (2004 [1992]) suggests listening out for the mood and atmosphere in cities as a method of studying everyday life, while Harrison (2000) argues that studying and explaining the unfixed, the unformed, and the sensate demands a change in styles of practising social analysis. Instead of directing attention to the body as a passive receiver and the embodiments per se, which is often seen in phenomenological analysis of the immaterial, the focus in this chapter is directed at exploring the collective and non-personal nature of sense and feeling by addressing the 'arenas of tensions' through which these are performed.

Second, the chapter contributes to the theoretical advancement of the existing stream of research on alternative food networks (AFNs). A common feature in most AFN research is the challenge of defining what an AFN is. Many definitions strive for a universal description of AFNs, denoting food systems that are different from, or downright counteract, the conventional systems. In such cases, AFNs are defined according to a peculiar form of reductionism, which can be said to actually enhance complexity, rather than reducing it, since AFNs are defined according to what the phenomenon is not, rather than what it is. Such oppositional definitions, with their bifurcation into two separate systems – conventional and alternative – are problematic partly because food systems in reality rarely operate within such artificial boundaries and partly because there is a long-term risk 'that scholarship tends towards "screening for authenticity" activities rather than engagement in deep, balanced, critical examinations of phenomena' (Tregear, 2011: 424). Broadly speaking, research on AFNs in Europe and North America has developed in two different directions (Goodman, 2003). Insightful studies from North America have shown how AFNs can be conceptualised as social movements, working in opposition to, inter alia, industrialised global food systems and/or economic globalisations (Lacy, 2000; Starr, 2010). Important European studies have shown how AFNs have inspired institutionalisation processes within European Union agricultural policies, for example, through national and regional food labelling (Fonte, 2008; Kjeldsen and Ingemann, 2009). Less has been done to create overarching theoretical and conceptual tools (Holloway et al., 2007), and we know very little about rural-urban territorialisation from the social and material processes associated with AFNs.

Finally, calls for including thorough consumer perspectives in AFN research continually surface in the literature (Goodman, 2003; Goodman and Dupuis, 2002; Tregear, 2011; Venn et al., 2006). Research on AFNs has developed from focusing primarily on the production and producer side of the networks to increasingly including consumer perspectives and consumer-and-producer perspectives. More recently, studies on the interactions between actors within AFNs have been added (e.g. Milestad et al., 2010); however, there is still a need for deeper engagement with the consumer side of AFNs and for understanding consumers more holistically as 'people' in all their complexity, ambiguity, and multiple social contexts (Tregear, 2011).

## The Danish territory of food provision

Alternative food provisioning was explored in the Danish capital, Copenhagen. Food production, food distribution, and food provisioning in Denmark, and Western societies in general, have been globalised, increasingly industrialised, centralised, distributed across greater distances, and increasingly marketed as consumer commodities since the 1950s (McMichael, 2009). Supermarkets have taken over food distribution on a large scale. In Denmark they were first established in the 1950s with aid from the Marshall Plan's productivity-enhancing programmes. Since then, increasingly more supermarkets have appeared and ever-larger supermarkets with longer opening hours have emerged. At the same time, smaller speciality stores and direct sales from producers and artisans have almost disappeared from the urban landscape. The general tendency thus has been for fewer and much larger supermarkets with long opening hours, self-service facilities, and ever-greater food selections to have replaced various smaller businesses (Nielsen, 2014). In 2012, 86% of all food products and other convenience goods sold in retail outlets in Denmark were distributed through supermarkets, department stores, and discount stores (Danmarks_Statistik, 2013). Food provisioning through supermarkets is notably popular in Denmark, particularly when compared to other Scandinavian countries. Danish supermarket consumers buy groceries very often: 97% every week, and 60% four times or more every week. The latter figure is 48% for Finland and Norway, and only 35% for Sweden (Konkurrence-og_Forbrugerstyrelsen, 2014).

As a technology, supermarket food distribution has accelerated. The underlying aim is to distribute as much food as quickly and cost-efficiently as possible, and new technological initiatives have been implemented, inter alia, twenty-four-hour supermarkets, self-service cash-desks, and most recently supermarket online commerce and the 'payless' supermarkets introduced by Amazon Go. Thus it is not only food selection in the supermarkets that becomes unlimited, but also the distribution and provisioning of that food.

## The case of alternative food provisioning in Copenhagen

Within the last ten years alternatives to supermarket food provisioning have (re-) emerged in Denmark, and around the Copenhagen area in particular. New markets and market halls, urban gardens and rooftop gardening projects, wild harvesting and foraging initiatives, local food co-op branches, plus a number of direct distribution initiatives – through box schemes and other internet-based initiatives – have all emerged in this period. Furthermore, a growing interest among urban residents to gather berries, mushrooms, herbs etc. to grow their own food, and to hunt and fish has been observed (Johansen, Hoff, and Jørgensen, 2015). The analysis carried out included material from two studies of alternative food initiatives in Copenhagen. The research included three types of data gathering:

- An ethnographic field study was conducted in one of the local departments of the Copenhagen food co-op (Københavns Fødevarefællesskab, KBHFF) from 2013 to 2016 by the second author as part of his PhD dissertation entitled 'Resisting the Supermarket'. The empirical material consists of ethnographic notes, participatory observations, interviews, pictures, and web materials, as well as a questionnaire survey of 519 KBHFF members (Hoff, forthcoming).
- An action research study – including an ethnographic field trip with people from Copenhagen who were active and engaged in non-supermarket food provisioning practices – was conducted in the summer and autumn of 2014 by the first author. The empirical material consists of participatory observations, participants' notes from three workshops, qualitative interviews, and pictures (Johansen et al., 2015).
- Finally, a phone survey of 601 citizens in Copenhagen was conducted in 2014 by the authors. The respondents were randomly selected from the inhabitants of four blocks in two neighbourhoods of central Copenhagen (Hoff, forthcoming; Johansen et al., 2015). The empirical material consists of 601 respondents' answers to thirty-nine questions about various alternative food provisioning practices.

When using the territorialisation approach the main emphasis in the analysis was on performance. Performances were conceptualised by the bodily and verbal actions that are practised through alternative food provisioning activities. The empirical material was analysed in terms of tensions between the performance that exposed the alternative and what this constituted an alternative to. By following a grounded approach involving an iterative process going back and forth between the empirical material and literature, three 'arenas' could be identified. These arenas are the sensorium, sociability, and everyday rhythms. The following three sections explain these arenas.

### *Sensorium*

One arena for re-territorialisation that could be identified by analysing the material for tensions was the sensorium. It is well accepted that food provisioning implies sensory perceptions and performances that are deeply embedded in cultural and social relationships (Howes and Classen, 2014; Korsmeyer, 1999; Rodaway, 1994; Vannini, Waskul, and Gottschalk, 2012). When exploring *alternative* food provisioning it thus becomes relevant to study more closely how re-territorialisation invokes the senses. We accept that sensing in general does not only involve touching, smelling, tasting, hearing, and viewing as suggested by Aristotle and the many scholars following in his footsteps. In recent decades it has been pointed out that more senses should be added, for example, kinaesthetic, balance, and thermoception (Vannini et al., 2012); however, for the analysis of alternative food provisioning we accept the five senses as a starting point. Anchored in this argument, the 601 randomly selected Copenhageners were asked about the role of senses in their food provisioning. The data indicate that Copenhageners who regularly engaged with certain alternative food provisioning practices attached greater importance to the possibility to touch, smell, and taste the produce before buying it than Copenhageners who never engaged with such practices. Fifty-eight percent of Copenhageners who bought produce at farm shops every month or more indicated that this sensory engagement with produce was extremely or very important to them. A comparable proportion (53%) of those who bought produce at food markets or market halls every week or more answered the same, whereas the corresponding figure for urban dwellers who never engaged in alternative food provisioning was only 27% (see also Figure 2.1).

The preference for multiple sensory perceptions among the Copenhageners who engaged in alternative food provisioning practices challenges the notion of 'hyper-consumption' which, according to Vannini et al. (2012), has reconfigured the sensory orders, resulting in a potential loss of senses and even senselessness. Material from the ethnographic study further indicates that Copenhageners would at times find inspiration for their multiple sensory performances from local farmers growing their produce in rural settings. For example, during introductory meetings at KBHFF, attendees were introduced to a local farmer via a six-minute video

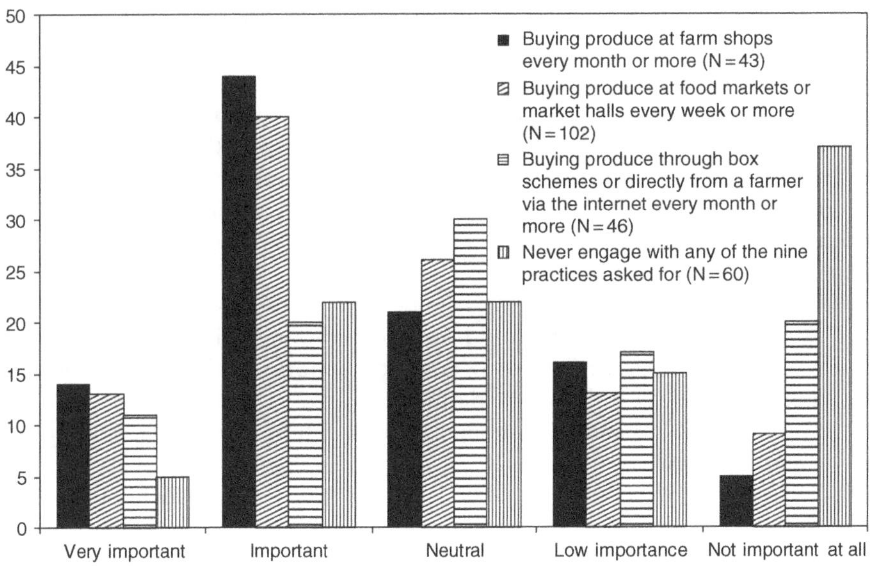


*Figure 2.1* The importance of being able to touch, smell, and taste produce before purchase in relation to (non)engagement in alternative food provisioning practices (in percentages)

clip. In detail and with great enthusiasm, the local farmer talked about the taste, the sense, and the look of the tomatoes he grew, about how to prepare them and how they are produced. Visually, the viewers were taken up close to the farmer's hand touching, caressing, and nursing the tomatoes. Through both verbal and nonverbal actions, he expressed multi-sensory engagement with the tomatoes, as he talked about, touched, smelled, and caressed them:

> Tomatoes are not just tomatoes. If you go to the supermarkets, then you can get a cherry tomato and you can get a regular tomato. And all the supermarkets have the same tomato. And that is, you know, deadly dull. Or at least you get tired of it. So in order to bring out the differences, I think it's fun to make something completely different. Here I'm holding the Berner Rose tomato.
>
> (KBHFF, 2013)

The Copenhageners' multi-sensory performances expressed in their alternative food provisioning practices involved re-configurations of the senses that might be seen as part of a re-territorialisation of food provisioning. Sociology and anthropology of the senses have pointed out how such sense configuration changes across space and time. For instance, Howes and Classen (2014) relate the example of how, historically, the upper classes used the grand department stores to escape the sensuous displeasures of the marketplace. This reconfiguration is carried over to contemporary supermarkets where the smell of the produce is often absent, which according to Rodaway (1994) has given rise to an 'olfactory silence'. Broadly speaking, commodification has eliminated odours from society, only to reintroduce them as 'packaged agents of fantasy, a means of recovering or recreating a body, an identity, a world from which one has already been irrevocably alienated' (Classen, Howes, and Synnott, 1994: 205). The ethnographic study found that smelling the ingredients was a rather important performance for the Copenhageners involved in alternative food provisioning practices. Observations from a local department of KBHFF during work shifts and during the weekly hand out of vegetables indicate very explicit appreciations of the smell:

> We unpack the vegetables and for the first time this year we're getting asparagus. This creates joyous, almost euphoric exclamations: 'wuuhuu asparagus!' and 'oh, how wonderful!'
>
> One takes a handful and smells them: 'Here, try to smell it', [sniffs] 'mmmmmmm'.
>
> (Field notes, 2014)

With alternative food provisioning practices, smelling the food ingredients is brought to the fore of the sensorium. This challenges a configuration of the senses, which places smell far below vision and hearing in the sensory hierarchy. According to Korsmeyer (1999) such a hierarchy of the senses is embedded in

Western cultures and in the acceptance of ways of knowing. Historically, vision and hearing are associated with the head and with rational thinking, because of the allowance for distance between the bodily anchored sensing organs (the eyes and the ears) and the object. The lower senses – smelling, tasting, and touching – because of the closeness between the bodily anchored sensing organ (nose, mouth, and skin) and the object, are associated with affective and emotional performances that are 'out of' rational control (Korsmeyer, 1999). Similarly, expressions of happiness, enthusiasm, astonishment, curiosity, and excitement are prevalent in alternative food provisioning practices. These types of affective and emotional performances seem to follow from smelling, tasting, and touching food. A member of KBHFF put this interconnection into words as she explained how she disliked the senselessness in supermarkets and how happy she felt when she sensed the vegetables from the weekly bag:

> It's very hard in the supermarket ... Everything is just packaged food, wrapped in plastic and I don't like packaged food. I can't touch it or sense it, you know? So sometimes of course I buy this stuff but I'm not enjoying it and it doesn't feel right. And I'm like 'uuuuhhh I want my fresh vegetables here'.
>
> (Interview, 2014)

Alternative food provisioning, then, re-territorialises (urban) food provisioning not only by reconfiguring the senses, but also by challenging the territory of the rational (ways of knowing about food).

### *Social interaction and informality*

A second arena that could be identified touches upon sociability. Supermarkets are organised to keep customers focused on the products, prompting them to buy as many products as possible. As opposed to traditional town markets, supermarkets with their tall sets of shelves and narrow aisles prevent most social interaction among customers and between salespeople and customers (Howes and Classen, 2014). Alternative food provisioning practices, on the other hand, often include engagement in informal social interaction. Observations made in food markets in Copenhagen found that social informality was pivotal to the practice of buying food at the market. Most sales and interactions between customers and the market stallholder included brief or longer conversations, often without regard to the build up of queues. These conversations were often related to different aspects of the food products: how they are produced, ways of preparing them, and former experiences with them. Furthermore, tasting samples were often handed out, sometimes engaging and activating children brought along to the market by their parents. Some returning customers praised specific products both to stallholders and other customers, and, in general, the atmosphere of these interactions was positive, supportive, and friendly.

> It was freezing cold today at the market, and one of the market stallholders didn't have enough warm clothing. One of the customers noticed this and asked insistently to help, offering to go home and get her some gloves and a scarf. Eventually, they arranged for the customer to act as market stallholder for a few minutes, while the market stallholder could go to a nearby shop and buy gloves.
>
> (Field notes, 2015)

This friendliness was also apparent from the farmers' market's Facebook page. Every week the organisers of the farmers' market posted pictures from the weekly market. These pictures almost consistently focused upon the products (via close-ups of the products), the interaction between market stallholders and customers (via close-ups of conversations), and the atmosphere (via overviews of the market). In one post accompanying such pictures, the caption reads: 'Thanks to all of you, you lovely customers who support us every Saturday. We have so much fun together with you' (Bondens Marked, 2016). In another post accompanying a picture showing the farmers and market stallholders from one specific Saturday market the caption reads: 'We are by far the toughest market stallholders, who show up in all kinds of weather – damn it, we are tough' (Bondens Marked, 2017). The reactions from customers, which are shown next to the picture, show a strong resonance. Customers express clear admiration, recognition, and appreciation. One customer writes: 'Respect! You are so cool and we love you for taking the trouble to come to Østerbro ♥♥♥'. Another writes: 'World class. We really appreciate your exciting stalls and especially your perpetual cheerfulness ☺'. To this, (one of) the organisers of the market replied: 'You're so sweet. Thanks a lot. One gets really touched. Hope for many great moments with lots of delicious food in 2017! See you!' (Bondens Marked, 2017).

The field notes and the Facebook interactions are illustrative of how the Copenhageners engaging in alternative food provisioning practices sought informal interaction with the local farmers. It might be argued that, by drawing on former rural-urban dynamics created by face-to-face sharing of knowledge about food and ingredients, alternative food provisioning re-territorialises the territory of the impersonal and almost absent social interaction in supermarkets.

Durkheim (1984 [1893]) explains how people arrange themselves around everyday social interaction differently in urban and rural settings and how, by the organisation of informal social interaction, they create a community identity. Put simply, urban social interaction is organic and arranged around a shared interest, while rural social interaction is mechanically organised around living in the same rural community. In the current case, alternative food provisioning was precisely such a shared interest which was used to build community identity in an urban setting. More specifically, some Copenhageners sought a community of interest created through engaging with KBHFF or other alternative food initiatives, knowing that fellow members took a similar interest in organic or biodynamic, local, fresh food. The survey among the members of KBHFF showed that, for about 40% of the respondents, the opportunity to meet new people was an important part of being a member and, for 47%, the community was very important or important. Interviews with members of KBHFF explain this preference for informal interaction and for 'belonging to' a community of interest. The answers support the Durkheimean understanding of urban social interaction:

> Of course I would like to meet people who also care about food, and food is important to them and very useful for our living ... So of course I'm doing this also for the people I'm going to meet and going to volunteer with. It's part of the daily life to find new people to be with.
>
> (Interview, 2014)

> To me it's wonderful to see and feel the energy of all the different people you meet here. In some way, it's very reassuring that so many people you don't know, or didn't know, also fight to make the world a greener place. Even if it's microscopic.
>
> (Interview, 2014)

> I think the sense of community is very much depending on how much energy there is in the local department to arrange activities beyond the weekly bag. In Vesterbro they have a communal dinner every Wednesday and it's very *hyggeligt* [enjoyable, cosy] so people stay around and get to know one another. There is something to gather around. And in the same way, in Amager they have all these different working groups, and small projects they've started up, like urban gardens and workshops about that and stuff.
>
> (Interview, 2014)

> Also when you're about in the city, and you meet someone with a KBHFF bag, then you're like [blinking]: 'so you're in the group'. That's really nice ... Because you can relate to that person in another way, even if you don't know him or her. And you know what they will have for dinner the next week [laughing].
>
> (Interview, 2014)

> I think some of it has to do with an imagined community. That you feel affiliated even if you don't know people that well ... many of the members who are not active any more said that they still feel like members. Because, they want to support the good cause. And people like to tell the story about KBHFF. This story ... there's also a sense of community in telling people that this is something WE do. It's important for all people to have something to feel a part of.
>
> (Interview, 2014)

The establishment of formal alternative urban food communities creates a forum for informal interactions between like-minded people; however, it also seems that these communities run into a problem produced at the intersection between informality and the degree of institutionalisation. The dilemma may be explained by Tönnies' suggestion of a difference in informalities between urban communities anchored in *Gesellschaft* and rural communities anchored in *Gemeinschaft* (Tönnies, 2001 [1887]). Some of the members found that the increasing formal institutionalisation of sociability removed an important form of informality. A member of KBHFF reflected upon a change in the organisation of voluntary work, so that it would now be mandatory and part of a contract between the members and the co-op:

> Now there will most definitely be some people who quit KBHFF because they have tightened up and everything. So now people will have to do the mandatory work. They can no longer just talk about it. And then it's probably the majority who ... they would stop coming here as much because now they have to participate. And that's just ... I mean they were just contributing to their own little community, and their own family, right? I mean that's not very social.
>
> (Interview, 2014)

Another example that illustrates Copenhageners' informality dilemma is found in the action research project. As part of the action research programme, Copenhageners were invited on a field trip to visit a number of local farms, producers, and other local initiatives in a region south of Copenhagen. The field notes show Copenhageners realising that they might learn from rural ways of organising social events. After the visits, one urban dweller reflected on the local rural community:

> I was in particular pleasantly surprised by the visit to the local village hall (Hellested Forsamlingshus). It was really impressive to meet a local community, who are capable of bringing together busy everyday lives around *hyggelige* food evenings putting the social in focus. We could learn a lot from this in my owners' association in Nørrebro.
>
> (Reflections, 2014)

Thus it may be that urban alternative food provisioning re-territorialises by its informal social interaction performances with farmers in the marketplaces; however, it does not take advantage of the possibility to re-territorialise through everyday informal social interaction with other urban dwellers in the marketplaces. Being social during food provisioning becomes just another explicit urban project rather than an integrated and tacit part of everyday life.

### *Everyday rhythms*

The third arena that was identified by analysing for tensions was everyday rhythms. Food provisioning practices are composed of diverse rhythms – they are polyrhythmic. In *Rhythmanalysis*, Lefebvre (2004 [1992]) emphasises the underlying tensions between linear time scales and cyclical rhythms, in the production of everyday life. According to Lefebvre, rhythms can be primarily linear or primarily cyclical, but no rhythm is exclusively cyclical (it always involves some degree of linearity) and, similarly, no rhythm is exclusively linear (since it then no longer becomes rhythmic). Predominantly cyclical rhythms are usually found in the natural world: seasons, day and night, plant cycles, growth and decay, etc. The linear on the other hand generally originates from human and social activities, particularly from the movements of work (Lefebvre, 2004 [1992]). It is often linked to capitalist societies, as it measures and schedules, is goal-oriented, and produces, inter alia, the rhythms of working days. Thus, in capitalist societies, where 'time = money', cyclical rhythms have been subordinated to the goal-oriented and rationalised linear time (Lefebvre, 2004 [1992]).

As a starting point, such tension between cyclical rhythms and linear time is manifested in the actual food made available through supermarkets and alternative food networks, respectively. In supermarkets, consumers have grown accustomed to a selection of foods which is basically unlimited. There is no significant seasonal impact on the food selection and the life cycles of food are prolonged to the greatest extent possible, often through use of more or less 'natural' additives. From a Marxist metabolic understanding, this is an example of how capitalism alienates humanity from the rest of nature (Foster, 1999). Finally, the variety of food products available in supermarkets has grown enormously (Kneafsey et al., 2008). Conversely, most alternative food networks submit to limitations imposed on food selection by (local) seasonal rhythms and natural life cycles. This shift from the unlimited availability of foods to a more natural and seasonal limitation on food selection can prove difficult and challenging. In winter months, the homogeneity and repetitiveness of foods included in the weekly vegetable bag from KBHFF would cause challenges to some members of the co-op:

> The first winter, I tell you, there was kohlrabi every single week. And there was parsnip and parsley root and parsley root, parsnip, parsley root and it was . . . it was heavy . . . Yes, I made a lot of soup and bread with kohlrabi in it . . . And grated potatoes in. . . . But then it just makes so much more sense. To eat all these heavy things in the winter and then eat all the delicious stuff in the summer. It's just really cool!
>
> (Interview, 2014)

As suggested by the quote, however, these challenges were often seen as positive and filled with purpose and meaning. Following, adapting to, or synchronising with the local seasonal rhythm is potentially a movement from a state of arrhythmia towards eurhythmia (Lefebvre, 2004 [1992]).

> I would actually love to ... work more with food and be devoted to the passion I have for food. I just love when it's season for ... er ... then there are rosehips and you make rosehip marmalade. It's just so nice. And it creates some kind of connection, somehow.
>
> (Field notes, 2015)

Besides the appreciation of such a felt and perceived '(re-)connection' with the seasonal rhythms, submitting to the local seasonal rhythms also leads to another form of re-connection. Kneafsey et al. (2008) argue that (supermarket) consumers have been disconnected from their food and its production, referring both to the structures and relationships within the food system, and also to perceptions and feelings about the food system, 'as most consumers in developed market economies do not know where (or how) much of their food is produced' (Kneafsey et al., 2008: 6). In this respect, we could add a temporal dimension as well, as most consumers do not know when much of their food is produced.

> It is definitely a positive thing to be forced to try some new and other vegetables, and that there are some seasonal limitations to what you take home with you. Absolutely! Okay, so late in the season I'm also sick of root crops, right? [laughing] ... So, I cheat and go to Irma (high-end supermarket) and buy a courgette ... But in general I think it's an eye opener to find out that now it's season for this, and now it's season for that.
>
> (Interview, 2014)

Thus the alternative food provisioning practices involve a re-territorialisation in which seasonal rhythms are followed (partly optionally) for the sake of personal inspiration and education as well as more intangible perceptions and feelings of 'being connected'.

In addition to tensions related to the rhythms of the food and the production of food, tensions in the organisational and distributional rhythms related to food provisioning practices were identified. Recently, Hartmut Rosa has pointed to social acceleration as the most essential dimension of modernity (Rosa, 2003). Part of this social acceleration is the acceleration of the pace of life, which shows a tendency to 'compress' actions and experiences, i.e. 'to do and experience more within a given period of time' (Rosa, 2003: 9–10). While the advances of technology and technological acceleration ought to make time abundant, there are strong indications that time becomes increasingly more scarce. Data from the telephone survey of 601 Copenhageners pointed to similar tendencies (see Figure 2.2), as more than half of respondents would grow more food if they had the time and possibility, more than half of respondents to a greater degree would collect berries and mushrooms, fish or hunt if they had the time and possibility, and more than half of respondents to a greater degree would go to the countryside and shop in farm shops if they had the time and possibility.

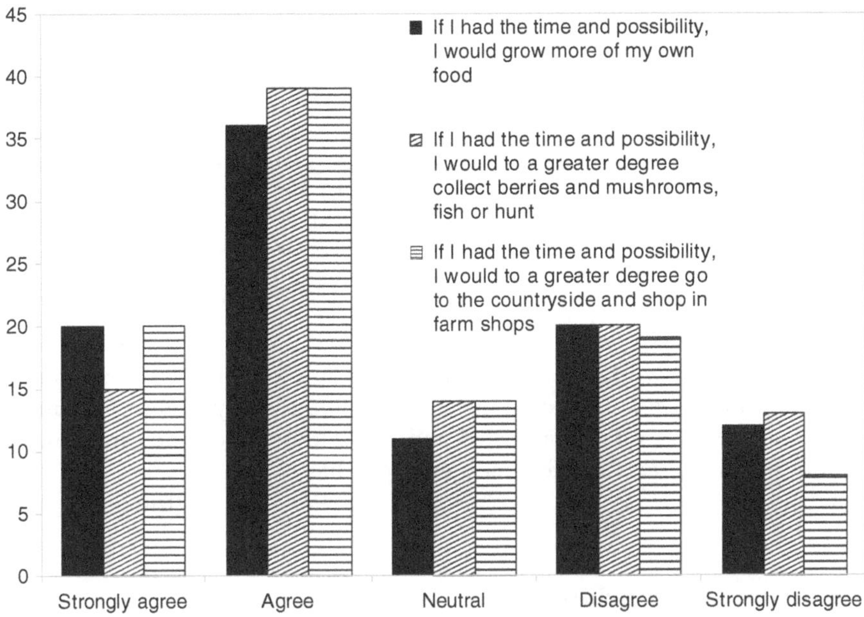


*Figure 2.2* Level of agreement with statements about engagement in alternative food provisioning practices (in percentages; N = 601)

Perhaps in less deliberate ways, the alternative food networks provided an alternative to this form of limitlessness as well. The specific dates and opening hours of farmers' markets and farm shops, and the specific dates and hours for both work shifts and picking up the vegetable bags at KBHFF, imposed spatial and temporal limits on the distribution and provisioning of food. But this fixation of time and space proves a challenge to many alternative food networks. In KBHFF, synchronising active and continual participation – both working three hours every month and picking up the vegetables within a two-hour time slot every week – with the urban pace of life rhythm has posed ongoing challenges and has been at the centre of much debate within the co-op. Data from the KBHFF members' survey show that the timing of the work shifts (either 12.30–15.30; 15.30–18.30; or 18.30–20.00) was the greatest challenge in relation to taking shifts (see Table 2.1). These numbers seem to indicate a challenge of reconciling the tendency to 'compress' actions and experiences with the fixed work shifts at KBHFF. The challenge of reconciling the acceleration of the pace of (everyday) life with the rhythms of KBHFF was an ongoing struggle in the development of the co-op. It was sought to be overcome, inter alia, by implementing a new team structure, with team coordinators that could better organise and supervise the work shifts, and thus make sure that members were actually showing up and taking part in the community work.

*Table 2.1* Challenges highlighted by KBHFF members in relation to work shifts (N = 519)

| | |
|---|---|
| The time of the work shifts makes it impossible for me to participate | 35% |
| I can't cancel if something comes up | 14% |
| There is no person in charge to ask questions | 13% |
| I don't know how to sign up for the work shifts | 7% |
| There are too many members so it's difficult for me to get a work shift | 6% |
| Because of the team structure it is always the same people | 4% |
| Because there is not a team structure it is always new people | 1% |

> And that is also what we're struggling with right now. We need to structure our work in a way that makes it easy for members. Families with children for instance. I mean three hours every month isn't much, but it still has to be coordinated and run without too much friction, and not be a huge concern for one's everyday life.
>
> (Interview, 2014)

## Discussion and conclusion

This chapter aimed to answer three questions about alternative urban food spaces: in what ways they can be said to be alternative; how they are produced; and why alternative food spaces are designated specifically as urban. The analysis focused on tensions created by the re-territorialisation performances of alternative food provisioning in an existing territory of (conventional) food provisioning for making explicit the specific arenas of performances.

In response to the first question, the analysis initially identified three arenas: sensorium, sociability, and everyday rhythms. The first arena pointed to a reconfiguration of the senses as constituting an alternative to conventional food provisioning. This reconfiguration implied a flatter hierarchy of the five basic senses and brought the smelling, tasting, and touching of food ingredients back to the food provisioning space. In this way the reconfiguration of the senses constituted an alternative to a traditional hierarchical structure of the senses in which the look of the food ingredients was most significant. These sensory performances were furthermore enveloped in feelings of happiness and curiosity and thus also presented an alternative to feeling annoyed, senseless, and emotionally detached by food provisioning. The second arena pointed to the informality in social interactions as constituting an alternative. The informality experienced in social interactions with the farmers reintroduced interactions known from former town markets. Performances were facilitated by the design of the marketplaces with overview and room for sociability between and across stalls. Together this constitutes an alternative both to the one-way communication between producers and consumers on food labels and to being directed through supermarket aisles with a tunnel view preventing social interaction between customers. Some

Copenhageners performing alternative food provisioning sought informal interactions with other active Copenhageners as a way of strengthening their sense of belonging. The third arena pointed to various rhythms related to food provisioning as constituting an alternative. The food items made available through alternative food networks were confined by (local) seasonal rhythms and natural life cycles, representing a clear alternative to the almost unlimited selection of foods made available in supermarkets. While limiting the food selection was difficult and challenging, often purpose and meaning were ascribed to this limitation. Furthermore, the organisational and distributional rhythms of alternative food provisioning constituted an alternative. With limited opening hours and specific dates for markets, spatial and temporal limits were imposed on the alternative food provisioning. This likewise constituted an alternative to the non-stop availability of supermarket foods. Taken together, these findings about what constitutes the alternative in alternative food provisioning supplements and supports the literature on alternative food networks in various ways. The findings recognise the hybrid nature of the networks and, instead of taking the alternative for granted, we point to particular aspects of the food provisioning that constitute specific alternatives to conventional food provisioning.

In response to the second question, the analysis found that different tensions/intersections, across the three arenas, took part in the production of alternative urban space. Through a reconfiguration of senses, through smelling, tasting, and touching the food ingredients, Copenhageners were 'taken' to the fields where the crops were grown, leaving a sense of the rural in their urban veins. Thus affective, multisensory performances took part in producing the alternative urban food space, and these performances included a sense of the rural. As such, our analysis points to an opening up of the apparently 'irrevocable alienation' related to the elimination of, inter alia, odours from society (Classen et al., 1994). Through seeking and facilitating informality in social interactions, alternatives to social interaction in conventional food provisioning were produced; however, since these initiatives gathered Copenhageners around a shared interest in alternative food provisioning and distribution of locally produced food, major attention was directed towards how to formally organise the alternative distribution, rather than how to create a platform for informal social interaction. Thus, it may be argued that the alternative distribution system is a democratic alternative to a profit-oriented distribution system, but institutionalisation of the social interactions that are embedded in the alternative food distribution system does not produce an alternative for enhanced informal interaction.

In response to the third question, the analysis found that, although the place-based informal interaction that may be found in rural communities served as inspiration for creating an alternative distribution system based on informality, it did not seem to be able to overcome the contract-oriented organisation of sociability in urban settings. The fact that the alternative urban food space is anchored in a shared interest in a specific way of performing food provision rather than being anchored in a shared performance of everyday life calls for a socially specific organisation. This organisation should be able to deal with the many different everyday lifestyles and values that are all part of the production of an urban setting.

In the introduction we argued that the chapter contributes to the understanding of the everyday production of alternative urban spaces by introducing the notion of 'arena'. Our exploration of the alternative food provisioning in Copenhagen focused on the unfixed, the unformed, and the sensate as they were being performed. For getting a hold on these fluid and affective entanglements of alternative food provisioning we suggested drawing on Foucault's notion of power to let the arenas be created by these tensions. The three arenas that the exploration led to should be seen also as suggesting a novel analytical approach to studies of the urban, the alternative, and food movements.

We suggested that the alternative food provisioning space may be framed as *rurbal* because it re-introduces a rural-urban social dynamic that has disappeared in the modern supermarket's focus on profit. The findings point to the conclusion that the *rurbal* space may be more urban than rural and that urban dwellers performing alternative food provisioning may be confronted with a dilemma. They are experiencing an accelerating everyday urban lifestyle in which alternative food provisioning may be just another urban project which happens to draw on rural everyday life qualities. They are, in other words, introducing alternative elements into urban life by drawing creatively on the rural as a constitutive outside.

## References

Bondens Marked (2016). 28 January. Available at: www.facebook.com/BondensMarkedIKobenhavn (Accessed: 9 November 2017).

Bondens Marked (2017). 7 January. Available at: www.facebook.com/BondensMarkedIKobenhavn (Accessed: 9 November 2017).

Classen, Constance, Howes, David, and Synnott, Anthony (1994). *Aroma: The Cultural History of Smell*. London: Routledge.

Danmarks_Statistik (2013). Detailhandlens omsætning fordelt på varegrupper, 2012 [Retail Trade Turnovers Divided into Product Categories, 2012]. Available at: www.dst.dk/pukora/epub/Nyt/2013/NR606.pdf (Accessed: 20 October 2016).

Deleuze, Gilles, and Guattari, Felix (1987). *A Thousand Plateaus*. Minneapolis: University of Minnesota Press.

Durkheim, Emile (1984 [1893]). *The Division of Labour in Society*. London: Macmillan Press.

Fonte, Maria (2008). Knowledge, Food and Place. A Way of Producing, a Way of Knowing. *Sociologia Ruralis*. 48(3). 200–222.

Foster, John Bellamy (1999). Marx's Theory of Metabolic Rift: Classical Foundations for Environmental Sociology. *American Journal of Sociology*. 105(2). 366–405.

Foucault, Michel (1982). The Subject and Power. *Critical Inquiry*. 8(4). 777–795.

Goodman, David (2003). The Quality 'Turn' and Alternative Food Practices: Reflections and Agenda. *Journal of Rural Studies*. 19. 1–7.

Goodman, David, and Dupuis, Melanie (2002). Knowing Food and Growing Food: Beyond the Production-Consumption Debate in the Sociology of Agriculture. *Sociologia Ruralis*. 42(1). 5–22.

Halfacree, Keith (2006). Rural Space: Constructing a Three-Fold Architecture. In: P. Cloke, T. Marsden, and P. Mooney (eds). *Handbook of Rural Studies*. London: Sage.

Harrison, Paul (2000). Making Sense: Embodiment and the Sensibilities of the Everyday. *Environment and Planning D: Society and Space*. 18. 497–517.

Hoff, Hannibal (forthcoming). Resisting the Supermarket. PhD dissertation. Odense: University of Southern Denmark.

Holloway, Lewis, Kneafsey, Moya, Venn, Laura, Cox, Rosie, Dowler, Elizabeth, and Tuomainen, Helena (2007). Possible Food Economies: A Methodological Framework for Exploring Food Production-Consumption Relationships. *Sociologia Ruralis*. 47(1). 1–19.

Howes, David, and Classen, Constance (2014). *Ways of Sensing – Understanding the Senses in Society*. Abingdon: Routledge.

Johansen, Pia Heike, and Chandler, Thomas Lund (2015). Mechanisms of Power in Participatory Rural Planning. *Journal of Rural Studies*. 40. 12–20.

Johansen, Pia Heike, Hoff, Hannibal, and Jørgensen, Ask Greve (2015). *Land og By og Mad* [*Rural and Urban Food*]. Odense: University of Southern Denmark.

KBHFF (2013). *KBHFF besøger Bakkegården I Ringsted* [*KBHFF Visits 'Bakkegården' in Ringsted*]. Available at: https://vimeo.com/77567885 (Accessed: 9 February 2018).

Kjeldsen, Chris, and Ingemann, Jan Holm (2009). From the Social to the Economic and Beyond? A Relational Approach to the Historical Development of Danish Organic Food Networks. *Sociologia Ruralis*. 49(2). 151–171.

Kneafsey, Moya, Cox, Rosie, Holloway, Lewis, Dowler, Elizabeth, Venn, Laura, and Tuomainen, Helena (2008). *Reconnecting Consumers, Producers and Food – Exploring Alternatives*. New York: Berg.

Konkurrence-og_Forbrugerstyrelsen (2014). Fremtidens detailhandel: Konkurrence-og Forbrugeranalyse 01 [The Future of Retail Trade: Competition and Consumer Analysis 01]. Available at: www.kfst.dk/media/2829/20140410-analyse-fremtidens-detailhandel.pdf (Accessed: 9 February 2018).

Korsmeyer, Carolyn (1999). *Making Sense of Taste: Food and Philosophy*. New York: Cornell University Press.

Lacy, William B. (2000). Empowering Communities through Public Work, Science, and Local Food Systems: Revisiting Democracy and Globalization. *Rural Sociology*. 65(1). 3–26.

Lefebvre, Henri (2004 [1992]). *Rythmanalysis: Space, Time and Everyday Life*. Translated by S. Elden and G. Moore. London: Continuum.

McMichael, Philip (2009). A Food Regime Genealogy. *Journal of Peasant Studies*. 36(1). 139–169.

Milestad, Rebecka, Bartel-Kratochvil, Ruth, Leitner, Hedrun, and Axmann, Paul (2010). Being Close: The Quality of Social Relationships in a Local Organic Cereal and Bread Network in Lower Austria. *Journal of Rural Studies*. 26(3). 228–240.

Nielsen, Jørgen Kiel (2014). Detailhandel (Dansk detailhandels udvikling – Efter 1960) [Retail Trade (Danish Retail Trade Development – After 1960)]. *Den Store Danske*, Gyldendal. Available at: http://denstoredanske.dk/index.php?sideId=63746 (Accessed: 9 February 2018).

Rodaway, Paul (1994). *Sensuous Geographies: Body, Sense and Place*. Abingdon: Routledge.

Rosa, Hartmut (2003). Social Acceleration: Ethical and Political Consequences of a Desynchronized High-Speed Society. *Constellations: An International Journal of Critical and Democratic Theory*. 10(1). 3–33.

Roy, Ananya (2016). What Is Urban about Critical Urban Theory? *Urban Geography*. 37(6). 810–823.

Simmel, Georg (2002 [1903]). The Metropolis and Mental Life. In: G. Bridge and S. Watson (eds). *The Blackwell City Reader*. Oxford: Wiley-Blackwell.

Starr, Amory (2010). Local Food: A Social Movement? *Cultural Studies ↔ Critical Methodologies*. 10(6). 479–490.

Tarde, Gabriel (1903). *The Laws of Imitation*. New York: Henry Holt and Co.

Tönnies, Ferdinand (2001 [1887]). *Community and Civil Society*. Cambridge: Cambridge University Press.

Tregear, Angela (2011). Progressing Knowledge in Alternative and Local Food Networks: Critical Reflections and a Research Agenda. *Journal of Rural Studies*. 27(4). 419–430.

Vannini, Phillip, Waskul, Dennis, and Gottschalk, Simon (2012). *The Senses in Self, Society, and Culture: A Sociology of the Senses*. New York: Routledge.

Venn, Laura, Kneafsey, Moya, Holloway, Lewis, Cox, Rosie, Dowler, Elizabeth, and Tuomainen, Helena (2006). Researching European 'Alternative' Food Networks: Some Methodological Considerations. *Area*. 38(3). 248–258.

# 3 Framing alternative urban spaces in unstable contexts

## A view from Beirut

*Christine Mady*

### Introduction

Unstable contexts due to wars, political conflicts, or socioeconomic or religious divides are no longer characteristic of cities only in the global south (Mady, 2013, 2017). In all such cases, the security of urban spaces is jeopardised, and their social practices emerge elsewhere, for example, in commodified, temporary, or alternative spaces. Investors are interested in the exchange value, and the generation of activities in a location is pursued with this purpose in mind. This occurs in shopping malls and other commodified spaces with heightened, privately provided, security services conditioning the activities that take place there (Mady and Chettiparamab, 2016). But this chapter instead examines alternative spaces, which are orientated towards use value and the support of inclusive living. What is not much explored in the literature is how the transformative potential of these spaces in unstable contexts (Mady and Chettiparamab, 2016) is communicated through encounters, participation, and the generation of work opportunities. To this end, framing theory is used to explain how individuals collaborate and transform shared experiences according to common values, beliefs, and goals (Goffman, 1974). The organisers of alternative spaces reframe a certain reality and highlight opportunities that serve to mobilise people for a shared cause (van der Stoep, 2014; Desrosiers, 2015).

Following this introduction is an overview of public spaces in unstable contexts, highlighting the role of social movements in meeting collective needs through framing alternative spaces. Next is an explanation of framing theory to examine how the organisers of alternative spaces build meaning to re-signify spaces and meet collective needs. After providing a contextual background, the chapter presents the case of Souq El Tayeb, a non-governmental organisation (NGO) that started initially as a farmers' market, then developed spin-offs covering various activities within and outside Beirut. Framing theory is used to explore the NGO's actors, the frames developed to provide alternative spaces, and their impact on people in an unstable context. The last part presents the challenges and opportunities of this approach not only in the Lebanese context but also for a broader spectrum of cities.

## Urban spaces in unstable contexts

Unstable contexts are characterised by unpredictability and the loss of urban rhythms. Instability is often due to political turmoil, conflict situations, and social divides across religious or other affiliations (Mady and Chettiparamab, 2016). Instability becomes a condition that affects how people use urban spaces, making them adapt their lives to cope with it (Borell, 2008). Despite interruptions to the daily routine of urban living, collective needs still have to be met, one being the provision of urban spaces for encounters. In unstable contexts, planning authorities can have limited ability to provide public spaces, allowing for other possibilities to emerge such as market-led development, provision by third parties, or provision by social movements.

In the case of market-led development, reference is made to neoliberal urbanism reflected in the privatisation of services, orientation towards speculation, and the commodification of space (Peck, 2014: 397); this indicates an emphasis on the exchange value rather than the use value of space (Lefebvre, 1991). Third parties, particularly political parties, often play the role of governments when providing these services to their followers through various kinds of *clientilism* (Seidman, 2012 gives an example from Lebanon). The third possibility focuses on 'de-commodified spaces' (Montagna, 2006: 296), where use value and social practices are the motives of individuals and groups to act in urban spaces, meet collective needs, and sustain urban rhythms in shared spaces (Montagna, 2006). This possibility corresponds to alternative spaces discussed in this chapter.

Trade and exchange of goods persist in unstable contexts, and could either be driven by pure profit or serve to enable encounters (Mady and Chettiparamab, 2016). Markets as places of exchange are either provided by local authorities or private investors as commercial spaces. Alternatively, they are collectively organised as public spaces to facilitate the possibility for encounters and exchange (Watson, 2006). Encounters have a transformative potential (Watson, 2006; Merkel, 2015), establishing relations among users of a space through affinity and complementarity (Merrifield, 2012: 271), familiarity, and co-presence, as well as sharing and nurturing sociability (Iveson, 2007; Janssens and Sezer, 2013; Ünlü-Yücesoy, 2013). Encounters are much needed to reconcile diverse publics in societies undergoing instability. Also, markets generate an aesthetic experience or a 'sensory delight' (Watson, 2006: 1; see also Chapter 2 in this book), which, according to Dewey (1980), is derived from the atmosphere generated by the interaction users have with a space and with the objects in that space (Lehtovuori, 2008). This leads to an absorption of the users within a space, whereby a positive, enjoyable experience is generated (Stroud, 2014).

On the one hand, through the aesthetic experience, markets re-signify a relational space with use value (Lefebvre, 1991) based on its activities and social practices. On the other hand, markets are one livelihood opportunity for newcomers to cities (Ünlü-Yücesoy, 2013) as opposed to shadow economies (Samers, 2005); note that unstable contexts are characterised by population displacement, migrants, and refugees who are faced with limited job opportunities. Specifically, low intensity production markets support small-scale producers (Bialski et al., 2016). Particularly during periods of instability, interest in these spaces is related to their ability to connect people and spaces, and the ability to spread into different locations and expand beyond being merely a coping mechanism (Samers, 2005; Ferreri, 2015). Markets within this category are part of a social economy contributing to public wellbeing (Gibson-Graham, 2008; Amin, 2009; Pearce, 2009). Existing alongside spaces from the other two categories, alternative spaces provided by social movements are in a constant struggle to maintain themselves as relational spaces (Knierbein, 2015) without tipping the balance to the other side and promoting market-led development (Ferreri, 2015). They succeed in developing a shared capacity to create an envisioned future in various locations (van der Stoep, 2014).

## Framing urban spaces for change

To study this complexity, and while having an understanding of the history and specificities of an unstable context (Jessop et al., 2008), this research builds on framing theory and concepts, and spatial approaches to social movements (Snow and Benford, 1988; Benford and Snow, 2000). It explores how the positionality of the social actors (Martin, 2003) and the processes for communicating new meanings (Desrosiers, 2015) lead to re-signifying spaces (cf. Jessop et al., 2008; Leitner et al., 2008). In relation to markets and social practices, a sociological standpoint of framing provides an integrative approach to understanding how different perspectives on space (Leitner et al., 2008) reinforce one another. Reference is made to Goffman (1974: 21), who refers to framing as the 'schemata of interpretation' of life events that are identified and interpreted to guide action towards change. This approach refers to communication and explains the relations between the framer, the frame, and the receiver (Desrosiers, 2015), and their roles in establishing alternative spaces. For framing to lead to transformative change, 'alignment' and 'resonance' must occur. Alignment refers to clarifying the perspective of the framer for the receiver. Resonance occurs when the frame echoes what the public already believes and experiences within a specific context (Desrosiers, 2015: 128). The context in this case is an unstable one stemming from social, economic, or political turbulences, where public spaces are overlooked, encounters are limited, and social needs are unmet. Although framing does not affect structural issues directly, it could influence how these are perceived and potentially lead to opportunities for change (Desrosiers, 2015). Framing enables both the identification of the problem and the proposal of a corresponding solution (van der Stoep, 2014; Desrosiers, 2015). An examination of the framer follows.

The framer in this case is the organiser of the social movement seeking to provide alternative spaces. Being insiders, the organisers are aware of contextual specificities, including unmet needs, and have knowledge about lived experiences, existing beliefs, cultures, and values (Desrosiers, 2015: 128). The organisers proceed through mutual support with the public by working together and sharing knowledge and skills (Pickerill and Chatterton, 2006) to build 'new imaginaries' (Leitner et al., 2008: 163) that are aligned with collective needs (Desrosiers, 2015). The organisers are able to connect to users emotionally (Bradley, 2012) by providing within spaces the atmosphere and aesthetic experience perpetuated through encounters.

Another trait of the organisers is their positionality, which allows them to transform their roles and generate new interpersonal relations (Leitner et al., 2008). The organisers' horizontal interaction with the public is required to understand their needs, and generate frames whose meanings resonate with the receivers (Desrosiers, 2015); while networking at other scales (Leitner et al., 2008: 160) is necessary to negotiate and associate the frame (Kurtz, 2003), and achieve the required alternative space. The organisers have the ability to scale up and empower themselves (Leitner et al., 2008), depending on contextual constraints and the required action, and to decide upon the stakeholders who should be engaged.

Scaling up affects the construction of the required frame. This is influenced by the context and by actors at various levels (Borah, 2011), such as governments, local authorities, organisations, the public, or individuals. The organisers' creative thinking (Desrosiers, 2015) enables them to combine different considerations (Gibson-Graham, 2008) that lead to generating alternative spaces. They perform a selective organisation of the information to deliver alternative or new interpretations or meanings of an existing space that would afterwards enable people to interact with and reconfigure it according to their needs (Martin, 2003; Borah, 2011). The frames acquire an assemblage of meanings, which resonate with the needs of different user groups within a context (Desrosiers, 2015). The tools of integrating the meaning and message comprise but are not limited to language, images, metaphors, and catchphrases (Borah, 2011: 249). This allows for the identification of windows of opportunity, which with the right process, could lead to transformation by instating use value and meeting collective needs away from the unstable reality.

Frames focus on the qualities of a space and accompanying social relations (van der Stoep, 2014). By selecting specific locations for spatial interventions and connecting them topologically through shared meanings, organisers enable spatial practices to stabilise in terms of their rhythmic repetition (Lefebvre, 2004). This enables the perpetuation of activities at other locations and contexts, allowing for use value to persist irrespective of the location's specificities (Leitner et al., 2008). Leitner et al. (2008: 162) refer to this quality as the 'immutable mobile', making the approach applicable without compromising it at different scales and locations, and eventually allowing for the generation of spin-offs (Lehtovuori, 2012). This mobility of alternative spaces and their ability to appear 'unexpectedly' (Leitner et al., 2008: 165) generates contextual dynamics conducive to change.

By reframing or 're-signifying place' through self-organised activities, the space is contested with interests in its exchange value (Montagna, 2006: 296).

The activities are based on unified themes shared among diverse individuals (Martin, 2003). This conversion of space leads to place attachment through the generated aesthetic experience (Lehtovuori, 2012: 80). Lehtovuori places equal importance on the void and the built environment, which together generate the atmosphere, affecting interactions in a space through its volumes, materials, and engagement with the senses, for instance, smells and light. He mentions how the history of a location, the space or building, is used as an anchor to preserve it, how scaling up empowers organisers to claim a space and how the 'new publics' (Lehtovuori, 2012: 77) appropriate the space for activities that are different from its initial or possible market-led ones. In this sense, 'sites and buildings can indeed be seen with new eyes, as something more independent and powerful than just pieces of land to be developed, property to be re-vamped or spots to insert a cool design' (Lehtovuori, 2012: 84). Using this conceptual approach, the spaces provided by one NGO are investigated in the Lebanese context to examine the extent to which they have led to change in an unstable context.

## The Lebanese context

Throughout history Lebanon has been at a crossroads of Eastern and Western civilisations due to its strategic geo-political location on the eastern Mediterranean basin; this has led to perpetual instability affecting the economy and use of public spaces (Salibi, 1998; Khalaf, 2006). The late Ottoman period in the early 1900s, followed by the French mandate period in 1920–1940, significantly impacted the country's planning in terms of centralising activities around the capital city and prioritising commerce. The Republic constituted in 1943 was a confessional one, reflecting the various religious sects or confessions and political parties ruling the country (Jones, 2007).[1] Beirut became the commercial, financial, and cultural centre, attracting both Lebanese and nationals from neighbouring countries (Saliba, 1998). By prioritising the private sector, planning focused on the facilitation of trade and commerce (Salam, 1998; Verdeil, 2011). Foreign investment from neighbouring Arab countries flowed into Lebanon (Khalaf and Kongstad, 1973) while other sectors such as farming were marginalised and remain so to present. In 2010 the Ministry of Agriculture (2010)[2] indicated a low percentage of employment in farming, let alone women's share of it.

Focusing on Beirut, the medieval city's public spaces included markets and water fountains as gathering spaces (Davie, 2001), which were eradicated with the modernisation introduced by the consecutive Ottoman and French planning authorities. Beirut's squares and few parks, for example, Martyrs Square, were managed and controlled by the consecutive authorities (Khalaf, 2006). The city was a mosaic of different backgrounds ranging from Lebanese of different sects to refugees and migrants from neighbouring countries (Khalaf and Kongstad, 1973; Saliba, 1998). Since 1943, and until the start of the civil war in 1975, influences of modernist planning resulted in the expansion of the street network and regulation of land use zoning, with little attention given to public spaces

(Salam, 1998). Instability affected the city in different periods, with the civil war being the longest (1975–1989) (El-Khazen, 2000). This war resulted in the closure and annihilation of the city centre, previously a public meeting place, the eradication of public spaces in Beirut (Khalaf, 1993, 2002; Khalaf and Khoury, 1993), the displacement of residents, and flow of migrants and refugees. Between 1989 and 2005, instability and the stronghold of private developers meant an ongoing neglect of public spaces within the prevailing market-led development (Roy, 2009). Yet, around the year 2005, following the assassination of the former Prime Minister Rafik Hariri (Sakr-Tierney, 2017), social movements in the form of associations and NGOs started appearing to reclaim public spaces and work towards local development and social integration. This was in solidarity with a national cause away from the sectarian differences (Khalaf, 2006), which addressed Lebanese artists, and farmers among others.

Regarding the current state of public spaces in Beirut, the streets are being taken over by vehicular traffic (see Figure 3.1), squares are either highly controlled (Monroe, 2011) or have been turned into traffic nodes, and the few existing parks have been enclosed (Shayya, 2010). No systematic planning and upgrading of public spaces was undertaken to accompany the densification that occurred with Beirut's population growth. Disparities between different city parts are evident (Bou Akar, 2012), with the reconstructed city centre providing gentrified real estate development (Sakr-Tierney, 2017) and controlled public spaces (Kabbani, 1998), while limited spaces in other parts of the capital's suburbs exist (Deeb and Harb, 2013). This situation has led to population segregation within areas dominated by the confessional and political affiliations surrounding the centre.

*Figure 3.1* Traffic in and around Beirut is taking over the streets

## Framing Souq El Tayeb's alternative spaces

Despite its elitist approach, the reconstructed city centre presented a spatial opportunity for the population, with their various affiliations, to come together on the basis of common interests. One opportunity was presented through Souq El Tayeb, a farmers' market established in 2004 with about twenty producers, which was the starting point for other spin-offs in Lebanon. Information on Souq El Tayeb comes from empirical work conducted on the market in 2007 and 2016. This included site observations, interviews with the market managers, and interviews with about fifty visitors to the market in each of 2007 and 2016. A comparative study of the market in this period is provided by Mady (2017).

The market was initiated by one person – KM – who wanted to support local small-scale producers, promote Lebanese food and culture, and gather people together. Findings on this market from previous studies indicate how the organiser's creative thinking led to 're-inventing' urban land through unpacking the property rights for a car park in Beirut's centre, allowing farmers to interact with visitors (Mady, 2012: 69). Locating the market in the centre was a conscious decision of selecting a gathering space that was not affiliated with the war-time divisions (Khalaf, 2002; Bou Akar, 2012). The purpose of the organiser focused on changing the war-time image of the country, promoting Lebanese food from small-scale producers including women, and providing a space for gathering and encounters at a time when insecurity meant that the Lebanese avoided gathering in public spaces (Mady, 2013). The market has also been studied in terms of its role in constructing space-related and interest-related identities that counteract the sectarian war-time divide (Mady and Chettiparamab, 2016: 7). In another study the market was analysed as a model of social economy for its innovation and ability to provide a livelihood for refugees and producers from different parts of Lebanon, persisting in a central location despite instability, and maintaining its role in bridging sectarian divides by providing a gathering place in Beirut (Mady, 2017). Despite the instability witnessed in Beirut between 2005 and 2016, the market continued and moved between several locations within Beirut's city centre. Both small-scale producers and market visitors participated in its activities. Moreover, through in-depth interviews conducted in 2017, this chapter explores the NGO following its establishment when the organiser KM partnered with another person: CC.[3]

The creative thinking of the organisers and their insider knowledge of the context and social needs formed the basis for scaling up to an NGO and framing its activities. Both organisers described the decision of becoming an NGO as a natural progression from being only a registered trade at the Lebanese Chamber of Commerce, since the market 'always functioned as a non-profit entity' (founder KM, personal interview 23 June 2017) and this change merely 'formalised' it: 'so we have official [vis-à-vis the authorities] existence' (founder CC, personal interview 23 June 2017). In fact, the organisers established interactions among civic, public, and private actors, which did not previously exist without the frame: connection to food. This formalisation is interpreted as aligning the NGO's aim and scaling up to enable addressing and collaborating with other actors. Depending on the actors involved, these collaborations were done either through verbal agreements with land owners to use the location, municipal permits to hold events, or contracts with other organisations to mobilise projects. Some examples were presented by the organisers, such as consultations with the Ministry of Agriculture on olive farming, the United Nations Development Programme (UNDP) for holding a market in Jordan, or the Jounieh municipality north of Beirut on planning a market, together with capacity building in Lebanese refugee camps (cf. founders KM and CC, personal interview 23 June 2017).

All the actors within Souq El Tayeb assumed different roles depending on the NGO's needs. The organisers KM and CC were a graphic designer and a legal consultant, respectively. The farmers assumed a role beyond harvesting and selling their produce, which involved educating visitors to the market on Lebanese food and heritage, and thus aligning with shared needs in that context. The managers of the various spin-offs had different backgrounds but were joined by a common vision; for example, the canteen in Beirut was managed by an engineer as stated by the founder CC. This founder explained how interest in and belonging to the NGO were built through the people involved. Collaboration and a creative combination and sharing of skills formed the engine for change by capitalising on differences and recognising the opportunities for learning from them:

> I think in recruiting we are very much open, and we don't have the 'needed' profile. You know anybody can be here, and it's other stuff we look for; for example, the empowerment that we apply a lot in people. We are giving the chance to people to make mistakes but also be responsible.
>
> (Founder CC, personal interview 23 June 2017)

Souq El Tayeb is an assemblage of meanings revealed through the activities and communication related to this NGO.[4] These meanings resonate with the experiences, perceptions, and values of different users, one being gathering over national food irrespective of sectarian and other differences. The market experience was coupled with the gathering table (Mady, 2013), providing a meeting place in Beirut's city centre on Saturdays and another location in Beirut on Tuesdays. Since its inception in 2004, the role of the market has been to provide a gathering place for encounters that was absent under instability. The table becomes the central object used in the different activities to gather people and encourage interaction. The organisers were also aware of the lack of opportunities for small-scale producers, specifically women among them, in a context dominated by chain food stores and restaurants, hence women's central role in the market.

The NGO's other activities comprised: food and feast, which were one-day events taking place in various parts of the country; capacity-building programmes particularly empowering women; and a series of canteens called 'tawleh' and guesthouses called 'beit'. The canteen or 'tawleh' is where women from different regions in Lebanon participate in cooking. The guesthouse or 'beit' is another activity highlighting local, natural and cultural heritage and employing locals. The geographic distribution of activities outside Beirut in urban and rural areas reflects a spread from the north to the south of Lebanon, along the coastal area and equally inland. While the locations have no direct relation to each other, their connection is established through the NGO's mission of local development. Regarding the distribution of activities, the organisers made sure they stated their mission clearly, aligning it prior to starting an activity in a new location. Regardless of the activity, while the locations were often proposed by municipalities or private owners rather than selected by the organisers, the message was always the same: promoting local Lebanese food, which was summarised by the organiser KM as: 'tradition, home, and women' (founder KM, personal interview 23 June 2017), and comprised an assemblage of meanings resonating with different users. The three terms resonate 'emotionally', generating an aesthetic experience and reflecting the organiser's insider understanding of what was lacking or had been suffered throughout the series of instabilities in Lebanon.

Regarding communication, there was an emphasis on using only Arabic language in a society that switches between Arabic, English, and French. The NGO used catchphrases such as its name 'Souq El Tayeb' – literally meaning the 'market for the delicious' – focusing on the vernacular and convivial living before the civil war. The names of the activities reflect the vision, as expressed by KM: 'the vision we have, it's just straightforward and simple' (founder KM, personal interview 23 June 2017). This was evident in the names of the activities that used the simplest terms, for example, 'tawleh' meaning table and 'beit' meaning house, coupled with the name of the activity's location in Beirut or Lebanon. A similar approach was used for the food and feast events focusing on what was local. Whether it was on the NGO's website, the flyers, or the social and communication media, the organisers creatively combined graphic depictions with their choice of words to resonate with the local culture and traditions embedded in Lebanese people of different backgrounds, away from the war-time divides. For example, the visuals depicted traditional Lebanese dress, stylised farming produce, and the heritage features of each location.[5]

In terms of re-signifying spaces, and depending on the location, the organisers always arranged the space to allow for gathering, and sought in a context its natural and cultural heritage traits, along with what the local people could offer. Place-based interests were capitalised (Mady and Chettiparamab, 2016). The organisers gave the example of the *tawleh* in Beirut, which was a canteen that used to be a car repair garage (see Figure 3.2). The space was screened with greenery to provide 'seclusion' from the hustle and bustle of the city.

*Figure 3.2* Three views of the *tawleh* in Beirut showing its green wall and the interior of the converted garage

> We created a green wall that didn't exist before to protect ourselves [from noise] even more and to create a cocoon. And the space itself, the high ceiling is quite amazing; the light is amazing. You get to this place . . . and you're nurtured, it brings something positive.
>
> (Founder KM, personal interview 23 June 2017)

The various locations of the farmers' market were car parks sometimes with trees as shading devices, or shading provided within the food stalls (Mady, 2017). The guesthouses were selected for their heritage value, alluding to old traditional Lebanese houses: 'We look at the history, the culture of the place or the house where it is, the environment, the people themselves . . . so it's a combination' (founder CC, personal interview 23 June 2017).

The organiser KM indicated that at least two qualities should be present in a location for it to be approved for framing by the NGO: it should be 'nurturing' and it should 'say something' (founder KM, personal interview 23 June 2017). These criteria were explained as follows: the location should 'address all the senses', 'be aesthetically pleasing', 'bring something positive to the users', and 'add something to their life' as an experience not found outside in the broader context. The organisers explained that tables in restaurants were there to serve the food, yet in this NGO, the table was the tool for enabling encounters among people: producers and visitors, through the atmosphere and the message behind the offered food.

## Challenges to positive change

Two main challenges were evident in the NGO's mission in terms of constructing frames that resonate in the unstable Lebanese context. The first was mitigating the structural, confessional division in Lebanese society (Hanf, 1993), which had been further exacerbated by perpetual conflicts. Targeting different locations for the activities and being called upon by municipalities across the country, were indications of welcoming the NGO to intervene for the sake of meeting collective needs, despite geographic, religious, or sectarian differences. The NGO presented one approach to mitigate this structural constraint by 'gathering' people with interests revolving around food and heritage (Mady and Chettiparamab, 2016), in other words, 'universalising' the themes (Martin, 2003: 738). It highlighted specificities of areas related to natural aspects and objects such as apples, cherries, pine trees, or culture through architectural heritage. Also, the NGO empowered local producers of different sects. The food and feast events emerged 'unexpectedly' and mobilised people to visit and explore different parts of the country irrespective of their backgrounds, reflecting a change in their perceptions of geographic and administrative locations in the country (Kurtz, 2003).

The second challenge was resisting market forces and security issues. The interest of private developers to call upon the organisers to promote their locations and increase their exchange value was an eminent threat to converting some of the NGO's activities to commodified ones. But this threat was countered, for example, in the case of the farmers' market by providing the opportunity to small-scale producers, comprising less privileged Lebanese and refugees (Mady, 2017), to actively participate in urban life in one of the most prestigious and often inaccessible locations in the capital city:

> just look at the farmers' market on Saturday, it's the fanciest, and most expensive, neighbourhood in Beirut, and we have farmers who cannot wish to sell there who cannot even come and visit, [they are] present and active, not only present, they are not visitors, they are selling there, so they are part of the function of the activity of this fancy part of town.
>
> (Founder KM, personal interview 23 June 2017)

The founders had implemented an alternative economy for the small-scale producers by interpreting the prevailing economic practices and providing new spaces for work, encounters, and exchange. All this took place amidst Beirut's highly securitised context (Fawaz et al., 2009; Monroe, 2011). Other examples include activities outside Beirut, which did not follow conventional business models:

> We follow a different vision, which is the woman, the farmer, the celebration of food. Business-wise it doesn't make sense maybe, but we make sense out of it in a different way. A regular business would create

> value for shareholders ... We don't, we follow a different vision, which is the woman, the farmer, the celebration of food.
>
> (Founder CC, personal interview 23 June 2017)

As explained by the founders, the danger of losing the balance and tipping towards commodification was partly countered by: being selective and focusing on small-scale producers only and not resellers; maintaining the quality of locally offered produce; taking advantage of developers to gain access to specific locations, yet keeping the low profile of the market even within high-end locations; strongly sticking to the values and mission of the NGO, and maintaining its 'identity, its soul' (founder CC, personal interview 23 June 2017); making sure each person was responsible for what they did and spreading ownership of the activities horizontally among the NGO members (Pickerill and Chatterton, 2006; Leitner et al., 2008); equally seeking opportunities in what could be done further, maintaining flexible frames that adapted to needs (Benford and Snow, 2000); and learning from the system within which the NGO functioned in order to perpetuate this approach for future generations. One of the founders stated: 'I mean we need to transmit it because we may go one day. Strategy for me is this: how to maintain the soul of what we made' (founder CC, personal interview 23 June 2017). This was supported by the organisers' insistence on the NGO members taking ownership of the activities they were involved in. As KM explained:

> They definitely have ownership each of their project ... I just develop a project and then I follow up on what's happening and that's it. It's setting the proper system, and then you know, just grow as a system and the people who are holding the system ... We don't help them, we do it together let's say, because that is a successful model.
>
> (Founder KM, personal interview 23 June 2017)

## The re-signified spaces and transformative potentials

Some of Souq El Tayeb's effects include establishing new relations and causing the perpetuation of similar activities not related to it. The organisers emphasised that, although the NGO's activities start with their ideas, these ideas are developed and realised by this network of activities through a complex set of relations among several actors and disciplines, on various scales from the international to the national to the non-governmental, from the developer to the producer but also the users, or the 'new publics' (Lehtovuori, 2012). As the activities are being framed to provide new interpretations through an assemblage of meanings, they get deciphered by different publics, each according to their interests and needs (Mady and Chettiparamab, 2016). Through scaling up, the NGO instigated changes in attitude that were evident in the various requests to implement the model and attempts to imitate it. This is reflected, for example, by the detail of traditional Lebanese dishes, habitually prepared only at home, now being widespread among caterers at social events:

> Souk el Ard, souk el Akl are independent entities trying to imitate Souq El Tayeb ... see how many people imitate, then that is already proof of something that works, and that there is demand for it; it means that you already changed the mindset or the attitude ... Now you know the Lebanese cuisine is trendy, you know the typical lentils with lemon.
>
> (Founder CC, personal interview 23 June 2017)

> I think we are creating trends ... It's a ripple effect which interests us, not just the project itself. Because our projects, no matter how many, are limited. But what's interesting is not only our projects, it's the ripple effect that will happen with others, which are not related to us at all.
>
> (Founder KM, personal interview 23 June 2017)

This 'ripple effect' was manifested in various parts of the country due to the flexibility of the frames used (Benford and Snow, 2000) and, at the same time, the universality in addressing different groups (Martin, 2003) and the ability to redefine scale and reconnect places across the country (Kurtz, 2003).

## Conclusion

This chapter has explored the role of alternative spaces in unstable contexts. Some of the challenges in such contexts include the absence of security, limiting encounters to controlled commercial spaces rather than public spaces, and accentuating differences within an atmosphere of uncertainty. The need for encounters in shared spaces becomes eminent and the threat of market-led commodification is augmented. Irrespective of the cause of instability, understanding the context is required prior to finding ways to provide alternative solutions (Knierbein, 2015); hence the significance of the organiser being an insider, who was able to understand and creatively reinterpret contingent socio-spatial conditions and realities. The chapter focused on Lebanon, a country with a record of instability, the loss of its public spaces, and an increase in social segregation not only from its past but also from its current events and influx of refugees. The research explored the case of one social movement instituted as an NGO. How one farmers' market became the nexus generating spin-offs was investigated through the organisers' framing, which enabled the connection of people with places, while building on the specificity of the location and collective interests, away from religious, social, and political divides.

The chapter discussed the positionality of the framer, and the processes of scaling up and networking to construct frames with multiple meanings. With these meanings, people's perceptions were affected, and the re-signified spaces responded to various needs related to working, exchange, and encounters.

This re-signification was manifested through the newly generated aesthetic experiences in the spaces and through the highlighted activities and objects, which were communicated through phrases and images resonating with the needs and experiences of the local people. The proposed model and system implemented in the NGO's activities in various and unrelated locations challenged the current market-led practices in Lebanon, by providing alternative interpretations. These re-signified spaces transformed the way markets and other conventionally business-oriented activities could support local development and induce interaction in societies within unstable contexts. The organisers or framers empowered small-scale producers and vulnerable people, and enabled encounters within conventionally inaccessible locations. This people-centred approach demonstrates the transformative potential of these alternative spaces. By addressing the challenge of social divides in Lebanon through establishing new spatial relations, mobilising people to see and experience the city centre in a different atmosphere, and equally visit other areas in the country, it allowed room to question and, to some extent, alter deeply rooted perceptions about refugees or sectarian divides within the local context.

In conclusion, the chapter has presented one approach leading to re-signifying urban spaces into alternative spaces that secure encounters within unstable contexts. This requires the combination of insider knowledge and the ability to join efforts and clearly frame a problem through appropriate contextual communication tools. The result comprises aesthetic experiences resonating with interests and spatial associations that could be sought both locally and internationally.

## Acknowledgements

I would like to thank the book editors, especially Jens Kaae Fisker, who have provided invaluable comments and guidance throughout the writing process. I would also like to thank the librarians at Notre Dame University for their support. My thanks also goes to the founders of the Souq el Tayeb NGO.

## Notes

1 The term 'confessionalism' reflects the government system, which is based on the distribution of positions relative to the sects within the two religions: Christianity and Islam in Lebanon. More information on how confessionalism has affected the country is available in Hanf (1993) and El-Khazen (2000).
2 www.agriculture.gov.lb/html/نتائج_الاحصاء_الزراعي_الشامل_/2010_تقرير_الاحصار_الزراعي/2010.pdf (Accessed: 11 August 2017).
3 Souq El Tayeb's organisation chart: www.soukeltayeb.com/the-organisation/structure-team.
4 Souq El Tayeb's website: www.soukeltayeb.com.
5 Souq El Tayeb's events: www.soukeltayeb.com/food-feast/events.

## References


Amin, A. (ed) (2009) *The Social Economy: International Perspectives on Economic Solidarity*. London: Zed Books.

Benford, R.D. and Snow, D.A. (2000) Framing Processes and Social Movements: An Overview and Assessment. *Annual Review of Sociology* 26, pp. 611–639.

Bialski, P., Derwantz, H., Otto, B., and Vollmer, H. (2016) 'Saving' the City: Collective Low Budget Organizing and Urban Practice. *Ephemera: Theory & Politics in Organization* 15(1), pp. 1–19.

Borah, P. (2011) Conceptual Issues in Framing Theory: A Systematic Examination of a Decade's Literature. *Journal of Communication* 61, pp. 246–263. DOI: 10.1111/j.1460-2466.2011.01539.x.

Borell, K. (2008) Terrorism and Everyday Life in Beirut 2005: Mental Reconstructions, Precautions and Normalizations. *Acta Sociologica* 51(1), pp. 55–70.

Bou Akar, H. (2012) Contesting Beirut's Frontiers. *City and Society* 24(2), pp. 150–172.

Bradley, Q. (2012) A 'Performative' Social Movement: The Emergence of Collective Contentions within Collaborative Governance. *Space and Polity* 16(2), pp. 215–232. DOI: 10.1080/13562576.2012.721504.

Davie, M. (2001) *Beyrouth 1825–1975 un siècle et demi d'urbanisme* [*Beirut 1825–1975. A Century and a Half of Urbanism*]. Beirut: Order of Engineers and Architects.

Deeb, L. and Harb, M. (2013) *Leisurely Islam: Negotiating Geography and Morality in Shi'ite South Beirut*. Princeton, NJ: Princeton University Press.

Desrosiers, M.-E. (2015) Tackling Puzzles of Identity-Based Conflict: The Promise of Framing Theory. *Civil Wars* 17(2), pp. 120–140. DOI: 10.1080/13698249.2015.1070449.

Dewey, J. (1980) *Art as Experience*. New York: Pedigree Books.

El-Khazen, F. (2000) *The Breakdown of the State in Lebanon*. Cambridge, MA: Harvard University Press.

Fawaz, M., Gharbieh, A., and Harb, M. (eds) (2009) *Beirut: Mapping Security*. Stuttgart: Diwan Series.

Ferreri, M. (2015) The Seductions of Temporary Urbanism. *Ephemera: Theory & Politics in Organization* 15(1), pp. 181–191.

Gibson-Graham, J.K. (2008) Diverse Economies: Performative Practices for 'Other Worlds'. *Progress in Human Geography* 32(5), pp. 613–632. DOI: 10.1177/0309132508090821.

Goffman, E. (1974) *Frame Analysis: An Essay on the Organization of Experience*. Cambridge, MA: Harvard University Press.

Hanf, T. (1993) *Coexistence in Wartime Lebanon: Decline of a State and Rise of a Nation*. London: Centre for Lebanese Studies in association with I.B. Tauris.

Iveson, K. (2007) *Publics and the City*. Oxford: Blackwell.

Janssens, F. and Sezer, C. (2013) 'Flying Markets' Activating Public Spaces in Amsterdam. *Built Environment* 39(2), pp. 245–260.

Jessop, B., Brenner, N., and Jones, M. (2008) Theorizing Sociospatial Relations. *Environment and Planning D: Society and Space* 26, pp. 389–401. DOI: 10.1068/d9107.

Jones, J. (2007) *Negotiating Change: The New Politics of the Middle East*. London: I.B. Tauris.

Kabbani, O. (1998) Public Space as Infrastructure: The Case of Postwar Reconstruction of Beirut. In Rowe, P. and Sarkis, H. (eds) *Projecting Beirut: Episodes in the Construction and Reconstruction of a Modern City*. London and New York: Prestel-Verlag, pp. 240–259.

Khalaf, S. (1993) Urban Design and the Recovery of Beirut. In Khalaf, S. and Khoury, P. (eds) *Recovering Beirut: Urban Design and Post War Reconstruction*. Leiden, The Netherlands: Brill, pp. 11–62.

Khalaf, S. (2002) *Civil and Uncivil Violence in Lebanon: A History of Internationalization of Communal Conflict*. New York: Columbia University Press.

Khalaf, S. (2006) *Heart of Beirut: Reclaiming the Bourj*. London: Palgrave Macmillan.

Khalaf, S. and Khoury, P. (1993) Preface. In Khalaf, S. and Khoury, P. (eds) *Recovering Beirut: Urban Design and Post War Reconstruction*. Leiden, The Netherlands: Brill, pp. xi–xxii.

Khalaf, S. and Kongstad, P. (1973) *Hamra of Beirut: A Case of Rapid Urbanization*. Leiden, The Netherlands: E.J. Brill.

Knierbein, S. (2015) Public Space as Relational Counter Space: Scholarly Minefield or Epistemological Opportunity? In Tornaghi, C. and Knierbein, S. (eds) *Public Space and Relational Perspectives: New Challenges for Architecture and Planning*. Abingdon and New York: Routledge, pp. 44–68.

Kurtz, H.E. (2003) Scale Frames and Counter-Scale Frames: Constructing the Problem of Environmental Injustice. *Political Geography* 22, pp. 887–916.

Lefebvre, H. (1991) *The Production of Space*. Translated by D. Nicholson-Smith. Oxford: Blackwell.

Lefebvre, H. (2004) *Rhythmanalysis: Space, Time and Everyday Life*. Translated by S. Elden and G. Moore. London and New York: Continuum.

Lehtovuori, P. (2008) Artifacts, Oeuvre and Atmosphere: Applying Lefebvre's Spatial Thinking in Urban Design. In Avermaete, T., Havik, K., and Teerds, H. (eds) *Into the Open: Accommodating the Public*. OASE 77. Rotterdam: Nai, pp. 58–70.

Lehtovuori, P. (2012) Towards Experiential Urbanism. *Critical Sociology* 38(1), pp. 71–87. DOI: 10.1177/0896920511407222.

Leitner, H., Sheppard, E., and Sziarto, K.M. (2008) The Spatialities of Contentious Politics. *Transactions of the Institute of British Geographers*, New Series 33(2), pp. 157–172.

Mady, C. (2012) Diversity in Conviviality: Beirut's Temporary Public Spaces. *Open House International* 37(2), pp. 63–71.

Mady, C. (2013) Social Entrepreneurs and Temporary Public Space Supply: Beirut. *Urban Design and Planning* 166(6), pp. 349–357.

Mady, C. (2017) Reading the Dynamics of Contemporary Urban Spaces in a Turbulent Era: A Case from Beirut. *Built Environment* 43(2), pp. 256–271.

Mady, C. and Chettiparamab, A. (2016) Planning in the Face of 'Deep Divisions': A View from Beirut, Lebanon. *Planning Theory* (Advance online publication), pp. 1–23. DOI: 10.1177/1473095216639087.

Martin, D.G. (2003) 'Place-Framing' as Place-Making: Constituting a Neighborhood for Organizing and Activism. *Annals of the Association of American Geographers* 93(3), pp. 730–750.

Merkel, J. (2015) Coworking in the City. *Ephemera: Theory & Politics in Organization* 15(1), pp. 121–139.

Merrifield, A. (2012) The Politics of the Encounter and the Urbanization of the World. *City* 16(3), pp. 270–283.

Monroe, K.V. (2011) Being Mobile in Beirut. *City and Society* 23(1), pp. 91–111.

Montagna, N. (2006) The De-Commodification of Urban Space and the Occupied Social Centres in Italy. *City: Analysis of Urban Trends, Culture, Theory, Policy, Action* 10(3), pp. 295–304. DOI: 10.1080/13604810600980663.

Pearce, J. (2009) Social Economy: Engaging as a Third System? In Amin, A. (ed) *The Social Economy: International Perspectives on Economic Solidarity*. London: Zed Books, pp. 22–33.

Peck, J. (2014) Entrepreneurial Urbanism: Between Uncommon Sense and Dull Compulsion. *Geografiska Annaler: Series B, Human Geography* 96(4), pp. 396–401.

Pickerill, J. and Chatterton, P. (2006) Notes towards Autonomous Geographies: Creation, Resistance and Self-Management as Survival Tactics. *Progress in Human Geography* 30(6), pp. 730–746. DOI: 10.1177/0309132506071516.

Roy, A. (2009) Civic Governmentality: The Politics of Inclusion in Beirut and Mumbai. *Antipode* 41(1), pp. 159–179.

Sakr-Tierney, J. (2017) Real Estate, Banking and War: The Construction and Reconstruction of Beirut. *Cities* 69, pp. 73–78.

Salam, A. (1998) The Role of Government in Shaping the Built Environment. In Rowe, P. and Sarkis, H. (eds) *Projecting Beirut: Episodes in the Construction and Reconstruction of a Modern City*. London and New York: Prestel, pp. 122–133.

Saliba, R. (1998) *Beirut 1920–1940: Domestic Architecture between Tradition and Modernity*. Beirut: Order of Engineers and Architects.

Salibi, K. (1998) *A House of Many Mansions: The History of Lebanon Reconsidered*. London: I.B. Tauris.

Samers, M. (2005) The Myopia of 'Diverse Economies', or a Critique of the 'Informal Economy'. *Editorial Board of Antipode* 37(5), pp. 875–886.

Seidman, S. (2012) The Politics of Cosmopolitan Beirut from the Stranger to the Other. *Theory, Culture and Society* 29(2), pp. 3–36.

Shayya, F. (ed) (2010) *At the Edge of the City: Reinhabiting Public Space toward the Recovery of Beirut's Horsh Al-Sanawbar*. Beirut: Discursive Formations.

Snow, D.A. and Benford, R.D. (1988) Ideology, Frame Resonance and Participant Mobilization. *International Social Movement Research* 1, pp. 197–217.

Stroud, S.R. (2014) The Art of Experience: Dewey on the Aesthetic. In Malecki, W. (ed) *Practicing Pragmatist Aesthetics: Critical Perspectives on Literature and the Arts*. Amsterdam: Rodopi, pp. 33–46.

Ünlü-Yücesoy, E. (2013) Constructing the Marketplace: A Socio-Spatial Analysis of Past Marketplaces of Istanbul. *Built Environment* 39(2), pp. 190–202.

van der Stoep, H. (2014) Stories Becoming Sticky: How Civic Initiatives Strive for Connection to Governmental Spatial Planning Agendas. PhD thesis. Wageningen: Wageningen University.

Verdeil, E. (2011) *Beyrouth et ses urbanistes. Une ville en plans (1946–1975)* [*Beirut and Its Planners. A City in Plans (1946–1975)*]. Beirut: Presses de l'Ifpo.

Watson, S. (2006) *City Publics: The (Dis)Enchantments of Urban Encounters*. Abingdon: Routledge.

# 4 New workspaces in Milan and Berlin

## Coworking spaces between defensive strategies and transformative potential

*Carolina Pacchi*

### Introduction

In the face of radical changes in labour patterns and labour market strategies in post-Fordist cities, workspaces are being transformed under the powerful influence of the diffusion of information and communication technologies (ICTs), the rise of knowledge workers, and job fragmentation and precarisation (Standing, 2011). Among such transformations, which concern both traditional activities and 'new' workspaces (Gershenfeld, 2005; Anderson, 2012), the emergence of coworking spaces stands out as a significant trend, with around 13,000 coworking spaces worldwide and an estimate of more than one million coworkers for 2017. Coworking started with some isolated pioneering experiences in the 1990s and has seen consistent growth since the first systematic data collection which counted 160 coworking spaces worldwide in 2008, 600 in 2010, and 2,000 in 2012 (Deskmag, 2017). These spaces are working environments in which people, not connected through any hierarchical or organisational structure, choose to work side by side to overcome isolation and to take advantage of proximity in order to enhance knowledge spillovers and embrace opportunities for cooperation, community building, and the strengthening of new working connections (Spinuzzi, 2012; Capdevila, 2013, 2014). They have been described as 'shared workplaces utilised by different sorts of knowledge professionals, mostly freelancers, working in various degrees of specialisation in the vast domain of the knowledge industry' (Gandini, 2015: 194).

This chapter investigates the transformative and alternative potential of such spaces through empirical research in Milan and Berlin. In particular, the chapter first introduces coworking spaces and their (functional, urban, and symbolic) role in contemporary urban spaces, and then critically discusses them from three different perspectives: (1) their embeddedness in evolving urban economies; (2) the role they play vis-à-vis the characters and evolutionary trends of the urban spaces they are located in; and (3) the potential for aggregation and construction of new forms of political representation for precarious workers. A concluding paragraph looks into the conditions under which coworking spaces might be seen as alternative urban spaces.

## Coworking spaces in the knowledge economy

The diffusion of coworking spaces worldwide has been connected by analysts and scholars to three (interlinked) phenomena:

- the diffusion of ICTs, which has significantly lowered transaction costs (McCann, 2008) and freed people from being located in a specific place, but with obvious problems and downturns (Isin and Ruppert, 2015);
- the rise in relevance of a knowledge economy (Scott, 2012); and
- changes in labour market structure, particularly those connected to the diffusion of jobs that differ from full-time regular employment (Allegri and Ciccarelli, 2013; Cappelli and Keller, 2013).

These three phenomena, combined in complex ways in the major urban and metropolitan centres, result in an increased diffusion of highly skilled free-lancers – workers who are forced to be always innovative – while at the same time the characters of the labour market make them a precarious and fragile segment of the job market (Allegri and Ciccarelli, 2013; Moriset, 2014). Zukin recaps this ongoing trend, also in relation to urban spaces:

> The rise of the symbolic economy, based on finance, information, fashion and other rapidly shifting forms of advantage, has pushed men and women to become entrepreneurial in the broadest sense. Many of the jobs in these industries are part-time or temporary, contingent on a project's success in pleasing clients, workers' self-investment and a firm's market success. Culturally, both individuals and groups aim to capture the temporary benefits of priority (the 'next new thing') and location (the 'unique' thing). For cities as well as individuals, this entrepreneurial behaviour is fuelled by economic pressure.
>
> (Zukin, 2006: 117)

In southern Europe, particularly in relatively poor cities (by German and European Union standards) like Berlin, the prolonged economic and financial crisis has worsened the living and working conditions of knowledge workers (Allegri and Ciccarelli, 2013; Moriset, 2014); workers who were already in difficult positions due to the precarisation of their jobs and exposure to low wages, notwithstanding their high level of skills and qualifications. Knowledge workers trade security for freedom, but this freedom can seldom be seen as an individual choice, since it rather tends to be a recurring condition of the labour market. Moreover, due also to the economic and real estate crisis, cheap office space has become extremely diffused, both in premises originally designed and marketed as offices or tertiary spaces, and in former industrial buildings or compounds (Mariotti, Pacchi, and Di Vita, 2017). The intersection of these two phenomena has played a significant role in the transformation of working spaces in general and in the emergence and diffusion of coworking spaces more specifically, particularly in large urban regions.

## Coworking spaces and urban economies

There is quite strong agreement in the literature on the fact that culture and context can be seen as important drivers which influence the development of coworking spaces (Klaas, 2013–2014: 13; Mariotti, Pacchi, and Di Vita, 2017). In analysing the transformative potential of new workspaces in their relationship with the urban dimension we look at the contexts in which such new workspaces emerge and diffuse, and in particular at the economic context and its evolution, since such phenomena tend in any case to be largely spontaneous and market driven (Deskmag, 2017). The public policy framework appears less relevant in shaping the coworking evolution, even if there are some targeted policies, which will be discussed in particular in the Milan case. Looking at these emerging trends, Milan and Berlin can be seen as examples of two very different development trajectories, having two very different forms of relationship between the emergence of urban cultural and creative productions as a relevant sector, and the consequent effects in terms of urban spatial transformation.

As is well known, Berlin quite abruptly transformed its economic basis after the fall of the Wall and the re-unification process, during the 1990s (Krätke, 2004). The situation of the city was already a sort of exception in the European and German panorama. In the decades leading up to World War II, Berlin had become a strong industrial city (with Siemens, AEG, etc.), but after the war and during the reconstruction period most major industrial groups moved their headquarters and their production sites to the then Federal Republic, while in the Democratic Republic, in the east, a completely state-owned industrial production system was developed (Colomb, 2012). In the subsequent decades, the eastern part of the city thus lived off this state industry, while the western part was heavily subsidised by the Federal Republic, as a sort of showcase of the Western lifestyle.

These two conditions in fact never permitted a full recovery of industrial production, and their 'artificial' nature abruptly came to an end after 1989–1990. This abrupt transformation caused very significant closures and job losses in both parts of the city, thus paving the way for a profound crisis from which the (now) reunified Berlin tried to re-emerge through the fostering of two economic sectors: the knowledge economy on the one hand and tourism on the other (Colomb, 2012). There has been a strong critical debate in the literature about the viability of this model (Krätke, 2004), the growing risks of social (and spatial) polarisation that this entailed (Holm, 2013; Mayer, 2013; Blume, 2014), and the overall governance of the 'new' Berlin (Kalandides, 2007; Novy and Colomb, 2013). Moreover, the risks of social polarisation and displacement of the existing population have been exacerbated by the fact that Berlin remained one of the most thriving but cheapest large metropolises in Europe from the beginning of the 2000s, and this in turn attracted to the city a large number of highly skilled workers in the knowledge sector and especially the creative and cultural sectors from across Germany, Europe, and beyond. The overall figures concerning the creative and cultural economy (including ICT and media) in Berlin today add up to around 36,000 companies, 270,000 employees, and an annual contribution to the city's GDP of around €30 billion (Senatsverwaltung für Wirtschaft, Energie und Betriebe, 2017: 4). At the same time, while the branding strategies that the Berlin Senate has been promoting in explicit support of this sector depict a very positive image, the reality of 'culturepreneurs' is different:

> Skilful alternation between unemployment benefit, temporary jobs, self-employment structures and new temporary network coalitions is practised by numerous young agents in the field of cultural production. Informal social bonds as well as network alliances have enabled the emergence of new creative milieus.
>
> (Lange, 2011: 4)

Looking at the use of space, Berlin has a long heritage of collective spaces (hackerspaces, community hubs, countercultural centres, squats, etc.), which is related to the rich context of social movements and grassroots groups active in the city. Since the 1970s, West Berlin has been the locus of grassroots mobilisation and experimentation, in different realms. One realm is housing struggles, as shown in the first wave of occupations and squatting in Kreuzberg in the 1980s (Hager, 2007; Holm and Kuhn, 2011; Perl and Steffen, 2015); the other is connected to the opening up of community and cultural centres such as the *Ufa Fabrik* in Tempelhof-Schöneberg, *Bethanien, Schokofabriek,* and many others again in Kreuzberg. Then a second wave of occupations took place mainly in Friedrichshain after the fall of the Wall, and, while some occupations have lasted to this day, the outcomes of that period are more ambivalent from an interpretative point of view (Holm and Kuhn, 2011; Gualini, 2015). It is exactly from the intersection between this cultural context and the emerging creative and cultural economy that different types of new workspaces, laboratories, and spaces for innovation emerged, taking different forms. In the beginning, being highly experimental and informal, such spaces – for instance, hackerspaces – were not necessarily codified, but today they are part of a trend of increasing codification into a smaller number of typologies, among which coworking spaces stand out as a very relevant one. This evolving context has led to the diffusion of new workspaces that are able, on the one hand, to use the vastly underused or abandoned built stock, and on the other, to host the emerging new professions, especially in the knowledge sector and for creative productions (Klaas, 2013–2014). Coworking spaces in the strict sense are as a matter of fact a subgroup of a wider array of new workspaces, which have been defined as 'innovation and creativity labs':

> environments conducive to creating and testing innovative ideas, alternative business practices and business models, new economic practices or flexible cooperation forms. They are experimentation fields that transform physical

> structures into spatial nuclei in which temporary practices for generating economic (product/process/organizational) innovations crystallize.
>
> (Schmidt, Brinks, and Brinkhoff, 2014: 232)

The fact that many coworking spaces originate from informal practices is a quite distinctive feature of the Berlin case, while in Milan, as we will see, most coworking spaces can be seen as a market response to emerging needs. The common element between the two urban contexts is the extremely small-scale, diffused, and bottom-up nature of the phenomenon, at least in the initial years and up to now.

In Milan, in turn, the economic situation evolved very differently. The most significant change in the development of the economic structure took place between the 1970s and the early 1980s, when the city experienced a radical transformation and a transition from an industrial to a post-industrial, tertiary, service-based economy (Magatti and Sapelli, 2012; Armondi and Di Vita, 2018), a shift which took place in many cities across Europe and North America. In Milan in particular, the main trends of change concerning the economy were accompanied by concomitant changes, such as the transformation of the social organisation and demographic structure of the city, and a complex process of political and administrative fragmentation (Pacchi and Pasqui, 2015), interpreted as a consequence of the change that took place in the local regulation system due to enquiries into large corruption scandals in 1992–1993 (Dente, Bobbio, and Spada, 2005). Moreover, in the last few years the economic trends have triggered tensions between decentralisation and recentralisation of economic activities (Bolocan Goldstein, 2018). Looking more closely, it is possible to highlight a series of relevant changes that the city underwent between the end of the 1980s and the beginning of the 1990s, which opened up a new phase (Organisation for Economic Co-operation and Development (OECD), 2006; Balducci, Fedeli, and Pasqui, 2011), with significant and lasting effects also in terms of the governance model.

For the economic dimension, the city (and, to a lesser extent, the metropolitan region) underwent a significant shift of the economic basis, from heavy and light manufacturing to a multi-faceted service economy, with growing strengths in the creativity sectors in general (fashion, design, media, etc.) and in finance (OECD, 2006). As far as the social dimension is concerned, the main trends have been the reduction of the population in the urban core, the ageing of this same population, a sharp increase in the number of migrants, a sharp decrease in the average household dimension, and in general, a weakening of the middle class – significantly worsened by the economic crisis that started in 2008 – and a retreat of the local welfare system, which had been one of the institutional strong points of the Milanese model and a test bed for inclusive citizenship in previous decades (Cucca and Ranci, 2016). Among large Italian cities, Milan has always had a distinct development trajectory and governance setting, characterised by the strong and effective presence of a multiplicity of diverse actors in the governance arena and a comparatively lesser role of local government in setting and actually implementing the urban agenda on many important issues (welfare, integration of migrants and disadvantaged populations, interventions in the urban peripheries, promotion of economic sectors and excellence, forms of innovation in labour and production, etc.). After the 1992–1993 rupture, for at least twenty years the governance regime was neatly directed at enhancing the global competitiveness of the city, through a mix of real estate development and providing (indirect) support to existing strengths in terms of the economic sectors.

After 2011, with a change in the political orientation of the city's government, a partial shift in attention occurred, putting some dimensions of social inclusion and the support of grassroots innovation back on the urban agenda. Within this context, in 2013 the Municipality launched a programme to support coworking spaces and makerspaces with measures both on the demand side (through vouchers) and on the supply side (through incentives for investment). The aim of the Municipality was to try at the same time to strengthen forms of innovation in the local economy and to facilitate the integration of precarious and disadvantaged workers, thus attempting to promote a peculiar form of innovation and inclusion (Polizzi and Vitale, 2017). Even if the economic basis of the Milan metropolitan region is still fairly diverse, and small- and medium-sized manufacturing industries are still present, in the urban core the tertiary economy is strongly prevalent, with a specific importance of sectors like creative industries and fashion, together with highly specialised services, such as health, higher education, research, and finance (Armondi and Bruzzese, 2017). As far as jobs are concerned, in 2011 the creative jobs in Milan amounted to 128,000, which was 16.5% of the total jobs (Bruzzese, 2015: 16–17).

It is in this economic and urban context that coworking spaces started to diffuse, initially as a totally private and market-led response to emerging needs, following a double trend of diffusion. In the first one, coworking started in smaller workspaces, frequently deriving from the reuse of existing architectural, design, or media firms, which needed to use their office space after the downsizing turn that took place after the 2008 crisis. The second trend concerned larger spaces explicitly devoted to coworking, often in conjunction with other new functions, such as makerspaces or start-up incubators (see also Chapter 5 in this book). One of the first examples in Milan was *Cowo*, opened in the Lambrate neighbourhood as early as 2008 by a communications agency, which then became the pivot of a large network of affiliated coworking spaces in Italy and Switzerland; but it was only after 2011 that coworking spaces started to be diffused within the city (Pacchi, 2018).

## Coworking spaces and urban space: location matters

A second line of enquiry in understanding the possible alternative paths of urban development associated with coworking spaces looked into the emerging features of coworking spaces as urban spaces, in terms of geographical location, forms of local clustering, and relationship with the surrounding neighbourhoods. Also in this case the picture which emerges in the two cities is considerably related to the main directions of urban development, showing context-specific signs of path dependency, while at the same time showing some remarkable similarities as well as some recurring features which definitely can be found across other European cities, but probably also beyond (Merkel, 2015). The distribution of coworking spaces in both cities is rather uneven. In Berlin, as shown by a map prepared within the *ProjektZukunft* (an initiative of the Berlin Senate Department for Economic Affairs, Technology and Research in 2016), coworking spaces tend to be clustered in a large area between Kreuzberg and Neukölln, in smaller numbers in Moabit and Wedding, and, more sparsely, across Prenzlauer Berg (Senatsverwaltung für Wirtschaft, Technologie und Forschung, 2016). They tend to be much rarer in the western areas of the city. As far as the figures are concerned, a survey also produced within the *ProjektZukunft* identified ninety-one coworking spaces in 2016. The spatial distribution of such spaces does not differ significantly from the distribution of the creative economy clusters, and it follows a quite recurrent path in which coworking spaces tend to be located in areas already 'colonised' by creative and cultural economy outposts.

Looking at some examples, one of the first spaces explicitly opened as a coworking space was *Betahaus*, which opened in 2009; its urban location is in the heart of Kreuzberg, near Oranienstrasse, where in subsequent years other coworking spaces opened (such as *Thinkfarm* and *Blogfabrik*), and near Moritzplatz where, in the same year, the grassroots community garden experiment of Prinzessinen Garten was started. The presence of a number of creative and cultural spots and grassroots initiatives in this area, together with a rich presence of retail outlets and cafés, makes the specific urban effects of each coworking space more difficult to isolate and detect; other coworking spaces have chosen less central and dense locations, as did *Agora*, opening off Hermannstrasse in Neukölln. Yet another model is *Factory*, a large coworking space hosting at the same time individual freelancers and corporate hubs, located in a highly symbolic location in Mitte, just off the former Berlin Wall. The picture that emerges is thus influenced at the same time by the attractiveness of specific urban locations in terms of creative and cultural milieu, and by the supply of rather cheap former industrial or tertiary space, thus involving real estate considerations. After the first pioneering coworking spaces opened up, there was a sensible facilitation effect, in that they triggered the establishment of similar spaces in the surrounding location.

In Milan coworking spaces tend to cluster in areas already characterised by the presence of cultural and creative industries, universities, and other centres of education and production of knowledge, and these functional features intersect with areas in which real estate prices are still relatively low, meaning that cheap vacant or semi-abandoned office or former industrial space is available (Mariotti, Pacchi, and Di Vita, 2017). The picture which thus emerges has some clusters located in particular in the northern part of the city, from Bovisa in the west, passing through via Padova-viale Monza, and touching the Lambrate area in the northeast. Parallel to this one, another much more central cluster aggregates around the quickly gentrifying area of Isola, from Sarpi to Garibaldi. In the southern part of the city the picture is different and much more scattered: there is a main agglomeration of coworking spaces in the Navigli-Savona-Tortona area, broadly corresponding to the existing creative production district, and minor ones (less significant in terms of clustering, even if individual coworking spaces are of a larger size) around Porta Romana-Tertulliano and Porta Vittoria.

Looking at specific locational geographies, an interesting spontaneous cluster emerged in the last few years around the Gorla neighbourhood, off Viale Monza in the northeastern periphery, in which *Sharewood, Unità di Produzione, Login*, and the first Milanese seat of *Talent Garden* (a much larger one opened up in 2016 in a former printing press in Porta Romana) found their location, together with makerspace *WeMake*. This former artisan neighbourhood offered a lot of empty industrial and tertiary space, and the diffusion of new workspaces has contributed to revitalising the area, bringing a dynamic urban population and enhancing exchanges (Mariotti, Pacchi, and Di Vita, 2017). Similarly to the Berlin case, it is more difficult to identify the specific urban effects of individual coworking spaces or clusters located in areas already characterised by a density of cultural and creativity operators, such as Isola or the Tortona area. In the latter in particular, the initiatives connected to *Fuori Salone* – the fringe events to the yearly furniture fair – have been significantly modifying the urban population and rhythms of use in the last few years, thus creating an urban environment specifically favourable to the diffusion of new workspaces. In both cities it is possible to read the overlapping geographies of coworking location and the diffusion of gentrification (Diappi, 2009; Holm, 2013; an de Meulen and Mitze, 2014; Giorgetta, 2017), but since the two phenomena have very different temporalities and rhythms of evolution (longer cycles for the diffusion of gentrification and shorter timeframes for the location of most coworking spaces in both cities), it is difficult to make grounded statements about causalities.

The total number of coworking spaces is not easy to define, in the absence of a univocal and shared definition of what such space is, nevertheless we can use as a proxy the number of spaces certified within a public register set up by the Milan City Council for the supporting measures we mentioned earlier, which is sixty-four (Comune di Milano, 2016). We can imagine therefore that in total the city hosts between 80 and 100 spaces devoted exclusively or jointly to coworking.

If we look more generally at the *urban* dimension, we can define urban here in two ways: one has to do with the geographical location and the relationship that each coworking space establishes with the surrounding urban environment, the other has to do with the intrinsically political nature of urban space and the urban dimension. From this perspective, Polizzi and Vitale think for instance that, in the Milan case, coworking spaces have had indirect urban effects because:

> Many of the fablabs and coworking spaces supported by the Milan Municipality did not produce only intrinsic effects, per se, in their direct functioning, on the contrary they generated sense, pressure and innovation

> in Milan in relational terms, because they have been used to make the professional training system evolve, to qualify it and to reduce drop-outs.
> (Polizzi and Vitale, 2017: 141)

At the same time, while such urban, indirect effects are extremely difficult to acknowledge and to assess, in both cities coworking spaces tend to share traditional features of office space, and to remain closed and quite separated from their urban environments, both on a small and a larger scale.

Lastly, if we look at *space*, its features, organisation, and role, it is notable that on a global level the number of small coworking spaces – those with less than ten members – decreased significantly over the last year (from 23% to 12%), while today nearly one in five coworking spaces has 150 or more members (one year ago it was 13%). This is another clear sign of the global trend, more visible in some countries than in others, towards the diffusion of larger coworking facilities, frequently associated with the presence of large market operators (in some cases from the real estate market sector) (Deskmag, 2017). This trend, if confirmed also in European countries (at the moment it is more readable in the United States), would imply a clear discontinuity with the starting phase of the coworking diffusion, in that the grassroots and small-scale nature of many spaces has clearly influenced the way in which coworking spaces are organised, the type of coworkers they attract, and the type of interaction that characterises such spaces (Mariotti, Pacchi, and Di Vita, 2017). In Berlin, coworking spaces emerged out of an intense phase of urban innovation and experimentation in different fields, and are therefore strictly connected with informality and creativity; in Milan, coworking spaces respond more clearly to market mechanisms, but in both cases they have shown the need to identify and invent distinctively new workspaces which correspond to new forms of labour. A common element between the two urban contexts is the need for precarious knowledge workers to find spaces-in-common as a sort of 'shelter' in the face of the difficulties of an extremely competitive but scarcely endowed labour market. This is extremely visible both in Milan and Berlin, because even if the economic bases and the development of knowledge-based, creative, and cultural production in the two cities has been extremely different, as we have seen, the emerging characters of the labour market for highly skilled knowledge workers are very similar.

## Coworking spaces and political emergence

The last question which characterises the Berlin and Milan contexts differently, but with great importance in both cases, concerns the role that knowledge workers play in the contemporary labour market and their ability to raise a voice and to build places of political representation. With the lack of traditional forms of political representation for freelance, precarious knowledge workers (Allegri and Ciccarelli, 2013), we can ask whether shared workspaces such as coworking spaces may contribute to strengthen forms of collective identification and facilitate the construction of new forms of (political) representation. We may look at the open tension between coworking spaces as a coping strategy for precarious (knowledge) workers, and as spaces of political opportunity to challenge labour market dynamics by building new forms of voice and representation.

In general, the rise of this new precariat is connected to the reorganisation of forms of labour in the knowledge economy, resulting, as mentioned in the introduction, in an increasing fragmentation of employment relationships and precarisation of the labour force. If this phenomenon concerns both ends of the labour market (low-skilled workers employed in the service sector as well as high-skilled ones, characterised by higher competences and networks), knowledge workers in fact share some features with a larger population of workers subject to permanent flexibility and 'desperately in search of emancipation and equality' (Allegri and Ciccarelli, 2013: 11). If we look specifically at urban and metropolitan contexts, in which knowledge workers tend to concentrate, the diffusion of start-ups and freelancers – the so-called 'lone eagles' (Moriset, 2013) – and the increasing definition of small and flexible management entities (Gandini, 2015) as the most diffused actors in a distributed labour context raise unprecedented issues concerning the right to the city – as a right to access, to be, and to participate in the city – and forms of local resistance for such a workforce (Marcuse, 2009; Pugalis and Giddings, 2011). Differently from what happened in the past, the struggle for basic rights connected to labour and the related forms of resistance tend to be developed at the moment on a purely individual level. These forms of resistance therefore have difficulties in resulting in forms of structured representation, in the forms which were typical of the industrial era, because a thorough process of collective identification of such actors is completely lacking: 'The price for freedom and serendipity paid by many freelancers and creative entrepreneurs – categories who represent the lion's share of coworking creators and users – is often precariousness: low or fluctuant income, fragile health insurance and retirement scheme' (Moriset, 2014: 20).

In the words of some coworking managers interviewed in Milan, freelance and precarious knowledge workers are so much under pressure in an extremely competitive and fragmented labour market that they are forced to overlook every possibility of raising a collective voice and of self-organising in terms of rights. This happens even when some possibilities of collective discussion would be at hand, such as the activities carried out in Milan by the freelance workers association ACTA. This organisation, which proposes meetings, training, and counselling activities across innovative and hybrid workspaces in Milan (and other Italian cities), is based, not by chance, in a coworking space in the city; moreover, other coworking spaces have been organising meetings and seminars targeting freelancers and their problems (like the spontaneous agglomeration of coworking and makerspaces located in Gorla, in the northeastern periphery). In all these cases, such initiatives remain sporadic and can be seen as exceptions, in a world usually characterised by an absence of forms of organised voice. In Berlin, in which, very differently from Milan, there has been the mobilisation of 'cultural producers' in many urban struggles, in particular those connected to urban regeneration, gentrification, and the commodification of culture (Novy and Colomb, 2013; Gualini, 2016), apparently the same intensity does not characterise forms of collective identification of knowledge workers generally. Cultural and creative operators, for instance, have been among those mobilising against the huge *MediaSpree* project (Gualini, 2016), a large and complex urban regeneration project aimed at transforming the two banks of the river Spree in Kreuzberg and Friedrichshain into a media district animated by large international corporate actors, combined with high-end housing; but the same intensity, in terms of ability to raise a voice, seldom can be found in precarious workers' representation.

## Conclusions: under which conditions can coworking spaces be considered alternative urban spaces?

In line with the questions which opened this chapter, and impinging on the short empirical explorations, the concluding remarks propose a critical discussion about the possibly alternative nature of coworking spaces, and some reflections about the conditions under which this may enact a transformative potential with effects which go beyond the individual workspace. The main question this chapter has attempted to answer by looking into the diffusion of coworking in two urban contexts is to what extent coworking spaces can be considered alternative to mainstream urban workspaces and which are the emerging features of this alternative dimension. Looking at the perspective this book proposes on the concept of 'alternative' in urban spaces, we can explore the possibility that coworking spaces may enact alternative paths 'through a more agonistic politics based on outreach and cooperation' (Fisker et al. in this book, p. 00). Literature on coworking has extensively discussed the centrality of horizontal and cooperative relationships among coworkers within such spaces (Moriset, 2013; Capdevila, 2014; Parrino, 2015), and it has also critically examined the real ability of such spaces to build shared spaces. In particular, Parrino (2015), in her in-depth study of different types of coworking spaces, underlines how physical proximity per se does not guarantee a significant flow of information and the strengthening of cooperative relationships among coworkers, but instead the proactive presence of an exchange platform and activities on the part of coworking mangers in this direction are necessary:

> On the whole, the results of the study contradict the image of coworking spaces as places for 'natural' relationships, collaborations and interactions among workers. Indeed, according to what has already been stated, elements of organisational and social proximity play a pivotal role in stimulating collaboration among coworkers and in promoting exchange of other forms of knowledge; however, on the contrary, we cannot say that these kind of connections arise within spaces characterised by the mere co-presence of coworkers.
>
> (Parrino, 2015: 271)

As far as processes of identification and representation of independent workers located in coworking spaces are concerned, we can say that at the moment they seem to be difficult to detect in both cities, with some small exceptions, being still at an embryonic stage. Thus, the emerging innovation is a double-edged phenomenon, because it is not clear yet to what extent coworking spaces have the potential to become places for a new collective identification and to produce forms of empowerment, or else if they will remain islands in a sea hostile to independent freelance knowledge workers, in which growing forms of social, professional, and economic polarisation will perpetuate and intensify. Looking at the two empirical contexts analysed in this chapter, it emerges that it is not the coworking model per se which may trigger a significant change in the development potential of these workers, but rather the (social, economic, and institutional) conditions and the type of urban environment in which coworking spaces are rooted that may determine a different trajectory. In particular, the differences in terms of scale (from a few seats to more than 1,000, with a significant trend of growth for the larger ones), sectorial specialisation (media, digital jobs, etc.), and mix of functions can play a significant role in articulating the question.

Even if the coworking phenomenon alludes to forms of cooperation and solidarity, the forms of resistance to domination and alienation for these workers, as we have seen in both Milan and Berlin, to the systematic expropriation of their resources, creativity, and freedom, are mainly carried out purely at the individual level, enacted through a strenuous defence of autonomy, independence, and freedom in their work models and in the patterns of relationships with their clients. There is thus a risk that coworking spaces, which originally emerged as a sort of 'sheltering' space for precarious knowledge workers, are in the course of becoming just another type of urban commodity, without having provided to those same knowledge workers a real arena for political discussion about their rights in an increasingly difficult labour market. If this trend proves to be real in the next few years, this in turn will open up questions regarding local authorities that support the diffusion of coworking spaces as a strategy to create and strengthen local jobs (even if in very small numbers) and the enthusiasm of knowledge workers themselves, who have not been using the possibility of coming together to raise a common, shared, political voice and might find themselves even lonelier in the future.

## References

Allegri, G. and Ciccarelli, R. (2013) *Il quinto stato. Perché il lavoro indipendente è il nostro futuro: Precari, autonomi, free-lance per una nuova società* [The Fifth State. Why Independent Labour is Our Future: Precarious Workers, Autonomous Workers, Freelancers for a New Society]. Milan: Ponte alle Grazie.

an de Meulen, P. and Mitze, T. (2014) Exploring the Spatial Variation in Quality-Adjusted Rental Prices and Identifying Hot Spots in Berlin's Residential Property Market. *Regional Studies, Regional Science*, 1(1), 310–328.

Anderson, C. (2012) *Makers: The New Industrial Revolution.* New York: Random House Business Books.

Armondi, S. and Bruzzese, A. (2017) Contemporary Production and Urban Change: The Case of Milan. *Journal of Urban Technology*, 24(3), 27–45.

Armondi, S. and Di Vita, S. (2018) Which Milan? Setting the Scene for Reflecting Urban Decline, Resilience, and Change. In Armondi, S. and Di Vita, S. (eds) *Milan. Productions, Spatial Patterns and Urban Change.* London and New York: Routledge, 7–35.

Balducci, A., Fedeli, V., and Pasqui, G. (2011) *Strategic Planning for Contemporary Urban Regions. City of Cities: A Project for Milan.* Aldershot: Ashgate.

Blume, J. (2014) Prekär aber selbstbestimmt? Fallstricke der Kreativwirtshaft [Precarious But Self-Determined? Pitfalls of the Creative Economy]. In Holm A. (ed) *Reclaim Berlin. Soziale Kämpfe in der neoliberalen Stadt.* Berlin and Hamburg: Assoziation A, 105–126.

Bolocan Goldstein, M. (2018) Urban Regionalization and Metropolitan Resurgence: Discontinuity and Persistence of a Spatial Dialectic. In Armondi, S. and Di Vita, S. (eds) *Milan: Productions, Spatial Patterns and Urban Change.* London and New York: Routledge, 36–47.

Bruzzese, A. (2015) *Addensamenti creativi, trasformazioni urbane e Fuorisalone: Casi milanesi tra riqualificazione fisica e trasformazione di immagine* [Creative Thickening, Urban Transformations and Fuorisalone: Milanese Cases between Physical Redevelopment and Image Transformation]. Sant'Arcangelo di Romagna: Maggioli.

Capdevila, I. (2013) *Knowledge Dynamics in Localized Communities: Coworking Spaces as Microclusters.* Available at SSRN: https://ssrn.com/abstract=2414121.

Capdevila, I. (2014) Coworking Spaces and the Localized Dynamics of Innovation. The Case of Barcelona. Working Paper presented at the XXIVe Conférence Internationale de Management Stratégique [24th Conference of Strategic Management]. 3–5 June, Paris.

Cappelli, P. and Keller, J.R. (2013) Classifying Work in the New Economy. *Academy of Management Review*, 38(4), 575–596.

Colomb, C. (2012) *Staging the New Berlin. Place Marketing and the Politics of Urban Reinvention Post-1989.* London and New York: Routledge.

Comune di Milano, Fondazione Brodolini (2016) Milan White Paper on Social Innovation. Accelerating Milan's Local Ecosystem for Social Innovation. Unpublished report.

Cucca, R. and Ranci, C. (eds) (2016) *Unequal Cities in Europe: The Challenge of Post-Industrial Transition in Times of Austerity.* London and New York: Routledge.

Dente, B., Bobbio, L., and Spada, A. (2005) A Tale of Two Cities. *DISP*, 162, 41–52.

Deskmag (2017) Global Coworking Survey 2017. Available at: www.deskmag.com/en/the-complete-2017-coworking-forecast-more-than-one-million-people-work-from-14000-coworking-spaces-s.

Diappi, L. (ed) (2009) *Rigenerazione urbana e ricambio sociale. Gentrification in atto nei quartieri storici italiani* [Urban Regeneration and Social Turnover. Ongoing Gentrification in Historical Italian Neighbourhoods]. Milano: Franco Angeli.

Gandini, A. (2015) The Rise of Coworking Spaces: A Literature Review. *Ephemera: Theory and Politics in Organization*, 15(1), 193–205.

Gershenfeld, N. (2005) *Fab: The Coming Revolution on your Desktop – From Personal Computers to Personal Fabrication.* New York: Basic Books.

Giorgetta, S. (2017) *Mapping the Change. An Analytical Approach to Identify Gentrification Processes in the Milanese Context.* Master's thesis. Politecnico di Milano.

Gualini, E. (ed) (2015) *Planning/Conflict. Critical Perspectives on Contentious Urban Developments*. New York and Abingdon: Routledge.

Gualini, E. (2016) Contentious Mobilization and the Challenge of Reflexivity in Strategic Urban Development Projects: Reflections on Planning Conflict in the Case of Mediaspree, Berlin. In Del Romero Renau, L. (ed) *Conflicts in the City. Reflections on Urban Unrest*. New York: Nova Publishers, 43–66.

Hager, C. (2007) Three Decades of Protest in Berlin Land-Use Planning, 1975–2005. *German Studies Review*, 30(1), 55–74.

Holm, A. (2013) Berlin's Gentrification Mainstream. In Bernt, M., Grell, B., and Holm, A. (eds) *The Berlin Reader. A Compendium on Urban Change and Activism*. Bielefeld: Transcript.

Holm, A. and Kuhn, A. (2011) Squatting and Urban Renewal: The Interaction of Squatter Movements and Strategies of Urban Restructuring in Berlin. *International Journal of Urban and Regional Research*, 35(3), 644–658.

Isin, E. and Ruppert, E. (2015) *Being Digital Citizens*. London and New York: Rowman & Littlefield.

Kalandides, A. (2007) *In Search of Berlin's Competitive Advantage – Marketing the Creative City*. Paper presented at the EUGEO2 2007 First International Conference on the Geography of Europe. 20–23 August, Amsterdam.

Klaas, Z. (2013–2014) *Coworking + Connectivity in Berlin*. Report Neurus Research Exchange (unpublished research exchange project). University of Illinois at Urbana Champaign.

Krätke, S. (2004) City of Talents? Berlin's Regional Economy, Socio-Spatial Fabric and 'Worst Practice' Urban Governance. *International Journal of Urban and Regional Research*, 28(3), 511–529.

Lange, B. (2011) Professionalization in Space: Social-Spatial Strategies of Culturepreneurs in Berlin. *Entrepreneurship & Regional Development*, 23(3–4), 259–279.

Magatti, M. and Sapelli, G. (eds) (2012) *Progetto Milano. Idee e proposte per la città di domain* [Project Milan. Ideas and Proposals for the City of Tomorrow]. Milano: Bruno Mondadori.

Marcuse, P. (2009) From Critical Urban Theory to the Right to the City. *City*, 13(2–3), 185–197.

Mariotti, I., Pacchi, C., and Di Vita, S. (2017) Coworking Spaces in Milan: Location Patterns and Urban Effects. *Journal of Urban Technology*, 24(3), 47–66.

Mayer, M. (2013) New Lines of Division in the New Berlin. In Bernt, M., Grell, B., and Holm, A. (eds) *The Berlin Reader. A Compendium on Urban Change and Activism*. Bielefeld: Transcript, 95–106.

McCann, P. (2008) Globalization and Economic Geography: The World Is Curved, Not Flat. *Cambridge Journal of Regions, Economy and Society*, 1, 351–370.

Merkel, J. (2015) Coworking in the City. *Ephemera*, 15(2), 121–139.

Moriset, B. (2014) *Building New Places of the Creative Economy: The Rise of Coworking Spaces*. Paper presented at the 2nd Geography of Innovation International Conference. 23–24 January, Utrecht University.

Novy, J. and Colomb, C. (2013) Struggling for the Right to the (Creative) City in Berlin and Hamburg: New Urban Social Movements, New 'Spaces of Hope'? *International Journal of Urban and Regional Research*, 37(5), 1816–1838.

Organisation for Economic Co-operation and Development (OECD). (2006) *OECD Territorial Reviews. Milan, Italy*. Paris: OECD Publishing.

Pacchi, C. (2018) Sharing Economy: Makerspaces, Co-working Spaces, Hybrid Workplaces, and New Social Practices. In Armondi, S. and Di Vita, S. (eds) *Milan. Productions, Spatial Patterns and Urban Change*. London: Routledge, 73–83.

Pacchi, C. and Pasqui, G. (2015) Urban Planning without Conflicts? Observations on the Nature and Conditions for Urban Contestation in the Case of Milan. In Gualini, E. (ed) *Planning/Conflict. Critical Perspectives on Contentious Urban Developments*. London and New York: Routledge, 79–98.

Parrino, L. (2015) Coworking: Assessing the Role of Proximity in Knowledge Exchange. *Knowledge Management Research & Practice*, 13, 261–271.

Perl, S. and Steffen, E. (2015) *Abriss und Aufbruch am Kottbusser Tor* [*Demolition and Protest at Kottbusser Tor*]. Berlin: FHXB Friedrichshain-Kreuzberg Museum, 1945–2015.

Polizzi, E. and Vitale, T. (2017) Governo collaborativo e catene relazionali di innovazione. Spunti a partire dal caso di Milano [Collaborative Governance and Relational Chains. Suggestions from the Milan Case]. *Quaderni Rassegna Sindacale*, 2, 129–147.

Pugalis, L. and Giddings, B. (2011) A Renewed Right to Urban Life: A Twenty-First Century Engagement with Lefebvre's Initial 'Cry'. *Architectural Theory Review*, 16(3), 278–295.

Schmidt, S., Brinks, V., and Brinkhoff, S. (2014) Innovation and Creativity Labs in Berlin. Organizing Temporary Spatial Configurations for Innovations. *Zeitschrift für Wirtschaftsgeographie*, 58(4), 232–247.

Scott, A.J. (2012) *A World in Emergence. Cities and Regions in the 21st Century*. Northampton: Edward Elgar.

Senatsverwaltung für Wirtschaft, Energie und Betriebe (2017) *Cluster IKT, Medien & Kreativwirtschaft. Auswertung der Berliner Wirtschaftsdaten für die Jahre 2014/2015* [ICT, Media and Creative Economy Cluster. Analysis of the Berlin Economic Data for the Years 2014/2015]. Available at: https://projektzukunft.berlin.de/fileadmin/user_upload/Wirtschaftsdaten_FINAL_Final.pdf.

Senatsverwaltung für Wirtschaft, Technologie und Forschung (2016) *Coworking Spaces in Berlin. An Overview*. Available at: https://projektzukunft.berlin.de/fileadmin/user_upload/pdf/Liste_Coworking/Liste_Coworking_Spaces_Mai_2017.pdf.

Spinuzzi, C. (2012) Working Alone, Together: Coworking as Emergent Collaborative Activity. *Journal of Business and Technical Communication*, 26(4), 399–441.

Standing, G. (2011) *The Precariat. The New Dangerous Class*. London and New York: Bloomsbury Academic.

Zukin, S. (2006) David Harvey on Cities. In Castree, N. and Gregory, D. (eds) *David Harvey. A Critical Reader*. Malden: Blackwell, 102–120.

# 5 *Deus ex machina*

## Makerspaces in Milan and their transformative potential

*Letizia Chiappini and Petter Törnberg*

### Introduction

Spaces organised around the practice of "making" are becoming an increasingly frequent sighting in cities around the world, in particular in Europe and North America. These "makerspaces" tend to provide access to a variety of equipment, including 3D printers, laser cutters, computer numerical control (CNC) machines, soldering irons, and even sewing machines, to feed the recent wave of do-it-yourself (DIY) culture. In the emerging literature, however, these spaces are portrayed as much more than merely a new locus for craftwork and urban social encounters. They have become the focal point for a growing discourse that claims urban economies of the future will be radically different from those of today and yesterday. In this discourse, the spaces are acclaimed as the driver of a fundamentally alternative mode of production, with its own distinctive spaces of work, and the potential to reinvent the industrial economy, the city, and urban governance structures.

It is hard to imagine that such narratives would not contain a hint of the exaggerated optimism and hyperbolic storylines that have often tended to surround the emergence of new technologies. But this is exacerbated by the lack of a competing and more serious social scientific understanding of the makerspace phenomenon. The literature broadly tends towards an over-reliance on theoretical speculation and conceptual discussion, and a lack of grounding in empirical evidence. Due to this, even the most fundamental questions – such as what even defines a makerspace – remain either unanswered or contested, leaving it far from clear what, if any, role these "makers" will play in shaping urban economies and urban life in the future.

This chapter aims to contribute to ameliorating this situation, by looking at the claims made in the literature in the light of an in-depth case study. The chapter first provides a brief overview of some of the narratives and claims made in the literature surrounding the maker movement and their suggested transformative potential. These narratives are then elucidated through an ethnographic case study on the maker movement in Milan – a city where makerspaces and maker-related activities have proliferated substantially in recent years. The fieldwork, conducted from 2013 to 2017, provides a detailed picture of how the maker movement has evolved in this particular urban context. This provides an empirical foundation for a more informed discussion of the claims and speculations regarding the nature and transformative potential of the maker movement, enabling us to begin moving towards a more nuanced and less hyperbolic understanding of the role of these emerging urban practices.

## Makerspaces and the dreams of a coming revolution

The attention given to makerspaces arguably has its origins in the more established peer-to-peer practices within software development, whose affordances and demands have enabled new forms of organisation and production processes. In software production, the hierarchical and top-down organisational characteristics of factory production generally have been replaced by decentralised peer practices, as epitomised by the open source movement. The emergence of technologies such as the 3D printer, capable of turning information into artefacts, implies the formation of a direct link that extends the logic of the information realm into the physical world. This development thus has been seen as poised to expand the logic and conditions of software production also into the realm of physical production. This has inspired several authors (e.g. Benkler 2006; Benkler and Nissenbaum 2006; Rifkin 2011, 2014) to associate peer production with a coming – or even ongoing – "third industrial revolution" (Hatch 2013; Troxler 2013), in which peer production is appropriated into various reformist liberal (e.g. Bauwens 2005) or revolutionary Marxist (e.g. Rigi 2013) grammars. This literature suggests that "these new producers will reinvent the industrial economy" (Anderson 2012: 229) and that they are "poised to overhaul our political economy in unprecedented ways" (Bauwens 2005: 1).

The literature on peer production as a technology network for useful social production is flourishing, particularly in the field of science and technology studies (Smith 2014). The argument here is that features of technology networks are relevant in practices such as participatory design and critical making (Tosh 2008; Ratto 2011; Disalvo 2012; Maxigas 2012; Smith et al. 2013). As such, the call for alternative production is embodied between prototyping activities and democratisation of production, in the so-called *critical making*. Again, Smith (2014: 6) insists "prototypes provided a practical means to engage people in political debate about the relationships of technology in society". This statement is based on the assumption whereby prototyping technology, for instance, producing software and microelectronics, remains a focal activity, but is presented as a catalysing device for mobilisation around associated political, economic, and social issues (Cooley 1987).

These narratives furthermore tend to forecast the replacement of top-down and disciplined production associated with large-scale factory production with a "locally organized, decentralized, scattered production in small production facilities" (Sylvester and Döring 2013: 223). The new factories will be a host of various forms of "open creative labs", such as coworking spaces, makerspaces, fablabs, and urban living labs. The common features of such spaces are said to be openness, peer production, knowledge-sharing, and collaborative practices (Schmidt et al. 2014, 2016), which delineate an alternative economic and spatial imaginary. Furthermore, when imagining the possibility of an alternative economic development, it is important to take into consideration the debate on the role of these new forms of shared-work spaces in the future of urban economies. The question of physical proximity in determining forms of collective innovation and distributed agency has been extensively discussed in economic geography literature and innovation studies (e.g. Hansen 2014; Capdevila 2013; Cohendet et al. 2014).

A central notion in this literature is that "open creative labs" in general, and makerspaces in particular, constitute local anchors for both local and global communities (Capdevila 2014). In short, the spaces function as meeting spaces that enable communities to be bound together, thus providing platforms for the formation of new forms of collective agency. This local anchoring enables them to constitute the basis for the development of social practices that also go outside the realm of production, and into other aspects of (urban) social life. The spaces are thought to be the foundation for a movement of grassroots activism that would bring the spaces into relevance also within the realm of governance, education, and welfare, laying the ground not only for new forms of production, but also for "an emerging collaborative age" (Rifkin 2011: 5). Some authors, in other words, see makerspaces as providing bottom-up and decentralised alternatives to traditional top-down government-organised services (e.g. Bauwens 2005; Gershenfeld 2005, 2012; Rifkin 2011). Peer production is seen as enabling a form of self-organised welfare system, which may provide an alternative to the current forms of welfare. One may thus extract three claims regarding the role and transformative potential of the maker movement from this literature, which we will make more explicit in order to enable them to be put under empirical scrutiny.

First, makerspaces are seen as *alternative social spaces* that bring a new transformative potential to urban social life. This claim goes beyond merely the provision of a meeting space, in that an alternative social space should also provide some form of protection from the pressures of market forces (Bathelt and Cohendet 2014: 3). The notion of an alternative social space implies not only the potential for meetings, but also that there is some level of protection from the powers that be (Benkler 2006; Rifkin 2011; Anderson 2012). Such social spaces are seen as central for creating the possibilities to develop alternative practices and foster oppositional virtues and consciousness.

Second, makerspaces are seen as providing an *alternative mode of production* that is thought to fundamentally transform the economic system or, at the very least, the economic imaginary (Smith 2014). While this claim comes in a number of different versions, we extract from them the common claim that the mode of production supported by makerspaces is challenging the current economic system. The decentralised and collaborative form of production associated with makerspaces is thus not merely a continuation of current economic conditions, but something fundamentally alternative (Dougherty 2012; Maxigas 2012; Troxler 2013).

Third, the spaces are seen as providing alternatives also outside of the realm of production. The maker movement is suggested to be capable of providing an alternative to existing systems for the provision of public services by organising services, for example, for education, healthcare, and care for the elderly (e.g. Dawkins 2011; Torri 2017). Again, we take this to imply that the maker movement is not merely a continuation of, but a *challenge* and *alternative* to, the current welfare regime.

It is primarily these three claims that we will cast light on through the following case study on makerspaces in Milan.

## Makerspaces in Milan

We will now look in detail at the maker movement as it has played out in Milan. This section is based on an ethnographic study combining participant observation (documented in field notes), document analysis, and qualitative interviews conducted in Milan between 2015 and 2017. The main data were collected from qualitative interviews; the informants were makers, civil servants, and aldermen within the Milanese metropolitan area. The section refers also to several interviews about the maker movement concentrated in Milan, conducted between 2013 and 2017, and partially used in Chiappini and d'Ovidio (2017), Chiappini and Anselmi (2017), and Anselmi and Chiappini (2017). All included quotes from interviews and statements have been translated from the original Italian by the authors.

### *The Milanese context*

In the past decade, urban governance in Milan has been characterised by the significant and widespread involvement of civil society (i.e. non-governmental organisations (NGOs), charities, foundations, and other third sector – voluntary, community, non-profit – organisations) compared to other Italian cities. Moreover, the private sector occupies an important position in terms of investments and agenda-setting within Milanese urban governance. Private actors tend to play a crucial role in the project implementation process, in particular in policy areas such as welfare, culture, and urban services (Chapter 4 in this volume; Armondi and Bruzzese 2017). The recent transformation of Milan has been supported by strong political action and the definition of a new urban agenda, in which coworking and makerspaces have become policy subjects (see also Chapter 4). In this context, the maker scene has been subsumed within a wider political strategy oriented towards revitalisation of the local economy and enhancement of social cohesion.[1]

In 2013 the first open call addressed to the new phenomenon of making was created under the label of "Creative Maker". The Municipality of Milan initiated significant investment in the development of coworking and makerspaces: in 2015 the Central Directorate for labour policies, economic development, and universities, Economic Innovation Sector, Smart City, and University allocated €500,000 for measures in favour of coworking and €300,000 for makerspaces and fablabs. The local authority furthermore has adopted soft policy tools to support the dissemination of makerspaces, fablabs, and coworking spaces. First, the Municipality provides direct economic and financial subsidies: delivery of economic incentives in favour of individual subjects to set up the lab and delivery of economic incentives in favour of suppliers of services already qualified (i.e. support to the space, improvement of machinery, etc.). Second, there is a list of qualified spaces within the city of Milan, inclusion on which constitutes an important source of public visibility and credibility for the makerspace. The requirements for inclusion on the list are: the availability of digital manufacturing equipment; training courses for the use of machines; public opening times of at least twenty-five hours per week; and a website with information on services, initiatives, timetables, fares, etc.[2]

The intervention by the local state apparatus is twofold. It includes the development of productive and cultural renewal of the city and encouragement of extensive processes of urban regeneration (d'Ovidio and Rabbiosi 2017), with the ultimate hope of creating job opportunities. In general, the new urban economy is considered by the local state and by makers as an alternative driver of urban development, pertaining to the organisation of work and the production and provision of goods and services on an urban scale. This refers, in particular, to the horizontal organisation of work, low-intensity production for local markets (Bialsky et al. 2015), non-commercialised cultural activities, digital manufacturing, and "prosumption". Makerspaces are, by these terms, new productive centralities located in urban areas. In the case of Milan, makerspaces are often scattered public-private hubs, community labs, and open-creative *ateliers* (Armondi and Bruzzese 2017). The local government deploys different existing urban resources, like abandoned buildings, brownfield sites, and former ex-industrial sites, both in central urban areas and outside of the inner city. Beyond the widely explored question of the transformation of and spatial opportunity provided by the large areas made available by the downsizing and re-localisation of Fordist production plants, today there is a need to deepen the phenomenon of reuse of minute and diffused spaces present in the mixed urban fabric in relation to the settlement demand for new types of companies: hybrids between research, production, and consumption of various kinds of goods and services, among which the maker laboratories are also situated.

The political strategy implemented in Milan, as a whole, is framed through the notions of a "smart and sharing city", in which a need to define a new urban agenda with a medium-term horizon emerges (Vitale and Polizzi 2017). At the same time, in view of the establishment of the new Metropolitan City of Milan, the urban policy system – supporting innovation – requires an expansion on a scale appropriate to the recent socioeconomic and spatial dynamics. This is necessary in order to take advantage of the spread of new workplaces as an opportunity for territorial rebalancing and, therefore, for containing an uneven metropolisation process that penalises many sectors of the Milanese urban region.

### *The role of makerspaces in Milan*

In Italy overall, 27.5% of makerspaces are concentrated in the larger cities: 20.8% are located in Milan, Rome, and Bologna, and the rest are distributed among seventy-five small- and medium-sized cities. The Milanese metropolitan area has the highest concentration of makerspaces of any metropolitan area.[3] There are ten makerspaces registered in the official list on the municipal website, but there are also additional creative *ateliers* and open creative labs that are not part of this list. Besides the makerspaces that had their origin in private initiatives, there are also spaces initiated by institutions, such as the Polifactory within the campus of the Polytechnic University of Milan located in the former workers' district of Bovisa, and the Tinkering Zone at the National Museum of Science and Technology in the central area of Sant'Ambrogio.

Looking at the geographical distribution of the makerspaces (Map 5.1) allows us to see whether makerspaces cluster in specific types of neighbourhoods. In the design district (Zona Tortona/Porta Genova) southeast of Milan, we can clearly observe a small cluster of makerspaces and several coworking spaces located within the same area.[4] Furthermore, we have collected data to complement the map with information about the kinds of buildings used to house these spaces. For instance, WeMake and OpenDot are located in ex-industrial areas that now form a residentialised part of the city, yet close to railroads and infrastructural nodes, which provide a high level of accessibility. When asked why they chose this location, one of the co-founders of WeMake motivated it with the low rents and the availability of spacious facilities. Unlike the two above-mentioned makerspaces, the new Digital Arts and Manufacturing Academy (D.A.M.A.) is located in the core of the city.

Despite the physical proximity between maker labs, the creation of the community and build up of their individual reputations through self-branding activities primarily takes place online. As one of the interviewees claimed:

> We are part of many online networks, like MakeinItaly, FabAcademy, and FabLabNet, also the global events like hackaton, Fab10 in Barcelona, MakerFaire around the world are front stage in which you can show your products ... We are different in terms of skills and missions. In Milan, a makerspace focuses more on training, workshops. We do not do that much. Our main business is prototyping, we are good at that.
>
> (Interviewee no. 3 – MioCugino makerspace)

Makerspaces are far from uniform entities, but rather notably heterogeneous. If we sketch out a simple typology of three Milanese makerspaces, we notice that they differ not only in size and participation, but also in more fundamental

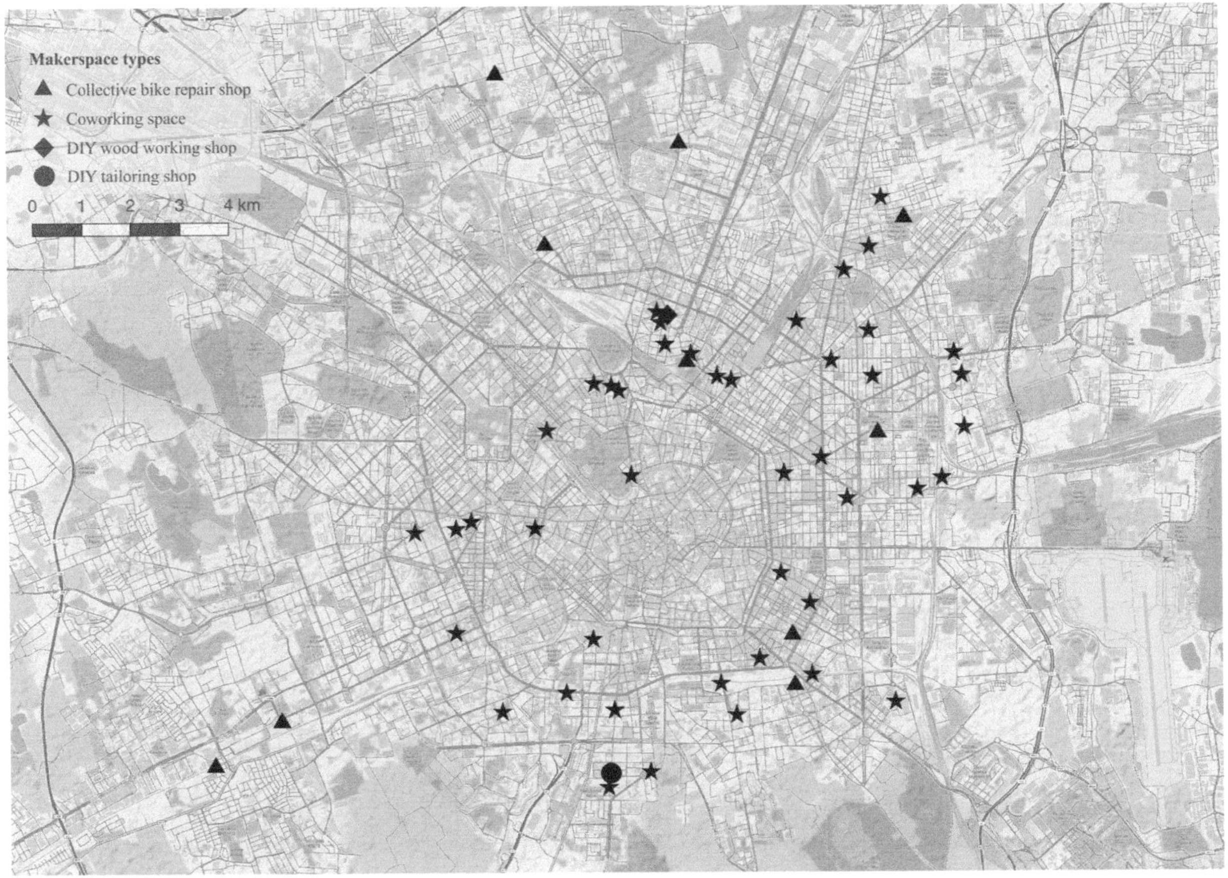


*Map 5.1* Spatial distribution of makerspaces in Milan

aspects, such as their material stakeholders, their functioning, output goals, and the type of activities that they organise (see Table 5.1). One may distinguish two main categories: makerspaces that are community-oriented and those that are market-oriented. The majority of our informants, however, suggested that all makerspaces share an associative side; the internal governance, in principle, is based on horizontal and informal organisation of work. For instance, OpenDot is a makerspace with many founding members and a variegated portfolio of projects, during an interview one of its founders asserted:

> The associative side is how you manage it. There are informal rules. For example, if you need a machine, say so. So if you want to use the same machine the same day, you know that it's not available. If you are not able to use that machine, you start a basic training course here and if you have doubts ask, we are always around. You pay a card for management fees and the insurance. Plus, free workshop and training for the dissemination of culture.
>
> (Interviewee no. 5 – OpenDot makerspace)

Besides this common focus on the associative side, makerspaces generate part of their profit through membership, workshops, and training courses. They are a fortiori shared-work spaces; just as the majority of the coworking spaces require you to pay for a desk, in the makerspace you sign up for membership depending on your needs. If you want to produce your own

*Table 5.1* Characterisation of selected Milanese makerspaces

| *Makerspaces* | *Functioning* | *Material Stakeholders* | *Current Output* |
|---|---|---|---|
| **WeMake (2013)**<br>Private funds from two co-founders (+ funds from Municipality) | Association with membership and Ltd. Voucher and "candies" for using machinery | *Login* coworking space. Lombardy region. Cultural foundations | *OpenCare* (EU – Horizon 2020). *PublicProduct* workshop |
| **OpenDot (2014)**<br>Private funds and many co-founders | Ltd + membership and estimated budget for using machinery | *Trotec, Makerland,* etc. SMEs. Design and architecture studios | *EduFrame* – children's education. *Makeat* – new craft exhibition. *Lift-Bit* – sofa prototype |
| **Yatta! (2013)**<br>Public funds from the Municipality, "Creative Maker" open call – three years' use of free space | Association with membership and estimated budget for using machinery | Secondary schools and universities. Cultural foundations. Associations | Education, life-long learning, training, workshops, and events. *Yatta! School* internship and stage |

artefacts and use a particular machine, you might also pay for the "time machine", i.e. the number of hours for which you use the machine to create your object. Training courses, management fees, and external commissions are vital to generate enough income to maintain the labour force and the space.

> It is better to have a company because you can bill, and make consultancy for other firms. It's a low profit company, it's not just an association. But the goal is not profit in itself, our goal is to create social wealth. We create jobs, the people who work part-time and full-time are crucial because they run the space and offer a service to the community ... Plus, we reinvest the profit in our makerspace.
>
> (Interviewee no. 5 – OpenDot makerspace)

Makerspaces carry out a mixed array of projects, usually in partnership with cultural foundations, private actors, and knowledge institutions. For example, the project Digital Fashion Design Pro[5] is addressed to all those who want to work in the field of digital design and fashion, digital craftsmanship, and manufacturing 4.0. It is a free course that explores new open source approaches in fashion by the use of software adapted to create products with numerically controlled makerspace machines. This course is realised through the alliance of Fastweb Digital Academy and Cariplo Factory.

When you spend a day in a makerspace you realise that machines are scarce resources, and that there is a hierarchy governing the right to their use. During the ethnographic fieldwork in Milan, we observed how makers internally organise their activities. To use a certain machine you need a specific set of skills, and usually not all the makers can use all the available equipment, as some are specialised in the use of a specific machine. Since it is not possible to allocate workloads in relation to a formal role within a company, what occurs is a distribution of tasks between individual makers (and micro enterprises) as a function of the skills and level of reliability that the various actors have in the reputational peer system. As a maker explained in an interview:

> The advantage is that between an exchange of goods or knowledge there is always someone who gives something to someone who receives. In the exchange of knowledge you both earn; the gain is also in the relationships. Marco, our first customer, now works with us. He has extensive knowledge on manual and electronic practices.
>
> (Interviewee no. 1 – MioCugino makerspace)

In another interview, the importance of social relations within the space is clearly a feature that defines an alternative mode of production:

> In the past 30 years of a white collar job, I forgot the importance of doing things with my hands and creating practical knowledge to share

with your peers, you build social relationships and this is producing in a socially alternative way.

(Interviewee no. 7 – WeMake makerspace)

If we look at makerspaces more devoted to community, what kind of services do they provide? To what degree are they alternative/complementary in the provision of local welfare? The political aims of the more community-oriented makerspaces in Milan are particularly geared towards issues associated with ageing. They want to support healthy and active ageing within the population (i.e. health, participation, and safety), emphasising the role of new digital technologies in the field of sensors and home automation solutions (Torri 2017). These efforts find support with the Municipality, where the official responsible for a project called OpenCare stated:

> OpenCare happens in the context of the fourth industrial revolution. We are in the process of a relocation of production activities within our urban environment. Fablabs and makerspaces stand as new actors in the care ecosystem.
>
> (Renato Galliano, event OpenCare and Digital Social Innovation in Milan, 22th November 2017)

The local government directly supports the OpenCare project, emphasising the importance of improving the physical health and independence of an ageing urban population, especially in terms of accessibility and functionality of living environments and services in urban space. Social initiatives in the healthcare system, such as OpenCare,[6] or projects of digital fabrication in former prisons,[7] are examples of practical solutions for providing social security and equitable accessibility for the "unnecessariat". The social expression of these alternative, or complementary, efforts in traditional welfare provision is an attempt to provide an alternative social infrastructure in which technology is the main driver. In these kinds of projects, makers work together with vulnerable and marginalised communities, co-designing and producing disability devices, re-manufactured products, toys and playground equipment for children, community computer networks, etc. Through these projects, makers advocate for a more democratic relationship with technology. By furnishing tools to needy segments of society, they claim to operate within an alternative paradigm that prefigures a different role for technology in society. In practice, the social change is embodied in projects that aim at low intensity production for a local market, such as the DIY shoes developed together with kids at OpenDot, or non-commercialised cultural production, like the modular urban gardening for kids, created in collaboration with MUBA, the children's museum in Milan. In the same vein, the project "Mi-Generation Lab" consists of a free training course on the use of new technologies, with participants receiving a certificate of the attended internship.[8] The local government posits that such activities can constitute alternative forms of civic engagement, the novel spaces for digital fabrication described above represent new opportunities for citizen empowerment and the provision of alternative and complementary services that cover different social needs. In sum, the novelty lies in the digitisation of services that favour the means of sharing the experience of making and co-producing with local communities.

## Dreams of revolution in the cold light of the empirical

Having now looked at the makerspaces in Milan, we will use this empirical grounding for a more informed discussion of the previously reviewed claims about the makerspace movement. As we saw in the brief review, the literature suggests makerspaces provide: (i) alternative spaces that create the potential for social mobilisation; (ii) an economic alternative, by being part of an ongoing industrial revolution that will transform the economy to a decentralised and networked structure; (iii) a social alternative, by providing alternatives to the existing capitalist provision of public services. In this section we relate each of these claims to the Milanese experience and evaluate the extent to which Milanese makers are on the route to fulfil such potentials.

### *Alternative spaces for mobilisation*

Makerspaces clearly constitute new urban meeting places that enable the coming together of diverse urban dwellers. As we saw in the brief literature review, the literature takes this to imply more potential than merely opportunities for meetings, these spaces are seen as platforms for social organisation and the emergence of new collective agency. Such a claim, that social spaces may bring the potential for social mobilisation, is not without basis in the broader literature. The claim can be linked to a broad and sprawling social movement literature that discusses the phenomenon under names such as *safe spaces, social havens*, and *counterpublics* (e.g. Boyte and Evans 1986; Törnberg and Törnberg 2017). Such spaces have been characterised as protective shelters against prevailing hegemonic ideologies and as hubs for the diffusion of ideas and ideologies. A common example that shows the role such spaces can play is the way in which southern black churches – removed from white control and repression – functioned as protective pockets that nurtured and sustained southern civil rights protests in the 1950s and 1960s. Could it be, then, that makerspaces function like the black churches of the civil rights era: as a bridge between the ordinary world and the world of revolutions? Do they serve to foster a latent class consciousness among the disgruntled precariat of "creative" workers socialising within its midst, with potentially large-scale political consequences? While such potential is clearly impossible to firmly confirm or deny, some observations regarding the role of makerspaces as alternative social spaces can be made on the basis of the case study.

First, the case study does not point towards any development of a movement or mobilisation on the basis of the spaces. The maker movement itself does not yet seem to be converging towards any coherent interest or direction. Rather, as we have seen, the "movement" describes such a heterogeneous set of actors and institutions that quotation marks are warranted. While makerspaces tend to describe themselves as bottom-up and democratic spaces for knowledge production, all their protagonists do not necessarily share this vision. It is furthermore clear that the development of makerspaces in Milan seems to be part of an "institutional action" by the local state, rather than a spontaneous bottom-up mobilisation. Rather than accepting the self-positioning image of makerspaces as bottom-up urban processes, they should be seen as the outcomes of a much more complex process involving both top-down initiated policy frameworks complete with funding opportunities, and bottom-up initiatives taking advantage of available funding channels and political support to realise various urban projects. It is difficult to ascertain whether these initiatives attach themselves to maker discourses because they believe in the "revolutionary" potential of the maker movement or simply because it is an effective way of securing public funding and support.

This points towards a second observation: the spaces cannot be said to be *protected* from either the economic forces of the market or the political forces of the public sector, which puts into question the analogy with the free social spaces literature. The Milanese case study reveals an unholy trinity of makerspaces, market, and state. This dependence on government support is furthermore likely to crowd out some of the alternative interests that may be kindled in these spaces. This can be seen in the tension in the Milanese movement between the idea of making as a way to increase social cohesion, and making as a way to drive urban growth and increase territorial competitiveness.

These semi-traditional business models imply dependence either on government funds, for example, memberships, projects, or money from private donors, or on the market. Milanese makers therefore, to an important degree, have to operate as highly precarious private micro-entrepreneurs, in the sense that they are dependent on selling services and products on the market; makerspaces are spaces for starting your business and a platform for freelancers and designers. They sell services to companies, foundations, universities, and public and private bodies, developing design paths and highly complex training programmes, such as commissioned orders and prototyping for private sector commercial research and development, educational and social design services, and internships and apprenticeships for technical schools, and have strong ties to certain segments of the Milan fashion industry. These factors imply that, while makerspaces are clearly social meeting places, the fact that there is little sign of any coherent movement emerging from them, and that they cannot be said to provide *protected* spaces, implies that one should remain reserved as to the claims that they are likely to function as incubators for the mobilisation of urban alternatives.

### *Alternative mode of production*

The idea in the literature that makerspaces are heralding a coming industrial and economic revolution is based on the notion that makerspaces provide a new form of decentralised and democratic production, to replace the hierarchical discipline of traditional factory production (cf. Rifkin 2011; Troxler 2013; Smith 2014). We first note that such decentralisation of production does seem to be playing out, in that the work in Milanese makerspaces is informally organised through informal social groups. While these groups are not without hierarchies, these are primarily informally and reputationally organised.

The claim that this also constitutes a sign of an ongoing industrial revolution towards small-scale production, however, is significantly more dubious. It is a long-observed pattern that new business opportunities created by radical technological innovation tend to be first exploited by small firms, before they are brought into larger-scale industrial production. It seems, with this background, rather likely that the new technologies enabling the makerspaces will similarly increasingly be brought into large-scale factory production. Since makerspaces are furthermore at least in part dependent on being competitive as private enterprises, this may imply an undermining of their market niche.

The value creation associated with urban producers and makerspaces is not always as alternative as it seems, in that the focus on value creation is almost exclusively on exchange value (i.e. skills, and relational and symbolic capital). While, on the one hand, the makers are inspired by visions of the community and a democratic world, they always operate within the market, where profit is the main engine of strategic choice. It therefore becomes central for the organisations to hide their economic, self-entrepreneurship aspect by referencing themselves as a movement that creates symbolic value and a cultural milieu within urban space. They want to brand themselves as social and grassroots entrepreneurs to hide the fact that they are – like virtually everyone – part of the capitalist economic system.

But this does not change the fact that increasing automation in the form of technology like 3D printing will likely produce more decentralised and self-organised work processes. This should, however, be put in the right historical context: production has gone towards exchanging blue-collar labour with white-collar labour through automation since the 1970s, in part as an effort to undermine the negotiation position of unions (Dunford 2000). Information and white-collar labour do bring with them fewer hierarchical work processes, and the decentralised work organisation of makerspaces thus fits neatly into the story of post-Fordism and neoliberalism, rather than constituting a challenge or alternative. While DIY culture often embraces values of pleasure, self-realisation, and (consumer) choice, this transformative rhetoric often reproduces, as Dawkins puts it:

> neoliberalist rationalities and limiting the political potential of craft and community activism. Pleasure and self-fulfillment are often exchanged for what might otherwise be felt to be unstable, precarious, and even exploitative work … Contemporary craftwork produces postfordist labor subjectivities through the blurring of labor and leisure.
>
> (Dawkins 2011: 261–279)

***Alternative welfare***

According to the claim in the literature, the maker movement is suggested to be capable of providing an alternative to existing systems for the provision of public services, by organising services, for example, for education, healthcare, and care for the elderly. The claim that we are to discuss is that the maker movement is not merely a continuation of the current welfare regime, but an alternative and a challenge to it (e.g. Dawkins 2011; Torri 2017). We may begin by noting that it is clear that the maker movement in Milan is indeed providing various social services, including healthcare, childcare, and care for the elderly. It should be noted that previously these services generally have been provided by public investments or, in the case of Sunday schools, by the Catholic Church. The makerspaces are thus stepping in to fill a hole in welfare services left by shrinking government funds and, consequently, they are indeed providing important services to the community. While this is a notable ongoing change, it does not seem to be the case that it springs from the service provision of makerspaces being in any fundamental way "alternative" to their previous organisation. In fact, in the case of Sunday schools for example, there are – despite superficial differences – striking similarities between the practices and activities in the makerspaces and those of previous regimes, even though the children are now asked to bow under a 3D printer instead of an effigy of Christ. The difference is rather in relation to organisational structuring and the way in which the services are financed. These aspects, however, seem to fit neatly into the larger narrative of ongoing economic transformations, in particular the ways in which neoliberalism has affected welfare systems throughout the world. There has been a recent upsurge in public-civic co-production of welfare services in which public authorities soften the effects of their retreat from welfare provision by gradually transferring responsibilities to civic actors, often under the banner of empowerment (McGimpsey 2016). The private-public partnerships shown in the Milanese case study seem to be exactly in line with such neoliberal transformations of welfare, and it is indeed quite hard to see anything progressive or alternative about them. When a publicly financed system is being replaced by public-private-civil organisational hodgepodges, this is not a challenge against the mainstream capitalist current, but merely something that floats downstream. The makerspace type of welfare is best understood as part and parcel of the processes of welfare neoliberalisation.

## Conclusion

This chapter has looked at some of the narratives that surround the maker movement and their transformative potential. These narratives clearly contain a hint of the exaggerated optimism that has often tended to surround the emergence of new technologies. The literature was found to suggest that makerspaces constitute (i) an alternative space that creates the potential for social mobilisation; (ii) an economic alternative that is part of an ongoing industrial revolution that will transform the economy; (iii) a welfare alternative, providing an alternative to the existing capitalist provision of public services. The aim of this chapter was to discuss these claims on the basis of an in-depth ethnographic case study of makerspaces in Milan, in order to begin to separate the hype from the reality.

The case study suggested that these narratives indeed tend to be overly hyperbolic, in particular concerning the notion of makerspaces as an *alternative* or a *challenge* to the status quo. Seen through the lens of empirical observation, the maker movement seems less like a radical alternative and more like the next step on the current trajectories of capitalist exploitation. The decentralised and networked production processes characteristic of the spaces are typical of a post-Fordist restructuring of labour through, for example, automation, driven in part by the interest to undermine union power. The welfare provision is similarly typical of a neoliberal era in which holes in the welfare provision left by retreating states are filled by amorphous private-public-civil partnerships with weak ties and soft boundaries. These aspects are thus, rather than *challenges* or *alternatives*, part and parcel of the neoliberal and post-Fordist developments that have been ongoing since the 1970s. The notion that they would provide a sustainable or scalable "alternative capitalism", let alone an "alternative to capitalism" (Rogers 2014), does not find much support in the empirical case study. While makerspaces seem to be part of, or at least symbolic of, ongoing important transformations, they are going *with* the current, not against it.

There is certainly something to be said for the creation of social spaces, as they do afford the growing precarious class of freelancers and creative workers meeting places ripe for politicisation. As we have noted, makerspace activities and practices in this way could play a role in enlarging a critical space for the deconstruction of capitalist realism (Fisher 2009). The mobilisation of organised precarian labour struggles may still be nurtured in these spaces, but only if the makers themselves realise that all they have achieved so far is to reinforce their own precarisation. By engaging in welfare provisioning, Milanese makers have seen that they are in a position to make a difference for other, less privileged, urban dwellers; what they still need to see is that they can also make a difference for their own collective futures as urban workers. Social spaces bring the possibilities for precisely such realisations, enabling the mobilisation and creation of new collective agency by kindling common class interests and identities. What limits the potential of makerspaces in this regard, however, is that they are in no way protected from those cold winds of market forces and government interests that tend to quickly blow out any transformative flame that such kindling may ignite. For a social space to function as tinder for the ignition of a dormant class consciousness, protection from market forces and government interests would be warranted. This underwhelming transformative impact of makerspaces, together with their generally ill-defined and amorphous nature, suggest that a more productive focus of study for future research on this movement should perhaps be on their discursive and cultural aspects. We see two main directions for such future enquiries.

The first direction focuses on the interests underlying government engagement in initiating and funding the makerspace movement. The context for such a discussion comprises the changing conditions of the public sector, implying new selection pressures for government organisations. Under conditions of neoliberalism and economic decline, governments lack an adequate tax base for the funding of necessary social services, and are thus increasingly becoming forced to turn to private investments and alternative sources of income. Governments are therefore looking to international grant processes to fill the holes left by inadequate public funds. This has created the need for them also to become competitive in such grant processes, which is primarily a question of capacity to mobilise discursive resources and form convincing coalitions. The maker movement becomes a valuable discursive resource in such a field, precisely because of the hyperbolic narratives that surround it, since the strong branding of the spaces makes them useful discursive devices in grant applications. This way of understanding the role of makerspaces implies the existence of what we might call a "grant machine" of the city, resulting in "grant coalitions rather than growth coalitions" (Bernt 2009). This implies that, in fact, the points that have caused observers to conclude that makerspaces are "more than just empty rhetoric" – for example, collaboration, openness in urban governance, civic engagement, and grassroots entrepreneurship – in fact may be precisely part of a strategy in a new competitive realm of empty rhetoric.

The second direction unravels from the hard-to-ignore fact that making is in no way a new phenomenon. Indeed, community meeting spaces with sewing machines are not a new phenomenon; neither is community provision of childcare and care for the elderly. This begs the question: what is actually new about these spaces that could explain the sudden excitement? The answer is hinted at when considering the only reason why the international maker movement is highly male dominated is that the millions of women sewing, knitting, and weaving are not included in the term. Through this lens, the maker movement looks more like a cultural recasting of existing social practices. This type of process will not be news to urban scholars, as parallel processes have been observed and theorised in other parts of the urban economy. For instance, while the poor and marginalised have always reused and repurposed, these practices seem to attain a new value and different signalling when done by white "hipsters". Similarly, making seems to attain another value when done by male *makers*, armed with the latest technological gadgets, rather than female *crafters*. In this way, makers seem to fulfil some of the same cultural roles as "hipsters" in attracting that ever-sought-after creative class. The maker movement is drenched in the cultural values of Silicon Valley – male-dominated, technological, and innovative – and there is perhaps some aspect of "cargo cultism" to the state's interest in supporting these entities:

the government is essentially building an aeroplane runway of practices associated with the creative class, with the hopes of attracting the Western aeroplanes of "creative workers" and international capital. This type of cultural analysis may in fact prove to be a more useful way of understanding the makerspace phenomenon than an analysis that departs from speculative claims about their innovatory and revolutionary potential.

To conclude, makerspaces and their 3D printers seem like the latest iteration of the frequently recurring story where a new machine is envisioned to come upon the stage of capitalism to resolve its difficult plot situations. But if we wait for the godly intervention of such a *deus ex machina*, we will not only be in for a long wait, but also continue to fall for precisely the same traps that the makerspace dreamers fell for: we will mistake technological change for social revolution, individualism for freedom, and the reinvention of capitalism for revolution. If we are to change the plot of the tragedy in which we live, we cannot wait for the intervention of an imagined celestial scriptwriter – we will have to craft our own future.

## Notes

1 "Innovare per Includere" is a political slogan and a laboratory for public policy instituted by the public administration and an amalgamation of local knowledge composed of academics, storytellers, policy makers, and Cristina Tajani, Councillor for Labour Policies, Production Activities, Trade, and Human Resources. She is the main gatekeeper in crafting urban policies to support makers, social entrepreneurs, start-ups, etc. See the website: www.innovarexincludere.it.
2 See the list on the website: www.lavoroeformazioneincomune.it/wp-content/uploads/2015/10/Misura-A-elenco-al-9-giugno-2017.pdf.
3 It is three times more than in Rome and Bologna (5.2% each) and four times compared to cities like Modena (3.7%), Venice (2.9%), Padua and Parma (3.6%) (Manzo and Ramella 2015).
4 Cf. Chapter 4 in this volume.
5 See the website: www.fastwebdigital.academy/digital-fashion-design-pro.
6 Since 2016, WeMake has contributed to a series of health and care projects with a bottom-up approach through the European Union-funded OpenCare project. The mission of the makerspace is oriented to support citizens, institutions, and companies in the creation of projects and solutions with a high social impact. The core of the project is the progressive automation of care solutions: from sensors to replace people dedicated to assistance, through the complete automation of performance acquisition functions, to the development of diagnostic techniques, assisted by computer algorithms. Over the course of the project, more than 400 participants made a written contribution to the online debate. In November 2017, the platform hosting the discussions on OpenCare recorded 760 threads and 4,850 posts for a total of one million words. In addition to the level of verbal interaction and storytelling, WeMake acted at the prototyping level. The online and offline solutions proposed were effectively designed, tested, documented, and shared for a total of six projects. See the website: http://wemake.cc/opencare.
7 See the website: http://wemake.cc/2018/02/13/imprese-ristrette-la-digital-fabrication-attraversa-i-muri-del-carcere.
8 The Municipality of Milan, in collaboration with eighteen partners, launched the project of free training courses on new technologies dedicated to young students

and citizens aged from eighteen to thirty-five years with residence or domicile in Milan who have precarious jobs, with the aim being to develop new skills and business ideas. The makerspace Yatta! is one of the main partners in this project.

## References


Anderson, C. (2012) *Makers: The New Industrial Revolution.* New York: Crown Publishing.

Anselmi, G. and Chiappini, L. (2017) L'imprenditorialità diffusa del movimento maker: tra fiducia e reputazione [The Widespread Entrepreneurship of the Maker Movement: Between Trust and Reputation]. In d'Ovidio, M. and Rabbiosi, C. (eds) *Maker e Città. La Rivoluzione si fa con la stampante 3D?* Milano: Feltrinelli.

Armondi, S. and Bruzzese, A. (2017) Contemporary Production and Urban Change: The Case of Milan. *Journal of Urban Technology*, 24(3), 27–45.

Bathelt, H. and Cohendet, P. (2014) The Creation of Knowledge: Local Building, Global Accessing and Economic Development – Toward an Agenda. *Journal of Economic Geography*, 14(5), 869–882.

Bauwens, M. (2005) The Political Economy of Peer Production. *CTheory Journal*, 12(1). Available at: www.ctheory.net/articles.aspx?id=499.

Benkler, Y. (2006) *The Wealth of Networks: How Social Production Transforms Markets and Freedom.* New Haven, CT: Yale University Press.

Benkler, Y. and Nissenbaum, H. (2006) Commons-Based Peer Production and Virtue. *Journal of Political Philosophy*, 14(4), 394–419.

Bernt, M. (2009) Partnerships for Demolition: The Governance of Urban Renewal in East Germany's Shrinking Cities. *International Journal of Urban and Regional Research*, 33, 754–769.

Bialski, P., Derwanz, H., Otto, B., and Vollmer, H. (2015) "Saving" the City: Collective Low-Budget Organizing and Urban Practice. *Ephemera: Theory and Politics in Organization*, 15(1), 1–19.

Boyte, H. and Evans, S. (1986) *Free Spaces: The Sources of Democratic Change in America.* New York: Harper and Row.

Capdevila, I. (2013) Knowledge Dynamics in Localized Communities: Coworking Spaces as Microclusters. Available at: https://ssrn.com/abstract=2414121.

Chiappini, L. and Anselmi, G. (2017) Molto più di un bit . . . L'utilizzo della comunicazione online e offline della comunità dei maker [Much More Than a Bit . . . The Use of Online and Offline Communication in the Maker Community]. In d'Ovidio, M. and Rabbiosi, C. (eds) *Maker e Città. La Rivoluzione si fa con la stampante 3D?* Milano: Feltrinelli.

Chiappini, L. and d'Ovidio, M. (2017) Il potenziale dei makers: tra innovazione economica e coesione sociale [The Potential of Makers: Between Economic Innovation and Social Cohesion]. In Bidussa, D. and Polizzi, E. (eds) *Agenda Milano. Ricerche e pratiche per una città inclusiva.* Milano: Feltrinelli, 34–35.

Cohendet, P., Grandadam, D., Simon, L., and Capdevila, I. (2014) Epistemic Communities, Localization and the Dynamics of Knowledge Creation. *Journal of Economic Geography*, 14(5), 929–954.

Cooley, M. (1987) *Architect or Bee? The Human Price of Technology.* Second edn. London: Hogarth Press.

Dawkins, N. (2011) Do-It-Yourself: The Precarious Work and Postfeminist Politics of Handmaking (in) Detroit. *Utopian Studies*, 22(2), 261–284.

Disalvo, C. (2012) *Adversarial Design*. Cambridge, MA: MIT Press.

Dougherty, D. (2012) The Maker Movement. *Innovations: Technology, Governance, Globalization*, 7(3), 11–14.

D'Ovidio, M. and Rabbiosi, C. (2017) *Maker e Città. La Rivoluzione si fa con la stampante 3D? [Maker and City: Is the Revolution Made with the 3D Printer?]* Milano: Feltrinelli.

Dunford, M. (2000) Globalization and Theories of Regulation. In Palan, R. (ed) *Global Political Economy: Contemporary Theories*. London: Routledge, 143–167.

Fisher, M. (2009) *Capitalist Realism: Is There No Alternative?* London: Zero Books.

Gershenfeld, N. (2005) *FAB: The Coming Revolution on Your Desktop: From Personal Computers to Personal Fabrication*. Cambridge: Basic Books.

Gershenfeld, N. (2012) How to Make Almost Anything: The Digital Fabrication Revolution. *Foreign Affairs*, 91, 43–57.

Hansen, T. (2014) Juggling with Proximity and Distance: Collaborative Innovation Projects in the Danish Cleantech Industry. *Journal of Economic Geography*, 90(4), 375–402.

Hatch, M. (2013) *The Maker Movement Manifesto: Rules for Innovation in the New World of Crafters, Hackers, and Tinkerers*. New York: McGraw Hill Education.

Manzo, C. and Ramella, F. (2015) Fab Labs in Italy: Collective Goods in the Sharing Economy. *Stato e Mercato*, 3, 379–418.

Maxigas (2012) Hacklabs and Hackerspaces: Tracing Two Genealogies. *Journal of Peer Production*, 1(2), 1–10.

McGimpsey, I. (2016) Late Neoliberalism: Delineating a Policy Regime. *Critical Social Policy*, 37(1), 64–84.

Ratto, M. (2011) Critical Making: Conceptual and Material Studies in Technology and Social Life. *The Information Society*, 27(4), 252–260.

Rifkin, J. (2011) *The Third Industrial Revolution: How Lateral Power is Transforming Energy, The Economy and the World*. New York: Palgrave Macmillan.

Rifkin, J. (2014) *The Zero Marginal Cost Society: The Internet of Things, the Collaborative Commons, and the Eclipse of Capitalism*. New York: Palgrave Macmillan.

Rigi, J. (2013) Peer Production and Marxian Communism: Contours of a New Emerging Mode of Production. *Capital and Class*, 37(3), 397–416.

Rogers, C. (2014) *Capitalism and Its Alternatives*. London: Zed Books.

Schmidt, S., Brinks, V., and Brinkhoff, S. (2014) Innovation and Creativity Labs in Berlin – Organizing Temporary Spatial Configurations for Innovations. *Zeitschrift für Wirtschaftsgeographie*, 58(4), 232–247.

Schmidt, S., Ibert, O., Kuebart, A., and Kühn, J. (2016) *Open Creative Labs: Typologisierung, Verbreitung und Entwicklungsbedingungen [Typology, Distribution and Development Conditions]*. Erkner: Leibniz-Institut für Raumbezogene Sozialforschung.

Smith, A. (2014) Technology Networks for Socially Useful Production. *Journal of Peer Production*, (5), 1–9. Available at: http://sro.sussex.ac.uk/53574.

Smith, A., Hielscher, S., Dickel, S., Söderberg, J., and Van Oost, E. (2013) *Grassroots Digital Fabrication and Makerspaces: Reconfiguring, Relocating and Recalibrating Innovation?* Brighton: University of Sussex.

Sylvester, A. and Döring, T. (2013) Urban Development with FabLabs. In Walter-Herrmann, J. and Büching, C. (eds) *FabLab: Of Machines, Makers and Inventors*. Bielefeld: Transcript Verlag, 223–230.

Törnberg, A. and Törnberg, P. (2017) Modelling Free Social Spaces and the Diffusion of Social Mobilization. *Social Movement Studies*, 16(2), 182–202.

Torri, R. (2017) Milan: Challenging the Private Interest Government in Times of Austerity. In Cucca, R. and Ranci, C. (eds) *Unequal Cities: Economic Development and Social Cohesion in European Cities*. London: Routledge, 183–201.
Tosh, J. (2008) *Why History Matters*. Basingstoke: Palgrave Macmillan.
Troxler, P. (2013) Making the 3rd Industrial Revolution – The Struggle for Polycentric Structures and a New Peer-Production Commons in the FabLab Community. In Walter-Herrmann, J. and Büching, C. (eds) *FabLab: Of Machines, Makers and Inventors*. Bielefeld: Transcript Verlag, 181–198.
Vitale, T. and Polizzi, E. (2017) Governo collaborativo e catene relazionali di innovazione. Spunti a partire dal caso di Milano [Collaborative Governance and Relational Chains of Innovation. Ideas Starting from the Milan Case]. *Quaderni di Rassegna Sindacale*, 18(2), 129–147.

## Sitography

Innovare per Includere website: www.innovarexincludere.it (accessed: February 2018).
WeMake OpenCare: http://wemake.cc/opencare (accessed: February 2018).
WeMake Digital Fabrication Attraversa i Muri del Carcere: http://wemake.cc/2018/02/13/imprese-ristrette-la-digital-fabrication-attraversa-i-muri-del-carcere (accessed: February 2018).
Comune di Milano, Lavoro e Formazione website: www.lavoroeformazioneincomune.it/wp-content/uploads/2017/10/Elenco-Makerspace-FabLab-aggiornato-al-2-Ottobre-2017.pdf (accessed: February 2018).
Fast Web Digital Academy website: www.fastwebdigital.academy/digital-fashion-designpro (accessed: February 2018).

# Part 2

# Alternative urban spaces of dwelling

# 6 Producing refugee spaces

## Disruptive spatial practice and the everyday in Cairo

*Samir Shalabi and Lee Pugalis*

### Introduction

On account of its location at the crossroads between Asia, Africa, and the Mediterranean, Egypt historically has been an important destination for travellers, migrants, and refugees (Liszka, 2012). With the country presently hosting one of the largest urban refugee populations in the world, the majority of which congregate in Cairo, the image of cities as social melting pots would thus seem to fit the metropolis well (Goździak and Walter, 2012: 5). Indeed, as Sanyal argues, cities are particularly attractive sites for refugees, not only on account of the abundance of work opportunities they generate, but also because cities allow refugees to break away from the international humanitarian assistance regime and the social stigma associated with refugee identity through mixing with the host population. In addition, by learning to navigate the multi-layered networks and social relations that cities are necessarily made up of, refugees are able to engage in the struggles, conflicts, and claims-making that enable new forms of politics and spaces to emerge (Sanyal, 2014: 560–561, and 569).

The 2011 Syrian uprising, which developed into a civil and international war, created a humanitarian crisis of devastatingly huge proportions.[1] In quantitative terms, as of 2018, almost seven million Syrians have been displaced from their homes; nearly six million have escaped across Syria's border, with regional countries receiving the bulk of these refugees. According to the United Nations High Commissioner for Refugees (UNHCR), which is the main body responsible for determining Syrians' refugee status, 129,000 are residing in Egypt (UNHCR, 2018); however, such official statistics underestimate significantly the quantum of Syrians fleeing to Egypt, as many of them do not register with the UNHCR. Indeed, in a recent report, the UN indicated that Egypt presently hosts "nearly half a million Syrians" (UN, 2017: 6). Despite the scale of the issue, to date there has been limited research addressing the plight of Syrian refugees in Egypt. We, therefore, aim to address this scholarly void, especially the research lacuna pertaining to their role in the production of urban space, including the spatial interjections and everyday practices of the refugees themselves.

Manual Castells' view that space is a reflection of society serves as the ontological perspective informing this chapter: the significance of spatiality and, in particular, the notion that spatial processes are of fundamental importance to the formation, organisation, and experience of society.

> Space is not a "reflection of society", it *is society* ... Therefore, spatial forms, at least on our planet, will be produced, as all other objects are, by human action. They will express and perform the interest of the dominant class according to a given mode of production and to a specific mode of development. They will express and implement the power relationships of the state in an historically defined society. They will be realised and shaped by the process of gender domination and by state-enforced family life. At the same time, *spatial forms will be earmarked by the resistance from exploited classes, from oppressed subjects, and from dominated women*. And the work of such *a contradictory historical process on the space will be accomplished on an already inherited spatial form, the product of former history and the support of new interests, projects, protests, and dreams*. Finally, from time to time, social movements will arise to challenge the meaning of spatial structure and therefore attempt new functions and new form.
>
> (Castells, 1983: 4, emphasis added)

Moreover, the production of space is a contradictory process, whereby the relationship between society and space is mutually constitutive: the socio-spatial dialectic (Soja, 1980; Lefebvre, 1991 [1974], 2009 [1979]). Thus, we follow Lefebvre's comprehension of space as "both a product (a thing) and determinant (a process) of social relations and actions" (Zielniec, 2008: 60). Simply put: "(social) space is a (social) product" (Lefebvre, 1991 [1974]: 30). In view of Sanyal's (2014: 558) observation that "Refugee spaces are emerging as quintessential geographies of the modern, yet their intimate and everyday spatialities remain under-explored", the key concern of this chapter is to investigate how refugees negotiate prevailing socio-spatial configurations and, thus, produce space, by exploring the repurposing of inherited spatial forms for alternative urban uses (cf. Castells, 1983). By investigating the production of refugee spaces, we focus attention on the ways in which refugees perceive, adapt to, as well as adapt and transform urban space through engaging in practices in their everyday lives.

Partly to alleviate metropolitan urbanisation pressures, since the late 1970s Cairo has witnessed a remarkable spatial expansion along its desert fringes through the development of a host of new cities, initially part of a post-World War II international "new town movement" (Merlin, 1980; Stewart, 1996). One of these, 6th of October City, provides the broader empirical setting for this chapter in which the analysis zooms in further to focus on a poverty-stricken social housing estate located at the city's spatial, social, and economic margins. This case enables us to explore the everyday spatial tactics of people who recently have sought refuge from war-stricken Syria. The central thrust of the chapter is to uncover how this refugee community negotiates and disrupts prevailing socio-spatial relations by developing the notion of *hyperlocality*.

Drawing inspiration from Lefebvre's contention that "authentic knowledge of space must address the question of its production" (Lefebvre, 1991 [1974]: 388), we deploy critical urban ethnography to analyse the production of alternative urban spaces, identifying five hyperlocal spatial practices: miniature shops on balconies, bread ovens outside buildings, vegetable gardens and chicken breeding cages on pavement plots, hairdressing within private homes, and a day-care facility that occupied a private flat but was extended to the street pavement through a steel cage. These hyperlocal spatial practices are examples not so much of embracing "bare life", but rather of reclamation and mobilisation of space (Owens, 2009; Bhimji, 2016). We contend that the production of refugee spaces through hyperlocal spatial practices can be viewed "as important sites for articulating new politics" (Sanyal, 2014: 558).

## Theorising the production of refugee spaces

Spatial re(con)figuration is dialectically implicated in processes of contestation; social practices that Henri Lefebvre (1991 [1974]) documented at length in *The Production of Space*. The production of space is a complex social process that cannot be simplified as a mechanistic logic of capitalism, but rather unfolds as an often-dysfunctional process of social conflict, everyday relations, and discourse (Smith, 1984; Gottdiener, 1985; Merrifield, 2000; Liggett, 2003; Mitchell, 2003; Watkins, 2005; Garmany, 2008; Zhongyuan et al., 2008; Leary, 2009). The strength of a Lefebvrian focus on how space is produced rather than space per se – i.e. space as process instead of space as object – is that it brings to the fore power relations. Embedding the infinity of meaning, plural perspectives, and the multidimensionality of social spaces in this work, we view urban space as the composite of multi-socialities, diverse flows and dynamic networks, fragmented spatialities, and spatio-temporal openness. This is a position that considers space, time, and social life as co-productive entities. The Lefebvrian triad represents the space of material social practice, conceived representations, and lived imaginations as process; continuously produced and reproducing in inseparable, yet shifting, historical, physical, political, and socio-economic contexts. This relational process is less a consistent temporal progression, but more spatial, broken by sporadic moments which transform, reinterpret, or recode a historical spatial formation. Thus, the production of space is simultaneously process and outcome, flow and thing, an inseparable conflictual process of creation (Lehtovuori, 2010).

Our understanding of the production of space cannot be reduced to a mental construct alone; it is also a tool for action, a means of production, and a means of control. It is the process and product of diverse social and political relationships of power. Lefebvre's theory of space sensitises us to experience simultaneously the productive and debilitating aspects, making it possible to interrogate spaces of inclusion and exclusion. Spaces of refuge can be seen as specific variants of the production of space; the number of refugees worldwide is in the millions, yet discussions about them in the public and academic realms largely "fall 'outside' the debates on 'normal' societies" (Sanyal, 2014: 558). Although light is modestly beginning to be shed on refugees and refugee spaces in urban studies, there is still "a prominent silence" on the issue within the field (Sanyal, 2014: 558).

It is a difficult task to theorise refugees in view of their "abnormal" status in society. As displaced persons, they differ from their "hosts", yet they are also similar, in terms of needs and desires. Camp spaces or "campscapes" have played a prominent role in spatial theorisations, raising pertinent questions about how to theorise and define such an emergent form of urbanism (Malkki, 2002). Turner (2015), for example, explores the relationship between space and refugee populations, identifying how refugee camps can be instrumentalised by host governments to serve economic objectives, such as a cheap supply of labour. Arguing against the conventionally held view of camps as sites aiding in the distribution of humanitarian assistance, as spaces of radicalisation and militancy, or as a means for governments to handle potential security threats, Turner (2015: 388) maintains that they also represent a "tool through which states spatially segregate those refugees, of certain socio-economic classes, those deemed surplus to labour market requirements". Focusing on how the Jordanian and Lebanese governments economically exploit Syrian refugees, the author stresses how the spatial concentration of refugee populations in camps helps states regulate their labour markets according to particular needs. Contrary to Turner's structural perspective, which highlights state-driven exploitative arrangements that can benefit host country economies, Kılıçaslan (2016) and Sanyal (2014) have directed their research efforts towards the agency of refugees in the production of space.

While a large part of the literature on refugees focuses on refugee camps under the official auspices of the UN or a host nation, it also should be remembered that refugees across the world increasingly *settle* in non-camp spaces (Stevenson, 2017), which has prompted research concerned with the integration and assimilation of refugees into "normal" society (Fabos and Kibreab, 2007), whereas scholarly debate on the politics of presence in urban-city spaces – what we might term urban self-settlement – is more recent (Darling, 2017). Those studies of refugee urban self-settlement have typically examined topics, such as livelihood (Macchiavello, 2004), urban informality (Darling, 2017), intra-urban mobility (Zanganeh et al., 2016), legal rights (Jones, 2015), and social networks, coping strategies, and social resources (Fiddian, 2006; Palmgren, 2014).

Moving beyond the refugee camp/non-camp spaces of refuge duality, Sanyal argues that other spaces of refuge do not easily fit into this dichotomous frame. Informal settlements, for example, represent one of these complex emergent refugee spaces, which "blur the boundaries between camps and cities" (Sanyal, 2017: 124). Our focus in this chapter is the production of refugee spaces, which we consider to be a particular form of alternative urban space. It is necessary to point out that "refugee spaces" are distinct from "refugee camps". Whereas the latter are said to "fall within the remit of humanitarian protection and aid, and outside the national order of things, they are simultaneously within and outside the law" (Sanyal, 2014: 559), the former are typically beyond the purview of humanitarian protection and within the national order of things, albeit typically occupying a tentative position at the socio-spatial margins. Therefore, refugee spaces can be understood as spaces of urban marginality (Thieme et al., 2017); however, refugees also can be compared with, and juxtaposed to, the urban poor. While they both clearly form part of marginal populations in cities, the urban poor usually have significantly better access to the job market than refugees, who face legal or social barriers in their search for work. At the same time, refugees are often able to secure their basic sustenance through aid organisations; a privilege the urban poor rarely enjoy. As Sanyal rightly points out, such complex relationships between urban populations present significant challenges "for articulating a 'refugee urbanism'" (Sanyal, 2014: 568).

Refugee spaces are, at one and the same time, ordinary spaces, spaces of displacement, and spaces of curtailed rights. First, refugee spaces are ordinary spaces in the sense that on the surface they are not too dissimilar to other socio-economically marginal spaces. Second, refugee spaces are spaces of displacement, inhabited by a concentrated number of refugees. These spaces of displacement can be exploited and transformed into sites where urban struggles and politics can play out in order to reclaim lost agency and voice. Seeing refugee spaces as mere exceptions to "normal" city life "is not only disingenuous, but denies the possibility of articulating these new politics at the margins" (Sanyal, 2014: 570). Third, refugee spaces are spaces of curtailed rights relating to citizenship and economic rights – fundamentally the right to work.

## Critical urban ethnographies of refugee spaces

The social reproduction of urban space both informs and is informed by memories, understandings, and representations from diverse situated vantage points that collectively shape the perceived, conceived, and lived aspects of space (Lefebvre, 1991 [1974]). In this study, ethnography was used to capture such vantage points. It reflects our attempt to "see things the way group members do, and grasp the meanings they use to understand and make sense of the world" (O'Leary, 2007: 84). Our approach embodies the presupposition shared by critical ethnographers that all socio-cultural worlds exist in perpetual tension between domination and resistance. This tension is found and expressed in daily interactions, behaviours, social systems, structures, and artefacts in any given socio-cultural setting. Critical ethnographic research takes these "seemingly mundane events, even repulsive ones, and reproduces them in a way that exposes broader social processes of control, power imbalance, and the symbolic mechanisms that impose one set of preferred meanings of behaviour over others" (Thomas, 2003: 4).

As urban ethnographers, we also recognise the impact that urban environments have on the people living in them by incorporating this perspective into our analysis (Ocejo, 2013). As Venegas and Huerta (2010) argue, doing ethnographic fieldwork in contemporary urban spaces is qualitatively different from conducting research in other environments. What makes a city particularly unique is its complex power structures with "their particular focus on race and class-based inequalities" (Venegas and Huerta, 2010: 154). Combining these approaches, the study deploys critical urban ethnography.

The research material was derived from approximately six months of ethnographic fieldwork, including interviews with local residents and interaction with, and observation of, refugee spaces and their social production. The main method for collecting the primary data was semi-structured individual and group interviews with participants of two types. The first type included Syrian refugees living in Cairo's 6th of October City. Interviews were conducted with thirty-nine Syrians, including twenty-six males and thirteen females. Their ages differed: the youngest was seventeen while the oldest was seventy-two. The second type of study participant comprised employees or higher officials in organisations providing material or legal assistance to Syrian refugees in Cairo, as well as journalists, academics, and other specialists focusing on the Syrian refugee issue or Cairo's urban development. In total, nineteen interviews were conducted with this cohort. Observations, informal conversations, social media monitoring, and a research diary were also utilised.

## Socio-spatial polarisation and uneven development in 6th of October City

6th of October City is a first-generation Egyptian new town, its name an eternal reminder of the commencement day of the 1973 Arab-Israeli war, and part of a broader plan to develop the nation's "strategic vacuums" and create "a new map" of Egypt through various "higher planning authorities" (Sadat, 1974: 77–78, 82). Since then, the "new town" policy has become a key pillar of Egypt's spatial development strategy and some two dozen new desert cities have emerged as the key sites for the country's urban expansion (Stewart, 1996). Inaugurated in 1981, 6th of October City, located approximately 35 kilometres west of central Cairo, was planned as an economically independent "new urban community" with a projected resident population of between 350,000 and 500,000 people (Sims, 2012; World Bank, 2008). The city was originally envisaged as a series of zones: a large industrial zone to the west, a tourist zone to the east, and a central service and commercial spine, with residential areas located perpendicularly on both sides (Wahdan, 2009).

In the early 1990s, the original concept of the new towns and the associated land management policies underwent fundamental changes. Until this point, the main target demographic had been the working classes, which were housed in swathes of state-subsidised affordable housing estates. But, with former president Hosni Mubarak's "roll-out" of neoliberal urban economic policies (Peck and Tickell, 2002), which had begun under president Anwar Sadat's *infitāḥ* ("opening") programme two decades earlier, a more profit-driven "state capitalist" approach to desert development was adopted (World Bank, 2008).

This shift in policy resulted in a state sell-off of publically-owned land to private investors, which encouraged land speculation and accelerated the commodification of space. As such, the quest for profit became a driving force in the Egyptian state's spatial development policy. Globally, as well as in Egypt, neoliberal urban economic restructuring generated "new forms of social polarization, and a dramatic intensification of uneven development at all spatial scales" (Brenner and Theodore, 2002: 352). For 6th of October City, this meant a dramatic expansion of its geographical boundaries into the surrounding desert and the sale of large tracts of land to private real estate developers. As a result, the city now encompasses a vast geographical space spanning some 400 square kilometres. Yet, it lacks a public transportation system, and therefore, if one is unable to afford or access a private motor vehicle, one has to rely on paratransit in the form of privately operated minibuses, quarter trucks, and the characteristic black and yellow tuk-tuks (three-wheeled motorised rickshaws).

Neoliberal capitalist development, together with state planners subscribing to "high modernist" planning principles, wherein differential zoning is considered imperative, produced highly uneven spatial patterns of development in the city. Consequently, while areas in central 6th of October maintained high levels of economic development, remoter ones were left acutely underserved. Although formal public transport services are non-existent throughout the city, other services, such as markets, health clinics, schools, and restaurants are concentrated in the downtown districts, which also has prompted the development of informal transport networks there (Shalabi, 2018). This political economy of space and marginality has been generated, in part, by the government's elitist urban policies, but more prominently through the deregulation of Egypt's market for social services. As has been the case with downtown Cairo (Khalil, 2016), letting market forces dictate the provision of social goods, such as education, health, housing, and transport, which has led to a subtle process of gentrification of the city's desert suburbs. While both peripheral and central areas depend on services, only the latter have managed to attract capital investments, as it is there that profitability is the highest.

As 6th of October City is located relatively close to Cairo proper, people were initially discouraged from migrating there, instead preferring the daily commute. According to the 2006 census by Egypt's official statistics agency CAPMAS, over 60 percent of housing units in the city are empty (2006). As a result, 6th of October emerged as a key landing pad for refugees. Up until the influx of Syrians to Egypt after the outbreak of the Syrian crisis in 2011, the main refugee populations residing there were Iraqis and, to a lesser extent, Sudanese and Somalis, however, Syrians are now the city's dominant refugee group. The social housing estate of Beyt al-'Ayla (Arabic for "The Family's Home"), located in what on official maps is referred to as 'south of the residential districts' on the southern fringes of the city, is where some of the poorest and most underprivileged Syrian refugees have settled. As one informal transport operator commented: "there are mostly Syrians [in Beyt al-'Ayla], they're poor, very poor". Migrants from Sudan and poor Egyptians from rural areas also reside there.[2] Beyt al-'Ayla is made up of an area of about half a square kilometre and holds approximately 3,000 flats (two rooms of 63 square metres), ideationally planned to provide "all the basic services for citizens, whether it be schools, markets, playgrounds or green spaces" (Thabit, 2007).

## The double marginality of Syrians in Beyt al-'Ayla

> *As we make our way through the sixth district in the back of a tuk-tuk, we observe broken furniture and tiny, run-down stores and workshops litter the left side of the street. To our right passes a long line of what looks like used, or perhaps just very old, porcelain toilets. Houses are tall and brown, clothes hang to dry from the balconies and windows. As we approach the border of Beyt al-'Ayla, the clopping sounds of hooves sweep in from a passing horse pulling a wooden cart and soon fade away in the distance. The driver stops the tuk-tuk, we climb down, and watch as the vehicle turns around and drives back on the same dusty road from whence we came. It is quiet here, serene, or perhaps decadent. Some children play on the "empty" street at the neighbourhood's entrance. We take a few steps, listening to the children's cheerful voices, as we venture into this alternative space on the margins of the city.*

The neighbourhood is delineated by six *marāḥil*, or geographical zones. With the exception of the fifth zone that lies to the southwest, metal fences with barbed wire surround the remaining ones. Further, between each zone is a low-rise, but robust, metal gate. Gates like these are also found on the neighbourhood's border to the east that function as entrances. These perform important roles in the control, division, and regulation of space on micro scales (Massey, 2012). Material barriers such as fences and gates not only serve as spatial partitions, but also function as "visual barriers" that carry symbolic meaning (Habeck and Belolyubskaya, 2016).

The space of Beyt al-'Ayla should be understood not only as a residential area in which the built environment simply reflects the fulfilment of a social need for affordable housing. Rather, its spatial configuration and disposition can be read as physical manifestations of an urban planning regime that denies, or at least subtly threatens to deny, residents from organically and spontaneously moving between the neighbourhood's spaces. Through barbed fencing and metal gates, the space subtly signals authority and control that suggest the area's residents are under some apparent threat and/or the residents themselves represent a threat to each other, by way of internal zoning, or to communities living outside the enclosure.

For its Syrian refugee residents, Beyt al-'Ayla's marginality is about much more than geographical location and spatial form. Sulayman, a man in his thirties, for instance, explained that "we went to Beyt al-'Ayla because it is cheap, the rents are cheap compared to for example the first or the second districts". Bent slightly forward while laying his hands on his knees he proceeded to explain that the area was "cheap because it's far away from

[6th of] October and al-Ḥoṣary and those [downtown] areas, and since I didn't have a good and stable job we had to come here". His monthly income was between 1,500 and 2,200 Egyptian pounds and, with apartment rent standing at 750 Egyptian pounds and utility bills amounting to about 300 Egyptian pounds, it was difficult for Sulayman to support his family as he was the only breadwinner. "Right now I'm working in welding, but if I'd had the same job in Syria I definitely would've earned much more", he said with an expression of dejection on his face. Although his mother used to work as a dentist back in Syria she had not been able to work in Egypt as work permits were not easy to get.

The exploitation experienced by Sulayman and the labour market exclusion of his mother illustrate a second layer of marginality. Not only did they live on the geographical periphery of the city, as Syrians they were also exposed to exploitation by employers who were in a position to push down their salaries by taking advantage of their precarious situation. Syrians were not allowed access to Egypt's formal labour market. Although Egypt was a signatory of the 1951 convention for refugees, one interlocutor employed at UNHCR's Cairo office noted:

> [Egypt] had reservations on certain articles, including the article related to access to the labour market. This makes the work prospects and livelihood options very limited if not difficult and refugees therefore don't have access to the formal labour market and are forced to work in the informal sector where they are exposed to exploitation and vulnerable to abuse.
>
> (UNHCR official, email correspondence, June 2016)

This situation had direct implications for family life and household economies in the neighbourhood. Whereas the cultural ideal among the Syrian refugees was for husbands to provide and for the women to be stay-at-home mothers, the situation of exploitation and exclusion had pushed women to assist their husbands and sons in generating an income to cover their expenses. A woman who had lived in the area since 2013 explained the kinds of activities this involved:

> There are those working with hair, they opened hair dressing shops in their homes, there are those who get lollipops and wrap them [in paper] at home in order to work, may God provide for them. People also go to the factories and [work as] house [maids], there are many things they work with. ... Beyt al-'Ayla is where most [work], this is a poor area, but [the women] living in the seventh [more affluent district], [do you think] they would go work? No.
>
> (Syrian woman, interview, March 2017)

Exploitation, exclusion, and the economic hardships that follow are piled on top of the marginality that comes with a peripherally located neighbourhood devoid of any public transport system. With the tuk-tuk and the minibus as the only options for destinations beyond walking distance, residents were highly constrained in their daily mobility. Amira, a woman in her sixties, explained how it was difficult to go outside the area and get the things she needed: "Because I'm old and I don't mingle [with people a lot] . . . but if there was a transportation line that would pass by . . . because I pay five pounds for a tuk-tuk every time I [need to] get something". Like Sulayman, she was *compelled* (*iḍḍarrịna*) to move to Beyt al-'Ayla due to the unaffordable rents elsewhere in the city. But with marginality comes the need for transportation, because the neighbourhood was inadequately furnished with shops and services. The combination of being excluded on the one hand from adequate and fair employment, and on the other from accessing socially valued resources such as services and amenities, finds its spatial expression in people like Sulayman and Amira living on the city margins.

## Hyperlocal practices as disruptive interventions

> *As the sun begins to set over the dusty rooftops of Beyt al-'Ayla, a group of boys kick a football on the street in front of a non-descript apartment building. They let out joyful shouts as they kick the half-pumped ball over the grey asphalt. Night is looming over the neighbourhood and men are returning from their places of work in other parts of the city. The gnarling sounds of tuk-tuks moving in and out of the area resonate across its sombre soundscape while their honking horns flow in and out of the field of audibility, as drivers try to make eye-contact with potential customers. A few women sit on the steps to a building, chatting. One of them yells over to a boy playing football, instructing him to come home to do his homework. Further down the street two young girls stand in front of a balcony on the ground floor of a building making conversation. One of them reaches up and gives the woman on the balcony a couple of pounds in exchange for a soda. From inside the apartment to which the balcony is attached sounds of music emanate, the female vocalist singing in a Levantine vernacular. As we meander through the neighbourhood, we glimpse into balconies where we see cheese, eggs, bread, chips, and other foodstuff stocked in rows filling up the small spaces. Through one of the door openings to an apartment, a man sits on what looks like a chair of the type that's found in barber and hairdresser salons. The bottom half of his face is covered in white, foamy shaving cream and a man standing next to him uses a steel straight edge razor to shave his beard.*

The urban dwellers in Beyt al-'Ayla did not passively accept their arguably dire situation but did what they could to get by. They employed an array of spatial tactics to change their deprived conditions, alleviate their problems, and resist the pressures that threatened their existence. The practices portrayed in the vignette above are examples of how residents negotiated their location on Cairo's periphery, and how they dealt with the near absence of employment opportunities, local services, shops, and other amenities. Their solutions were not part of broader, strategic programmes but nevertheless point out the omissions and deficiencies that such programmes would have to address, should government agencies, non-governmental organisations (NGOs), or other such actors decide that something ought to be done.

We refer to the informal solutions implemented by residents as *hyperlocal* since they were implemented informally at a micro level below the scale of the neighbourhood or community.[3] Informal activities are here understood as practices that are not recognised or regulated by formal institutions and that take place outside contractual and legislative frameworks requiring registration and taxation. Informality is also taken to be the usage of public space in a way not conforming to how that space was originally intended to be used, as specified in a city plan and/or relevant national laws (see also Chapter 9 on the formal-informal divide). Five examples can be drawn out as outlined below.

*1. Miniature shops on balconies*

In the absence of well-stocked grocery stores, Beyt al-'Ayla residents with ground-floor flats have turned their households into miniature convenience stores. This activity takes place on balconies and even within the flats themselves. A variety of basic foodstuffs not available in the formal neighbourhood grocery store are sold here. A Syrian woman in one of the balcony shops explained that she had opened the store with her husband, because they knew that people preferred not to leave the neighbourhood to buy food. It supplied the family with an extra source of income to supplement her husband's salary as a factory worker. Other residents explained that, while these stores could not fulfil all shopping needs, they did provide an important supplement to the inadequate formal services.

*2. Bread ovens in the street*

In other cases, a shop was not even needed. One woman was simply sitting outside her home baking bread in a traditional Egyptian oven, discretely tucked away behind a cloth curtain. This practice was reported in the neighbourhood as a common way for women to supplement their husbands' income, as well as furnishing the family with bread for their own consumption.

*3. Vegetable gardens and chicken coops*

Yet another response to the lack of basic foodstuffs was to start hyperlocal agricultural production within the neighbourhood, wherever possible. One resident encountered during fieldwork was doing gardening in the street, where he had found a small plot of soil for his vegetables. He said that "the shops are so far away and the supermarket is expensive and the greengrocer doesn't always have what we need, so we grow things ourselves". When asked where he had learned the skill, he explained that he was from a village in Eastern Ghouta in the Damascus countryside where they used to have a farm and work the land so it came naturally for him to grow vegetables where he lived. The practice was quite common in the neighbourhood where it took place either on miniature plots or within fenced spaces adjacent to the homes themselves. Additionally, chicken coops in the form of small cages could be found in the streets.

*4. Hairdressing in private homes*

Beyond produce, residents were also left to fend for themselves where basic services such as a shave or a haircut were concerned. Women had opened hair salons in their homes and barbershops for men were readily observable from the streets. One barber explained that he was unwilling to commute in order to work in one of the commercial centres, preferring instead to stay in the neighbourhood to set up shop at home. He worked in the same profession before fleeing from Syria and now offered cheap haircuts to local residents who also saved the money and transport effort required to access the same service elsewhere.

*5. A day-care facility spilling into the street*

Childcare was another service not being catered for through formal channels in the neighbourhood. One informal day-care facility was particularly visible as it had been expanded from an apartment building and into the street itself. Located in an otherwise uninhabited area of Beyt al-‘Ayla, an iron cage had been installed outside the door to allow the children to go outside within an enclosed space. At first the facility gave no other indication of what it was, but after a while a sign with the word day-care (*ḥaḍāna*) and contact phone numbers was added to the exterior.

All of the hyperlocal solutions documented above are not just informal but constitute illegal activities according to Egyptian law. The authorities have responded, but only partially and selectively, singling out the convenience stores in ground-floor balconies for special attention. These have been forcibly and repeatedly shut down by the authorities, which give no explanation beyond pointing out that they are illegal. Yet, the other practices are allowed to continue even though they too occur within full visibility. This is indicative of a broader pattern. According to some estimates, Egypt's informal economy accounts for as much as 40 percent of GDP (European Bank for Reconstruction and Development, 2017). Egyptian authorities have therefore tended to target only the most visible expressions of informality, such as illegal shops and street vendors. In Beyt al-‘Ayla, the perceived necessity of clamping down on informal enterprises may have been exacerbated by the fact that the neighbourhood was part of the nationwide programme to provide affordable housing for low-income groups. Consequently, these areas needed to be as presentable and neat as possible. The shutting down of shops, however, was largely ineffectual. As soon as the authorities had left, shops were simply reopened, either in the exact same location or in neighbouring apartments and balconies. According to residents, this happened repeatedly, even as shopkeepers risked fines and imprisonment for repeated offenses.

## Defiance and diversion in the production of refugee urban space

It is tempting to consider the hyperlocal solutions in Beyt al-‘Ayla simply as everyday practices of coping with a difficult situation. Coping indeed is a relevant term, but it can only adequately capture the practices if coupled with the concept of defiance. Residents were not just coping, they were coping defiantly. The swift reopening of forcibly shut down balcony shops was the most obvious expression of such defiance. Swiftness was of key importance here, because it effectively undermined the power of the authorities in the eyes of residents when they saw how short-lived the effect of state intervention was. The symbolic expression imbued in these defiant acts was saying that state authority had no real power here. The fact that all the other informal practices had not been challenged only serves to reinforce this sense that residents, and not the state, were in control of the neighbourhood. What is at stake in Lefebvrian terms, then, is a claim by urban dwellers of their right to the city. This is achieved by challenging regulations pertaining to the *conception* and *usage* of formal city space.

More precisely, hyperlocal practices can be captured conceptually by the Lefebvrian concepts of *appropriation* and its closely related sister term *diversion*, which in the theoretical literature is sometimes referred to as *differentiation*. The appropriation of space, according to Lefebvre (1991 [1974]: 165) connotes "natural space modified in order to serve the needs and possibilities of a group". Closely associated with, but subtly distinguished from this term, is the spatial practice of diversion, which he understands as the putting to new use of an existing space that may have "outlive[d] its original purpose" (Lefebvre, 1991 [1974]: 167f). If appropriation is the effective use of the *natural* properties of a particular space in order to fulfil some human need, the diversion of space is thus a form of *re*-appropriation of a space, using it for another purpose than was initially intended. As should be clear at this stage, this definition is intimately linked to tensions between state-led production of urban space as seen in Egypt's desert new towns and the informal, hyperlocal practices discussed above.

Baking bread and cutting hair in one's own home in exchange for money, growing vegetables on a pavement plot for private and commercial use, breeding chickens in a cage on a street corner, keeping a vegetable stand in an empty spot outside a building, taking care of the community's children inside and outside a private apartment, and selling foodstuffs from one's balcony – these activities are in one sense mundane everyday acts which indeed may be seen as coping mechanisms, but they should also be appreciated as defiant expressions of how some of the formal, organised spaces of the neighbourhood have outlived their "original" purpose and have been re-appropriated, *diverted*, for new spatial practices. As these practices are informal, unregulated, and *illegal*, they are, in Lefebvre's (1991 [1974]: 33) words: "linked to the clandestine and underground side of social life" and thus to space as a directly lived expression of everyday life.

According to Manuel Castells (1983), the relationship between space and society simultaneously expresses and performs the interests of the dominant class. At the same time, the spatial forms that emerge from this process become points of convergence for "resistance from exploited classes" (Castells, 1983: 4).

In some instances, these focal points of resistance can develop into social movements that challenge the spatial status quo and attempt to restructure city space using new forms and functions. Although the situation in Beyt al-'Ayla cannot be said to represent an explicit attempt to reorganise the neighbourhood through a community-based social movement, it is nevertheless clear that the area's formal, *perceived*, and *conceived* space is being challenged by explicit interventions in the built environment of the neighbourhood-scape. Beyt al-'Ayla, then, has become a point of convergence for resistance, but not of the organised kind usually associated with social movements. Resistance is rather embedded intractably in everyday life, where it comes to be expressed through defiance and the diversion, or re-appropriation, of urban space.

## Conclusion

In the extended quote that opened this chapter, Manuel Castells introduced a sweeping dialectic according to which urban space is produced through the interplay of contradictory tensions between domination and resistance. This corresponds closely to the relations of domination built into the Lefebvrian triad of perceived, conceived, and lived space. Seeing the dialectic at work in Beyt al-'Ayla affords an opportunity to discuss some of the central points implied by both Castells and Lefebvre. For, as Edward Soja (1996: 46) has rightly pointed out, "all social relations become real and concrete, a part of our lived social existence, only when they are spatially 'inscribed' – that is, *concretely represented* – in the social production of social space". The dialectics involved in the production of urban space, then, can only be assessed through concrete analysis as exemplified in the critical urban ethnography carried out for this chapter.

First, the study has drawn attention to the agency of what Castells (1983) calls "oppressed subjects" and their role in the social production of space. According to Castells, the spatial status quo is only challenged when points of convergence for resistance coalesce into social movements. Such a view is at risk of under-appreciating the agency of other forms of resistance, not least those associated with the hyperlocal practices observed here. It may be worth asking whether the intractable ways in which these practices are embedded in everyday urban life do not reflect a strength of agency that may be more difficult to sustain in an organised social movement. Authorities that wish to counter resistance have no clear targets to single out and have to settle for the most visible expressions they can find. Evidently, this has had little to no effect. It may, in other words, not always be in the best interests of urban grassroots to coalesce into social movements. Their agency outside of movements, consequently, has to be seen not only as rational pursuits of material benefit, but also may be read as symbolic expressions of the insistence on upholding the rights of the local community to access different forms of social resources.

Second, the hyperlocal practices explored in this chapter are like links in a chain tied to the most physical aspects of corporeality, but they are also symbolic expressions of the *struggle over space* between, on the one hand,

Lefebvre's perceived and conceived space and, on the other, lived space. These small, hyperlocal acts of disobedience to the hegemonic "expert" discourses on how space should be defined, constructed, and experienced, thus also can be seen as representing inventive imaginations of other socio-spatial futures. As such they demonstrate how alternative urban imaginaries cannot be isolated from the materiality and corporeality of urban spatial practice. An alternative imaginary may be most easily identifiable when observed in discursive utterances such as text, image, or video, but it is equally present in the mundane act of growing vegetables in the street or selling groceries from a balcony, and even more so as, in these cases, the alternative is not only imagined but put into practice. The fact that the act is not accompanied by a political statement or embedded in a coordinated programme of action should not subtract from its status as an act of resistance through reappropriation, a small assertion of one's right to the city, and the clandestine agency that flows from the lived space of everyday life.

## Notes

1 Protests first erupted in the southern city of Dara'a in March 2011 after the authorities arrested some youngsters who had painted anti-regime slogans on a school wall. Having been met with brutal force by the regime, demonstrations spread across the country calling for the fall of the house of president Bashar al-Assad. The violent response by government forces to the initially peaceful protests prompted opposition groups and individuals to take up arms against the government, which thrust the crisis into a vicious civil war with strong international involvement.

2 In 2013, around 380 Syrian families were moved with the help of local UNHCR partner organisations from the neighbouring social housing estate Masakin 'Uthman to Beyt al-'Ayla due to protection issues, including cases of rape and sexual harassment of Syrian women. Since these 380 families moved in, Syrians in the ensuing years have continued to settle in the area. According to a Syrian aid distributer helping people in the area, in 2017 there were between 1,000 and 2,000 Syrian families living in Beyt al-'Ayla.

3 The term hyperlocal is borrowed from media studies where it has been used to designate new media production on, or directed towards, a minuscule scale, often involving citizen reporting, social media, and the use of mobile devices (Radcliff, 2012). We use it here in a broader sense that includes both material practices and symbolic acts or expressions occurring below the community or neighbourhood level.

## References

Bhimji, F. (2016) Visibilities and the Politics of Space: Refugee Activism in Berlin. *Journal of Immigrant and Refugee Studies*. 14(4). 432–450.

Brenner, N. and Theodore, N. (2002) Cities and the Geographies of "Actually Existing Neoliberalism". *Antipode*. 34(3). 349–379.

Castells, M. (1983) *The City and the Grassroots: A Cross-Cultural Theory of Urban Social Movements*. Berkeley and Los Angeles: University of California Press.

Central Agency for Public Mobilization and Statistics (CAPMAS) (2006) *General Census of Population, Housing and Buildings 2006: Final Results*. Cairo: CAPMAS.

Darling, J. (2017) Forced Migration and the City Irregularity, Informality, and the Politics of Presence. *Progress in Human Geography*. 41(2). 178–198.

European Bank for Reconstruction and Development (EBRD) (2017) *Private Sector Diagnostic: Egypt*. Cairo: EBRD.

Fabos, A. and Kibreab, G. (2007) Urban Refugees: Introduction. *Refuge*. 24(1). 3–10.

Fiddian, E. (2006) Relocating: The Asylum Experience in Cairo. *Interventions*. 8(2). 295–318.

Garmany, J. (2008) The Spaces of Social Movements: O Movimento dos Trabalhadores Rurais Sem Terra from a Socio-Spatial Perspective. *Space and Polity*. 12(3). 311–328.

Gottdiener, M. (1985) *The Social Production of Space*. Austin: University of Texas Press.

Goździak, E.M. and Walter, A. (2012) *Urban Refugees in Cairo*. Washington: Institute for the Study of International Migration.

Habeck, J.O. and Belolyubskaya, G. (2016) Fences, Private and Public Spaces, and Traversability in a Siberian City. *Cities*. 56. 119–129.

Jones, M. (2015) Legal Empowerment and Refugees on the Nile: The Very Short History of Legal Empowerment and Refugee Legal Aid in Egypt. *The International Journal of Human Rights*. 19(3). 308–318.

Khalil, O. (2016) Fada'at al-Qahira bayn al-irtiqa' wa al-'askara. [Spaces of Cairo between Upgrading/Gentrification and Militarisation]. *al-Safir*. 3 March. Available at: http://arabi.assafir.com/article/4326.

Kılıçaslan, G. (2016) Forced Migration, Citizenship and Space: The Case of Syrian Kurdish Refugees in Istanbul. *New Perspectives on Turkey*. 54(78). 77–95.

Leary, M.E. (2009) The Production of Space through a Shrine and Vendetta in Manchester: Lefebvre's Spatial Triad and the Regeneration of a Place Renamed Castlefield. *Planning Theory and Practice*. 10(2). 189–212.

Lefebvre, H. (1991 [1974]) *The Production of Space*. Oxford: Basil Blackwell.

Lefebvre, H. (2009 [1979]). Space: Social Product and Use Value. In: Lefebvre, H. Brenner, N. and Elden, S. (eds) *State, Space, World*. Minneapolis: University of Minnesota Press.

Lehtovuori, P. (2010) *Experience and Conflict: The Production of Urban Space*. London: Ashgate.

Liggett, H. (2003) *Urban Encounters*. Minneapolis: University of Minnesota Press.

Liszka, K. (2012) Foreigners, Pharaonic Egypt. In: Bagnall. R.S., Brodersen, K., Champion, C.B., Erskine, A., and Huebner, S.R. (eds) *The Encyclopedia of Ancient History*. Chichester: Wiley.

Macchiavello, M. (2004) Livelihoods Strategies of Urban Refugees in Kampala. *Forced Migration Review*. 20. 26–27.

Malkki, L.H. (2002) News from Nowhere. Mass Displacement and Globalized "Problems of Organization". *Ethnography*. 3(3). 351–360.

Massey, D.S. (2012) Reflections on the Dimensions of Segregation. *Social Forces*. 91(1). 39–43.

Merlin, P. (1980) The New Town Movement in Europe. *The Annals of the American Academy of Political and Social Science*. 451. 76–85.

Merrifield, A. (2000). Henri Lefebvre: A Socialist in Space. In: Crang, M. and Thrift, N. (eds) *Thinking Space*. London: Routledge.

Mitchell, D. (2003) *The Right to the City: Social Justice and the Fight for Public Space*. New York: Guilford Press.

Ocejo, R.E. (2013) *Ethnography and the City: Readings on Doing Urban Fieldwork*. New York: Routledge.

O'Leary, Z. (2007) *The Social Science Jargon-Buster*. London: SAGE Publications.
Owens, P. (2009) Reclaiming "Bare Life"? Against Agamben on Refugees. *International Relations*. 23(4). 567–582.
Palmgren, P.A. (2014) Irregular Networks: Bangkok Refugees in the City and Region. *Journal of Refugee Studies*. 27(1). 21–41.
Peck, J. and Tickell, A. (2002) Neoliberalizing Space. *Antipode*. 34(3). 380–404.
Radcliff, D. (2012) *Here and Now. UK Hyperlocal Media Today*. London: Nesta.
Sadat, A.M. (1974) *The October*. Working Paper Cairo: Ministry of Information (State Information Service).
Sanyal, R. (2014) Urbanizing Refuge: Interrogating Spaces of Displacement. *International Journal of Urban and Regional Research*. 38(2). 558–572.
Sanyal, R. (2017) A No-Camp Policy: Interrogating Informal Settlements in Lebanon. *Geoforum*. 84. 117–125.
Shalabi, S. (2018) City in Motion: Comparing the Spatial Distribution of Urban Transport Services in a Greater Cairo Suburb. *The Built Environment Observatory*. Available at: http://marsadomran.info/en/policy_analysis/2018/03/1485.
Sims, D. (2012) *Understanding Cairo: The Logic of a City Out of Control*. Cairo: American University in Cairo Press.
Smith, N. (1984) *Uneven Development*. Oxford: Basil Blackwell.
Soja, E. (1980) The Socio-Spatial Dialectic. *Annals Association of American Geographers*. 70(2). 207–225.
Soja, E. (1996) *Thirdspace. Journeys to Los Angeles and Other Real-and-Imagined Places*. Malden: Blackwell.
Stevenson, J. (ed) (2017) The Urban Refugee Crisis. *Strategic Comments*. 23(2). v–vii.
Stewart, D.J. (1996) Cities in the Desert: The Egyptian New-Town Program. *Annals of the Association of American Geographers*. 86(3). 459–480.
Thabit, H. (2007) Gawla gadida li-Mubarak fi itar al-mashro' al-qawmi li-al-Iskān [Mubarak on a New Tour in the Framework of the National Project for Social Housing]. *Masress*, 24 September.
Thieme, T., Lancione, M., and Rosa, E. (2017) The City and Its Margins. Ethnographic Challenges across Makeshift Urbanism: Introduction. *City*. 21(2). 127–134.
Thomas, J. (2003) Critical Ethnography. In: Lewis-Beck, M.S. Bryman, A. and Liao, F.T. (eds) *The SAGE Encyclopedia of Social Science Research Methods*. Thousand Oaks: SAGE.
Turner, L. (2015) Explaining the (Non-)Encampment of Syrian Refugees: Security, Class and the Labour Market in Lebanon and Jordan. *Mediterranean Politics*. 20(3). 386–404.
United Nations (UN) (2017) 3RP Regional Refugee and Resilience Plan 2017–2018 in Response to the Syria Crisis: Egypt. Available at: https://reliefweb.int/report/egypt/3rp-regional-refugee-resilience-plan-2017-2018-response-syria-crisis-egypt.
United Nations High Commissioner for Refugees (UNHCR) (2018) Syria Regional Refugee Response: Inter-Agency Information Sharing Portal. Updated 30 April 2018. Available at: http://data.unhcr.org/syrianrefugees/country.php?id=8.
Venegas, K.M. and Huerta, A.H. (2010) Urban Ethnography: Approaches, Perspectives and Challenges. In: Savin-Baden, M. and Howell Major, C. (eds) *New Approaches to Qualitative Research: Wisdom and Uncertainty*. Abingdon and New York: Routledge.
Wahdan, D. (2009) Planning Egypt's New Settlements: The Politics of Spatial Inequities. *Cairo Papers in Social Science*. 32(1). 76–77.

Watkins, C. (2005) Representations of Space, Spatial Practices and Spaces of Representation: An Application of Lefebvre's Spatial Triad. *Culture and Organization*. 11(3). 209–220.

World Bank (2008) *Arab Republic of Egypt: Public Sector Update*. Vol. 1. Report No: 44506-EG. Washington: World Bank.

Zanganeh, Y., Alireza, H., and Hosseinali, K. (2016) The Analysis of Factors Affecting the Residential Mobility of Afghan Immigrants Residing in Mashhad (Case Study: Municipality Regions 4, 5, and 6). *Asian Social Science*. 12(6). 61–69.

Zhongyuan, Z., Spicer, A., and Hancock, P. (2008) Hyper-Organizational Space in the Work of J.G. Ballard. *Organization*. 15(6). 889–910.

Zielniec, A. (2008) *Space and Social Theory*. London: SAGE Publications.

# 7 The struggle for the right to housing in Spain

*Vítor Peiteado Fernández*

## Introduction

The economic crisis, which was sparked in 2008, caused half a million Spanish families to lose their homes in a period of eight years (García-Lamarca and Kaika, 2016). These numbers resulted from a housing structure characterised by high levels of home ownership, product of policies and discourses that framed housing as a safe investment (López and Rodríguez, 2010), encouraging thousands of Spaniards to contract considerable debts to purchase overpriced houses. The easy access to credit, securitisation strategies, and tax policy fuelled the signing of these risky mortgages, turning the economic crisis into a social drama in which thousands lost their homes for not being able to pay their mortgages when the economy collapsed (García, 2010; Burriel, 2011; Colau and Alemany, 2012; Coq-Huelva, 2013; Sabaté, 2016).

In 2009, as a reaction to this critical situation, a group of activists in Barcelona formed the Platform of People Affected by Mortgages (PAH), an organisation that has confronted banks and politicians to guarantee the right to housing as protected in the Spanish Constitution. The success of PAH for gathering social support, stopping evictions, and influencing the political agenda has attracted attention from many scholars who have analysed the organisation from diverse perspectives such as empowerment, the creation of new forms of governance, and the articulation of social movements (Romanos, 2013; Flesher Fominaya, 2015; Gonick, 2016; Di Feliciantonio, 2016; García-Lamarca and Kaika, 2016; García-Lamarca, 2017); however, all these valuable accounts pay little attention to PAH's discourse, which remains mainly unresearched. This chapter attempts to start covering this lacuna by switching the focus from PAH as an organisation to the construction of a discourse around the right to housing. These discursive changes have shown the potential to open the political space to the development and implementation of alternative experiences and perspectives to the hegemonic commodification of housing.

That said, research on discourse creation as an isolated feature of social mobilisation would offer only a partial understanding of the process. As many social movements scholars claim, to fully comprehend the evolution of social mobilisation it is necessary to look at its key dimensions as intertwined

(McAdam et al., 1997), making it necessary to consider the mutual influence between them. Among these, discourse—researched within this body of literature mainly through frame analysis—and repertoire of collective action —the actions of social movements—have received most attention in research on social mobilisation (Della Porta and Diani, 2006; Tarrow, 2011). Unfortunately, despite the previously mentioned calls for integration, the studies focusing on these two dimensions traditionally have been limited to mechanistic accounts about how frames shape actions, thus oversimplifying what is in fact a more complex interaction. This chapter attempts to enrich this research by seeing instead frames and repertoire as permanently embedded in a dialectic relation (Ellingson, 1995), in which not only the former determines the latter, but focusing mainly on how the repertoire influences the discourse's evolution and construction of new meanings. In other words, the chapter investigates how an alternative definition of the right to housing, which confronts the hegemonic perception of housing as an asset, can be developed in relation to the social mobilisation articulated by PAH. The chapter is divided into four main parts. The first part describes the organisation, the second part develops the theoretical framework, while the third part analyses how PAH's struggle has evolved over time. The last section summarizes the main conclusions.

## Mobilising for housing rights

Although PAH grew fast by incorporating affected people who were not politicised before (García-Lamarca, 2017), its existence in the first years was limited to Catalonia and some big cities in the rest of Spain like Madrid, Valencia, or Murcia (Huerga, 2015). The 15M or Indignados movement in May 2011, of which PAH was one of the promoters, proved to be an important moment in its expansion, as PAH became one of the main organisations used by activists around the country to sustain their activism after the squares were abandoned (Abellán Bordallo, 2015). As of March 2017, PAH had 239 nodes that worked independently on a local basis, although coming together in regional and national assemblies to discuss general strategies and tactics (PAH, 2015a). These gatherings established an overarching framework for mobilisation through the launch of "campaigns" for a concrete goal and with a specific repertoire. Nonetheless, it is each local PAH which decides how to get involved and "against" whom to implement those campaigns depending on their context.

In general, PAH follows a hybrid strategy of conjoining an institutional and a more confrontational repertoire in order to advance its demands. This has been a common strategy of Spanish social movements after the 15M movement (Martínez López, 2016), although, in the case of PAH, the institutional strategy has exclusively taken the form of addressing and negotiating with institutions, refusing to enter them. Moreover, PAH has always defended its neutrality towards institutional actors, especially the political parties, so the more stable connection with the institutions is made through other mediating organisations like *Observatory Desc* (Weerdt and García, 2016), which are linked to PAH through the double militancy of some core activists.

The analysis in this chapter focuses on the five main national campaigns launched by PAH by 2017 and how they have influenced the definition of the right to housing. The data were collected both from primary and secondary sources. The primary sources were drawn from fieldwork in two chapters of the organisation: *PAH Barcelona*, the first and one of the most important nodes; and *Stop Desafiuzamentos Coruña*, a small PAH from the city of A Coruña, a mid-sized city in the Spanish context (around 250,000 inhabitants). This fieldwork was conducted as participant observation in both cities between March and December 2017. The data were retrieved by attendance at assemblies of affected people, coordination assemblies, thematic commission meetings, and protest actions implemented by both nodes. In addition, this fieldwork was complemented by online sources like the general website of PAH,[1] general communications, press releases, mailing lists, and social media, especially Facebook. Regarding the secondary sources, these mainly included previous studies on PAH and news from mass media.

## Theoretical framework

As a consequence of the multifaceted articulation of social mobilisation, the literature on social movements is vast and varied. It is beyond the scope of this chapter to discuss the advantages and pitfalls of the different approaches, instead the focus will be on the two key concepts within the body of research used here: repertoire of collective action and discursive frame analysis.

### *Repertoire of collective action*

The concept of repertoire of collective action, first coined as repertoire of contention by its creator Charles Tilly (1986), refers to "the whole set of means [groups] have for making claims of different kinds on different individuals or groups". Thus, although many of these means could be defined as unconventional, since they do not use the channels offered by the political system (e.g. elections), this consideration is not static, as such actions can be integrated and normalised by the system (Della Porta and Diani, 2006). Furthermore, Tarrow (2011) talks of the modularity of the repertoire of collective action to reflect how the actions that form the repertoire can be exported to other groups and episodes of contention through processes of adaptation to the goals and the new context. Nevertheless, this translation is not immediate, since the repertoire is embedded in specific political cultures that constrain the actions at hand for the movements, taking some time before innovative forms of protest become fully incorporated within the repertoire (Tilly, 2005). Moreover, the repertoire is dynamic, conjoining actions from different strategies at the same time and changing in the different phases of the wave of protest (Della Porta and Diani, 2006), as a reaction to the effects of multiple variables like interactions with authorities, the level of repression, or the development of networks (Diani, 2003).

One way to categorise these actions is by attending to their levels of confrontation, distinguishing between violent, contained, and disruptive behaviour (Tarrow, 2011). Violent action is the easiest to initiate, but is usually limited to small groups due to high costs for the activists. The contained are linked to the most institutionalised actions that can be accepted by the elites and are based on the creation of certain routines. Disruptive, on the contrary, try to break the normal use of certain space or the normal functioning of a certain institution, the economy, or the society in general, with the intention of disorienting the elites (Tarrow, 2011). The last two types are by far the most common, because they imply lower costs for mobilisation. An example of a disruptive action would be actions linked to civil disobedience, whereas contained actions refer to institutionalised ones, like petitions. Obviously, there is not a clear-cut separation of when an action is disruptive or not, so this is better seen as a continuum. Furthermore, the level of disruption of an action depends on spatio-temporal variations, which make it necessary to attend to the political, social, and economic context to categorise individual actions. Moreover, this characterisation does not come without problems, since the actions imply interaction between multiple actors, which can lead to unexpected developments (e.g. a peaceful demonstration turning into a violent one). The categorisation therefore should be used more as a guideline than as well-defined a priori categories. This categorisation of the modular repertoire of collective action provides a criterion to analyse the different campaigns implemented by PAH, defining their specificities and their impact on the definition of the right to housing.

### *Collective action frames*

Introduced for the study of social movements by Snow et al. (1986), frame analysis focuses on the "interpretative schemata that simplifies and condenses the 'world out there' by selectively punctuating and encoding objects, situations, events, experiences, and sequences of actions within one's present or past environment" (Snow and Benford, 1992: 137). These discursive frames explain and legitimise social mobilisation, including three main tasks: diagnosis, establishing the grievance, the undesirable situation to be changed, and those responsible for it; prognosis, describing the desirable future and the means for advancing towards that future; and motivational, offering the motives that work as the impetus for action (Snow and Benford, 1988; Haunss, 2007).

As it happens with the repertoire, frames are also culturally embedded, so their potential for mobilisation relates to the broader discursive context in which they are inserted (McCammon et al., 2007). To increase the frame resonance within that context is basic to implementing mechanisms of frame alignment, through which the frame is adapted and transformed to connect congruently the interpretive orientations of the social movement organisation and its potential supporters. Among the processes of frame alignment, Snow et al. (1986) distinguish four, according to the degree to which they rest on existing values or on alternative ones: *frame bridging*, understood as the linkage of two or more structurally unconnected frames regarding a particular issue or problem (Snow et al., 1986: 467); *frame extension*, meaning the extension of the boundaries of the primary framework to encompass objectives which can attract new adherents; *frame amplification*, defined as the invigoration of a frame that bears on a specific issue or event; and finally, *frame transformation*, which implies a change of the domain-specific interpretative frame or a change in a global interpretative frame in which one frame gains ascendance over others. These can be seen in a continuum from less to more ambitious in the attempt to change general values, with *frame transformation* being the most ambitious and central for developing a master frame that prevails over other secondary frames. This chapter argues that, in the case of PAH, the right to housing functions as this master frame, being mentioned since the beginning of the mobilisation, but changing its meaning as mobilisation advanced.

Regarding the combination of repertoire and discourse, despite the calls for integration from social movements scholars (McAdam et al., 1997), the analyses are limited almost exclusively to how discourse frames the repertoire or how structural variables influence contentious language adaptation (Steinberg, 1999; Haydu, 2012; Tarrow, 2013; Motta, 2015). Little attention has been rendered to specifically analyze how the repertoire influences a social movement's framing. Exceptions to this vacuum include Ellingson's (1995) research on the changes of abolitionist and anti-abolitionist discourses after the riots in Cincinnati in the 1830s, and Sewell's (1996) account of how the meaning of the word "revolution" changed after the taking of the Bastille. Both focus on events understood as "sequences of occurrences that result in transformation of structures" (Sewell, 1996: 843) and on dislocations that change the framing as the groups adapt to the contentious actions. Consequently, it is necessary to consider the temporality of events, their framing, and how they form historical series of connected events (Sewell, 1996). Thus, by following the temporality of PAH's campaigns as a series of connected events, this chapter reconstructs how the repertoire has been evolving as a reaction to the particular conditions created by the housing crisis, becoming an important factor in the transition from a framing around a vague opposition to evictions to specific measures against housing commodification. That said, there are two main differences between Ellingson's and Sewell's accounts and the one presented here: first, they focus on the impact of violent actions, ignoring the consequences of disruptive and contained actions; and second, they mainly focus on general cultural frame changing by actors external to the movement, while here the focus is on the discursive operations within the movement as intertwined with the repertoire implemented by the movement itself.

In summary, the actions are considered here not only as instruments for gathering support or pressuring rivals, but also as expressions of the protesters' demands that centre on the "right to housing", which becomes the master frame for mobilisation. The development, expansion, and contraction of the master frame are not purely discursive operations, but comprise a process influenced by extra-discursive mobilisation actions. Consequently, these aspects are dialectically interlinked, so the discursive frame is necessary to boost mobilisation, while at the same time the evolution of that contention shapes the way in which the frame is understood. The next section describes the mechanisms and dynamics that have determined this relationship in the case of PAH.

## An antagonist's right to housing

Already in its first documents, PAH explicitly referred to the right to housing, which was also part of its main slogan: "*De la burbuja inmobiliaria al derecho a la vivienda*" ("From the real estate bubble to the right to housing"). Thus, by showing the transition from the bubble mentioned in the first part of the motto and the need for overcoming this through the defence of the right to housing, the organisation started to fill the diagnostic framing task. This section analyses how this definition has been shaped by PAH's five main campaigns until it became the main master frame for the last campaign and the mobilisation in general:

1. *Stop Desahucios* (Stop Evictions). Officially started on 3 November 2010 (PAH, 2012), it was the first campaign organised by PAH. It is based on direct measures for protecting people from eviction for not being able to pay their mortgages. Thus, besides legal advice, when a local node learns about an eviction, it mobilises to stop it by peacefully blocking the entrance of the court representative executing the eviction. These actions reinforce the framing created in the assemblies, turning the problem from the individual shame of losing one's home into a collective problem caused by external actors. Furthermore, as García-Lamarca and Kaika (2016) relate, the direct participation in stopping evictions played a central role to create an identity by developing solidarity bonds among people suffering during the housing crisis, who then depend on each other's support.

   Even though the campaign remains active, the number of actions has been reduced, especially due to the willingness of the banks to negotiate when they learn that the affected person is supported by PAH. The launch of this campaign reacted to the emergency at the beginning of the crisis and can be labelled as defensive disruptive measures. Although the right is mentioned when framing these actions, its meaning is not discussed and the claim is limited to the right of people to keep their houses. Therefore, in the press releases linked to the first blockades in 2010 and 2011, mentioning of the right referred directly to the application of the Spanish Constitution and the Universal Declaration of Human Rights (PAH, 2010). The definition of this right is not discussed yet, but it exposes a reality that proves the failure of that constitutional protection.
2. Campaign for *changing the law* to guarantee retroactive nonrecourse debt. In 2011, PAH presented a Legislative Popular Initiative (ILP) to be processed by the Bureau of the Parliament to allow the collection of at

least 500,000 signatures to force Parliament to discuss its proposal for changing the law. After two refusals by the Bureau (PAH, 2011a), the collection started in February 2012, getting 1.4 million signatures and forcing Parliament to discuss it (PAH, 2013c). According to Spanish law, foreclosure does not imply the cancellation of debt unless the value of the house covers the debt entirely. This was the main point that PAH wanted to change, although its proposal included other measures as well. The right to housing appears only once in the proposal and the definition is vague. Moreover, the measures proposed are exclusively limited to the protection from foreclosures due to the impossibility of paying a mortgage and to guaranteeing a social rent for those facing eviction (PAH, 2011b). This represents a more institutionally-contained approach, according to Tarrow's (2011) typology, and can be labelled as legislative-palliative measures.

The beginning of the campaign coincided with the 15M movement. Together with the territorial expansion previously mentioned (Huerga, 2015), the politicisation started by the 15M movement also influenced PAH's discourse (Díaz Cortés and Sequera, 2015) by helping to reframe the housing issue more politically and to insert the housing crisis within the frame of regime and democratic crisis denounced by those occupying the squares (Flesher Fominaya, 2017). Thus, activists proposed a discourse of a new citizenship, which implied the defence of a set of rights (Gerbaudo, 2017), and questioned the definition of the rights within the representative liberal democratic regime. Through a process of *frame bridging* (Snow et al., 1986), this citizenship discourse was translated by PAH by questioning the definition of the right to housing as protected in the Constitution, which is understood now as a fundamental universal human right. Furthermore, with the expansion of the discourse, politicians (mainly from the conservative Partido Popular) were now included as being held responsible for the housing crisis, as they preferred to take the banks' side against the people affected when they did not take the law proposal under consideration (Flesher Fominaya, 2015). Thus, in her speech before the sub-commission of the Spanish Parliament for the reform of the mortgage system in connection with the discussion of the ILP, Ada Colau, spokesperson of PAH, made a final tirade in which she warned that time was running out and so was the social peace, so politicians should choose the right side (Alemany and Colau, 2011). Even the title of her speech, "Menos comisión y más democracia" ("Less commission and more democracy"), frames the confrontation between a delegitimised Parliament and the citizens. The right to housing is not yet the main master frame and its definition is still under construction, but the framing as a fundamental right becomes preeminent. This growing importance and the more confrontational discourse against the institutions imply a deepening of the disruption, as will be seen more clearly in the next campaign.

3. The failure of the ILP—withdrawn by PAH in 2013 due to the substantial changes made by the parties during the parliamentary discussion—was used to show the separation between the population and the politicians' interests.

Furthermore, it played a central role in legitimising a radicalisation of the repertoire, which affected the discourse. These developments led to open support for civil disobedience and more disruptive actions like bank blockades and occupations. The most relevant action in terms of visibility and disruption was the *campaign of escraches* that started in February 2013 (PAH, 2013e). *Escrache* is a civil disobedience action, popularised in Argentina, consisting of gathering in the streets for making noise with pots and other tools. In the case of PAH, the actions happened in front of houses and places where MPs were located, in order to pressure them to vote in favour of the ILP (Romanos, 2013). Once the proposal was rejected the campaign intensified, especially against members of the ruling party, those mainly responsible for the failure (Partido Popular). Nevertheless, the campaign stopped after a while, due to the high costs for the participants and because it started to divert the focus from the right to housing to the democratic legitimacy of actions (Flesher Fominaya, 2015), which could cause PAH to lose the initiative in terms of framing, as Ellingson (1995) showed in the case of anti-abolitionists in Cincinnati.

In this campaign, the task of diagnosis was prevalent, by expanding the rivals and the injustice to be challenged. This campaign indicates an evolution in the repertoire, as more disruptive civil disobedience appeared as a legitimate tool to achieve the right to housing, which, as a fundamental right, must be protected even by radical means. The rights discourse derived from the 15M movement appears fully integrated in PAH's framing, helping to reformulate the right to housing and to increase its importance as the master frame. Besides, the failure of the ILP reinforced the framing of the linkage between politicians and the financial sector, which was seen to impoverish democracy (PAH, 2013a, 2013b). As the right to housing emerged as the master frame, the causes of the housing crisis expanded from the high levels of debt to a whole crisis and corruption of the economic and political system, although the definition of the right to housing was still limited to the nonrecourse debt, the social rent for evicted people, and the stopping of evictions. Furthermore, this mobilisation—in opposition to *Stop Desahucios*—was not directed to the defence of individual families to remain in their houses, but was rather a political action for pressuring politicians who were marked as responsible for the housing problem. This campaign continued the transition to a more structural perspective, since the previous struggle for the right of specific individuals was transformed into a general claim for measures to guarantee a universal housing right for everyone as a basic feature for a democratic system, which was constantly ignored and must be protected even through radical actions. This paved the way for the expansion of the next campaign, which gained prominence within the press releases related to a reactivation of *escraches* for the European elections of May 2014 (PAH, 2014).

4. *Obra Social* (Social work) rehoused evicted people in empty apartments belonging to banks, as a way to pressure the banks to relinquish those houses for a social rent to those occupying them (PAH, 2013d). Even

though the campaign was launched in September 2011, it was after the failure of the ILP at the end of 2013 that it became generalised. Before that year it was concentrated in a few nodes in Catalonia (PAH, 2013d), but the number of occupied houses expanded greatly around the country after 2013. Although this did not disturb the normal functioning of the economy or an institution, it is considered here as a disruptive action because it attacked a core aspect of capitalism: private property.

While up to this campaign mobilisation had centred on the criticism of the promotion of indebtedness or political and legal aspects, now private property was specifically challenged. Therefore, this campaign implemented the direct confrontation of the system sketched in the end of the *escraches* campaign, evolving the discourse to a more antagonist perspective against the commodification of housing, and presenting occupations as a legitimate way to guarantee the fundamental right to housing (PAH, 2013d). This represents an important milestone, since what was challenged now was the very logic of capitalism because private property must be subject to people's needs. This increased the antagonism and allowed the right to housing to reinforce its position as the master frame, in which demands for social housing, which were not present in previous definitions, started to be included. The prevalent task of the framing here was prognosis, as this implemented some desirable measures to assure the right to housing.

Furthermore, this campaign confronted commodification by re-signifying squatting. Whereas in Spain traditionally squatting had a political dimension linked to anarchist and libertarian movements, now this was expanded as a housing solution for those who had been evicted by the system. During my fieldwork in Barcelona there were every week cases of people squatting who joined PAH in search of collective support. This created new imaginaries to resist the hegemonic practices that considered housing as a private property for being traded.

5. All these campaigns culminated in *Las 5 de la PAH* (The five of PAH), launched in November 2015, in which a clear definition of the right to housing was formulated. Even though the initial goal was to pressure the parties running for the general elections of December 2015 with five points to guarantee the right to housing (see Table 7.1), the demands became a general framework for the mobilization of local PAHs. The campaign evolved after the elections in a complementary campaign for the creation of a new housing law (PAH, 2015b), which culminated in the registration of the law proposal at the Spanish Parliament in January 2018. The campaign was still ongoing at the time of writing this chapter.

The definition of the right to housing is more concrete now than the proposal included in the ILP of 2011, emerging as the master frame over other secondary frames for all PAH's mobilisation. Furthermore, claims that were not part of the initial formulation of the right to housing are now included (PAH, 2017). Previous demands are now redefined and concretised, while

*Table 7.1 Las 5 de la PAH* (The five of PAH)

| *Retroactive nonrecourse debt* | *Affordable rent* | *Stop evictions* | *Social housing* | *Guaranteed electricity, water, and gas supply* |
|---|---|---|---|---|
| 1. Mechanisms for guaranteeing "second chances" to grant nonrecourse debt and write off that debt<br>2. Inability to seize a guarantor's home<br>3. Elimination of abusive clauses and economic compensation for them | 1. Reform of the Housing Law to provide security and stability<br>2. Extension to five years and/or formulas by which the contract can be terminated only in specific urgent cases<br>3. Create a regulatory framework for prices in accordance with the population's average income | 1. Moratorium of evictions from the main and only home<br>2. Mandate for banks and big real estate companies to offer a social rent to affected families prior to the execution of their eviction<br>3. Financial help for paying rent in cases where the landlord does not have many houses<br>4. Mandate to public administrations to offer resettling even in cases of squatting<br>5. Mandate for companies to offer settlement in the same municipality and neighbourhood in cases of resettling | 1. Use of empty houses through mandatory cessions<br>2. Increasing the offer of public housing<br>3. A maximum of 30% of a family's total income for stabilising social rents | 1. Caution principle: guarantee for not cutting off the basic supply of water, electricity, and gas without gathering information about the situation of the affected people<br>2. Social subsidy: payment according to purchase power<br>3. Refusal to cover the debts with public funds, forcing suppliers to assume the costs of families that cannot pay |

Source: PAH (2015b)

two new demands developed in connection with the evolution of the repertoire appear in the last two points. Thus, although Colau mentioned social housing already in a speech before the Parliament during the defence of the ILP in 2011, she exclusively framed it as the possibility of transforming empty houses belonging to banks into social housing for those facing evictions (Alemany and Colau, 2011). Now, through a process of *frame extension*, this appears reformulated and expanded as the demand for an active policy to increase the stock of social and public housing. Moreover, the fifth point incorporates a new demand previously disconnected from the right to housing, expanding the frame even further and connecting it with external demands. This is again an institutional-contained action in Tarrow's (2011) typology, although some PAH branches attach to it some actions like blockades, which approximates it more to the disruptive at certain moments and places.

It is necessary to clarify that, even though campaigns like *escraches* were launched for a specific time span, the actions attached to these campaigns were incorporated within the repertoire of collective action, being activated or reconfigured in specific moments by local chapters (e.g. *Stop Desafiuzamentos Coruña* organised on 31 May 2017 an action at the headquarters of Banco Popular to apply pressure against one eviction). Furthermore, although here the campaigns are presented chronologically attending to the moments when they picked up speed, they overlapped and influenced each other.

The politicisation produced by the campaigns, in which structural aspects progressively gained importance over the more individual resistance to evictions, has been enriching the master frame. Thus, in the first documents the frame is present but vague and not really connected to specific measures other than stopping evictions. In this stage, motivational and diagnostic frame elements appear as the main tasks filled by the frame. With the beginning of the mobilisation and the resistance to individual evictions the right was filled with meanings of non-recourse debt, which culminated in the campaign for the ILP with a proposal that focused purely on evictions. When the 15M movement's discourse of citizenship and democracy gained momentum, it increased the resonance of the right to housing as one of the main rights to be included within that renewed definition of citizenship and democracy. Besides, it initiated a transition towards a more structural conceptualisation, starting with the demand for deep legal changes to guarantee and expand the right to housing, although this was still vaguely defined. The subsequent radicalisation of the *escraches* introduced the further antagonist occupation of empty apartments as a solution for the lack of affordable housing. This led to the reference and inclusion of structural measures to control the market, such as the claim for the expansion of the stock of social and public housing demanded in the last campaign. As the movement advances and the implemented actions diversify, prognosis becomes a central task for the frame, although this prominence is not accompanied by a redefinition of "the desired future" in order to adapt it to the new scenario. Thus, this still refers just to people affected by mortgages, even when my fieldwork confirmed that PAH deals today with a large diversity of housing issues and not only foreclosures. For example, when doing fieldwork in PAH Barcelona, I detected that most of the new cases were of people facing rental eviction (PAH only started to adjust to this new scenario and explicitly refer to the rental crisis at the end of my fieldwork). Concurrently, this lack of reformulation limits the development of the motivational task, since new motives with the potential for mobilisation (i.e. the increase of rental prices) have not yet been fully incorporated within the master frame.

## Conclusion

The analysis has shown how the right to housing has emerged as the main master frame for mobilisation concerning housing, evolving from a vague restricted conceptualisation about the phenomenon of evictions to a more concrete and broader vision which points to the structural level. In this process, the repertoire has influenced the frame construction differently, depending on the type of collective action implemented. Thus, more disruptive contentious actions have influenced in a more prefigurative way (Yates, 2015), actualising potential new meanings for the frame, while the institutional actions fixed and abstracted that actualisation. The chronology of campaigns shows how disruptive actions precede institutional ones to create the conditions for changes in the frame that will be systematised by those changes. Thus, for example, the defence of social housing is prefigured by the occupation of houses through *Obra Social*, before this even becomes systematised as part of the right to housing. This confirms the value of the hybrid strategy of conjoining disruptive and contained actions for developing and extending the frame and, in this case, increasing its antagonism. This resonates with Sewell's (1996) findings about the word revolution, in which the French Parliament translated the meanings derived from actions, with the difference here being that the actors who create the conditions are the same ones who change the meanings. Moreover, this case seems to show a more limited effect than the one concerning the word revolution or the riots in Cincinnati (Ellingson, 1995), since the effective structural changes are more modest.

Besides, mechanisms of *frame bridging* and *frame extension* contributed to this evolution, being influenced by the actions implemented by the organisation in various ways, such as the direct interaction with authorities during the actions. In this sense, the fact that the master frame departs from a contradiction between the formal constitutional defence of the right to housing and the reality facilitates the diagnosis and agential task of the frame, presenting the authorities as a clear target to blame for not guaranteeing the right they are supposed to protect. Moreover, the total opposition by those authorities legitimated the challenge, first, to the regime due to its lack of democracy—*frame bridging*—and, second, to the whole economic system—*frame extension*—aspects which were incorporated in the right to housing by defining it as a fundamental right and by the need for social housing to confront speculation. Furthermore, the actions helped to expand the actors responsible for the housing crisis—one of the frame's tasks—by blaming not only the authorities but also economic elites—as exemplified in the framing of the *escraches*.

Concurrently, the previous account shows that attending to the influence of extra-discursive dimensions provides insights to better grasp social movements discourse formation mainly in three ways. First, it helps to explain how the discourse and the repertoire are embedded and influence each other; second, it shows also that the construction of the master frame implies an expansion of the frame meanings that relate it to new demands that are not directly linked to housing (the inclusion of guaranteed supplies is a good example); third, it demonstrates how the development of an antagonist master frame benefits from social mobilisation that reinforces it, making it necessary to consider it in the analysis to better understand the process of creating such a frame.

Moreover, this case provides an interesting example of how an antagonist conceptualisation of the right to housing can be developed and strengthened through the empowerment of people suffering during the housing crisis. This chapter has demonstrated the potential of bottom-up housing activism to challenge consolidated hegemonic housing regimes by developing and extending alternative perspectives of housing that question housing commodification discourses. Furthermore, the empowerment and the reformulation of the right to housing promoted by PAH politicised the housing issue, incorporating it into the public agenda. Therefore, without the path opened by PAH's struggle, it would be impossible to understand the proliferation of initiatives to rethink housing issues that would have seemed strange in the Spanish context not long ago but now pop up all over the country, as, for example, the promotion of co-housing or the creation of a tenants' union in Barcelona. As such the chapter contributes a more nuanced understanding of the dialectics between discursive and extra-discursive struggles in the production of alternative urban spaces of dwelling. This process can only be properly understood by considering the intertwined nature of extra-discursive activist performativity (the blockades to stop evictions, the occupation of empty houses, etc.) and the sustained discursive struggles necessary to produce counter-hegemonic urban imaginaries in which alternatives gradually begin to appear as real possibilities rather than vague utopian dreams.

## Note

1 afectadosporlahipoteca.com.

## References

Abellán Bordallo, J. 2015. De la red a la calle: El proceso de movilización previo a las manifestaciones del 15 de mayo [From the Net to the Streets: The Mobilisation Process before the Demonstrations of 15 May]. *ACME: An International E-Journal for Critical Geographies*, 14(1), pp. 10–29.

Alemany, A. and Colau, A. 2011. Menos comisión y más democracia real. Comparecencia ante la subcomisión para la reforma del mercado [Less Commission and More Real Democracy. Appearance before the Subcommittee for Market Reform]. Press release. PAH: Madrid. Available at: http://ibdigital.uib.es/greenstone/collect/cd2/import/PAH/pah0007.pdf.

Burriel, E.L. 2011. Subversion of Land-Use Plans and the Housing Bubble in Spain. *Urban Research & Practice*, 4(3), pp. 232–249.

Colau, A. and Alemany, A. 2012. *Vidas Hipotecadas* [*Mortgaged Lives*]. 1st edn. Barcelona: Cuadrilatero de Libros.

Coq-Huelva, D. 2013. Urbanisation and Financialisation in the Context of a Rescaling State: The Case of Spain. *Antipode*, 45(5), pp. 1213–1231.

Della Porta, D. and Diani, M. 2006. *Social Movements: An Introduction*. 2nd edn. Malden, MA: Blackwell Publishing.

Diani, M. 2003. "Leaders" or Brokers? Positions and Influence in Social Movement Networks. In: M. Diani and D. McAdam (eds) *Social Movements and Networks: Relational Approaches to Collective Action*. Oxford: Oxford University Press, pp. 173–203.

Díaz-Cortés, F. and Sequera, J. 2015. Geografías del 15-M: Crisis, austeridad y movilización social en España [Geographies of the 15M: Crisis, Austerity and Social Mobilisation in Spain]. *ACME: An International E-Journal for Critical Geographies*, 14(1), pp. 1–216.

Di Feliciantonio, C. 2016. Social Movements and Alternative Housing Models: Practicing the "Politics of Possibilities" in Spain. *Housing, Theory and Society*, 33, pp. 1–19.

Ellingson, S. 1995. Understanding the Dialectic of Discourse and Collective Action: Public Debate and Rioting in Antebellum Cincinnati. *The American Journal of Sociology*, 101(1), pp. 100–144.

Flesher Fominaya, C. 2015. Redefining the Crisis/Redefining Democracy: Mobilising for the Right to Housing in Spain's PAH Movement. *South European Society and Politics*, 20(4), pp. 465–485.

Flesher Fominaya, C. 2017. European Anti-Austerity and Pro-Democracy Protests in the Wake of the Global Financial Crisis. *Social Movement Studies*, 16(1), pp. 1–20.

García, M. 2010. The Breakdown of the Spanish Urban Growth Model: Social and Territorial Effects of the Global Crisis. *International Journal of Urban and Regional Research*, 34(4), pp. 967–980.

García-Lamarca, M. 2017. Creating Political Subjects: Collective Knowledge and Action to Enact Housing Rights in Spain. *Community Development Journal*, 52(3), pp. 421–435.

García-Lamarca, M. and Kaika, M. 2016. "Mortgaged Lives": The Biopolitics of Debt and Housing Financialisation. *Transactions of the Institute of British Geographers*, 41(3), pp. 313–327.

Gerbaudo, P. 2017. The Indignant Citizen: Anti-Austerity Movements in Southern Europe and the Anti-Oligarchic Reclaiming of Citizenship. *Social Movement Studies*, 16(1), pp. 36–50.

Gonick, S. 2016. Indignation and Inclusion: Activism, Difference, and Emergent Urban Politics in Postcrash Madrid. *Environment and Planning D: Society and Space*, 34(2), pp. 209–226.

Haunss, S. 2007. Challenging Legitimacy: Repertoires of Contention, Political Claims-Making, and Collective Action Frames. In: A. Hurrelmann, S. Schneider, and J. Steffek (eds) *Legitimacy in an Age of Global Politics*. London: Palgrave Macmillan, pp. 156–172.

Haydu, J. 2012. Frame Brokerage in the Pure Food Movement, 1879–1906. *Social Movement Studies*, 11(1), pp. 97–112.

Huerga, C. 2015. Desde V de Vivienda a la PAH, la lucha por el derecho a la vivienda [From V de Vivienda to PAH, the Struggle for the Right to Housing]. *Viento Sur*, 138, pp. 57–62.

López, I. and Rodríguez, E. 2010. *Fin de ciclo: Financiarización, territorio y sociedad de propietarios en la onda larga del capitalismo hispano (1959–2010)* [*End of Cycle: Financialisation, Territory and Society of Owners in the Long Wave of Spanish Capitalism (1959–2010)*]. Madrid: Traficantes de Sueños.

Martínez López, M.A. 2016. Between Autonomy and Hybridity: Urban Struggles within the 15M Movement in Spain. In: M. Mayer, C. Thörn, and H. Thörn (eds) *Urban Uprisings: Challenging Neoliberal Urbanism in Europe*. London: Palgrave Macmillan, pp. 253–281.

McAdam, D., Tarrow, S., and Tilly, C. 1997. Toward an Integrated Perspective on Social Movements and Revolution. In: M. Irving Lichbach and A.S. Zuckerman (eds) *Comparative Politics: Rationality, Culture, and Structure*. Cambridge: Cambridge University Press, pp. 142–173.

McCammon, H.J., Sanders Muse, C., Newman, H.D., and Terrell, T.M. 2007. Movement Framing and Discursive Opportunity Structures: The Political Successes of the US Women's Jury Movements. *American Sociological Review*, 72(5), pp. 725–749.

Motta, R. 2015. Transnational Discursive Opportunities and Social Movement Risk Frames Opposing GMOs. *Social Movement Studies*, 14(5), pp. 576–595.

PAH 2010. Comunicado de la PAH para denunciar el desahucio de una familia en Lleida, y los más de 20 diarios que se producen en Cataluña [PAH's Press Release to Report the Eviction of a Family in Lleida, and the More Than 20 Evictions That Take Place in Catalonia Everyday]. Barcelona. Available at: https://afectadosporlahipoteca.files.wordpress.com/2010/10/comunicado-desahucio-lleida-28-nov-2010.pdf.

PAH 2011a. Presentación de la iniciativa legislativa popular para reformar la ley hipotecaria [Presentation of the Popular Legislative Initiative to Reform the Mortgage Law]. afectadosporlahipoteca. Available at: http://afectadosporlahipoteca.com/2011/03/22/presentacio-de-la-iniciativa-legislativa-popular-para-reformar-la-ley-hipotecaria (Accessed: 20 April 2015).

PAH 2011b. Proposición de ley de regulación de la dación en pago, de paralización de los desahucios y de alquiler social [Law Proposal for the Regulation of Nonrecourse Debt, for Stopping Evictions and for Social Renting]. Available at: http://afectadosporlahipoteca.com/wp-content/uploads/2012/01/ilp_dacic3b3n-en-pago-retroactiva_moratoria-de-desahucios_alquiler-social.pdf.

PAH 2012. #Stopdesahucios cumple dos años y se acerca a los 500 desahucios paralizados! [Stop Desahucios Makes Two Years and Approaching 500 Evictions Stopped!] Available at: http://afectadosporlahipoteca.com/2012/11/03/stopdesahucios-cumple-dos-anos-y-se-acerca-a-los-500-desahucios-paralizados-y-que-sean-muchos-mas (Accessed: 14 September 2015).

PAH 2013a. De Ciudadano a Presidente [From Citizen to President]. Available at: http://afectadosporlahipoteca.com/2013/05/04/de-ciudadano-a-presidente-pah-rajoy (Accessed: 20 October 2013).

PAH 2013b. El escrache a Rajoy clausura la campaña Hay Vidas en Juego [The Escrache to Rajoy Closes the Campaign There Are Lives at Stake]. Available at: http://afectadosporlahipoteca.com/2013/05/14/el-escrache-a-rajoy-clausura-la-campana-hay-vidas-en-juego (Accessed: 14 May 2013).

PAH 2013c. Iniciativa legislativa popular (ILP) [Popular Legislative Initiative]. Available at: http://afectadosporlahipoteca.com/2013/02/12/iniciativa-legislativa-popular-ilp (Accessed: 14 September 2015).

PAH 2013d. La Campaña Obra Social de la PAH cumple un año en plena forma! [The Campaign Social Work Makes One Year in Great Shape!] Available at: http://afectadosporlahipoteca.com/2013/01/24/la-campana-obra-social-de-la-pah-cumple-un-ano-en-plena-forma-juntas-podemos (Accessed: 14 September 2015).

PAH 2013e. Nueva campaña de la PAH: Escraches [New PAH Campaign: Escraches]. Available at: http://afectadosporlahipoteca.com/2013/02/04/final-ilp-campanya-escraches (Accessed: 14 September 2015).

PAH 2014. Protocolo de la campaña de escraches [Protocol for the Escraches Campaign]. Available at: http://afectadosporlahipoteca.com/wp-content/uploads/2014/05/protocoloescrache.pdf (Accessed: 9 May 2014).

PAH 2015a. From the Housing Bubble to the Right to Housing. Available at: http://afectadosporlahipoteca.com (Accessed: 21 October 2015).

PAH 2015b. Las 5 de la PAH [The Five of PAH]. Available at: http://las5delapah.com (Accessed: 1 December 2015).

PAH 2017. La PAH comparece para rechazar la proposición de Ley del PdeCat de desahucio exprés en los casos de ocupación sin garantizar realojo [PAH Rejects the Law Proposal Made by PdeCat for Express Eviction in Cases of Occupation without Guaranteeing Rehousing]. Press release. Available at: http://afectadosporlahipoteca.com/2017/06/06/la-pah-comparece-para-rechazar-la-proposicion-de-ley-del-pdecat-de-desahucio-expres-en-los-casos-de-ocupacion-sin-garantizar-realojo (Accessed: 6 June 2017).

Romanos, E. 2013. Evictions, Petitions and Escraches: Contentious Housing in Austerity Spain. *Social Movement Studies*, 13(2), pp. 296–302.

Sabaté, I. 2016. Mortgage Indebtedness and Home Repossessions as Symptoms of the Financialisation of Housing Provisioning in Spain. *Critique of Anthropology*, 36(2), pp. 197–211.

Sewell, W.H. 1996. Historical Events as Transformations of Structures: Inventing Revolution at the Bastille. *Theory and Society*, 25(6), pp. 841–881.

Snow, D.A. and Benford, R.D. 1988. Ideology, Frame Resonance, and Participant Mobilization. *International Social Movement Research*, 1(1), pp. 197–217.

Snow, D.A. and Benford, R.D. 1992. Master Frames and Cycles of Protest. In: A.D. Morris and C.M. Mueller (eds) *Frontiers in Social Movement Theory*. Oxford: Yale University Press, pp. 380–412.

Snow, D.A., Burke Rochford, E. Jr., Worden, S.K., and Benford, R.D. 1986. Frame Alignment Processes, Micromobilization, and Movement Participation. *American Sociological Review*, 51(4), pp. 464–481.

Steinberg, M.W. 1999. *Fighting Words: Working-Class Formation, Collective Action, and Discourse in Early Nineteenth-Century England*. Ithaca, NY: Cornell University Press.

Tarrow, S. 2011. *Power in Movement: Social Movements and Contentious Politics*. 3rd edn. New York: Cambridge University Press.

Tarrow, S. 2013. *The Language of Contention: Revolutions in Words 1688–2012*. New York: Cambridge University Press.

Tilly, C. 1986. *The Contentious French: Four Centuries of Popular Struggles*. Cambridge, MA: Harvard University Press.

Tilly, C. 2005. *Regimes and Repertoires*. Chicago, IL: University of Chicago Press.

Weerdt, J.D. and García, M. 2016. Housing Crisis: The Platform of Mortgage Victims (PAH) Movement in Barcelona and Innovations in Governance. *Journal of Housing and the Built Environment*, 31(3), pp. 471–493.

Yates, L. 2015. Rethinking Prefiguration: Alternatives, Micropolitics and Goals in Social Movements. *Social Movement Studies*, 14(1), pp. 1–21.

# 8 The production of slums

## Old Fadama as an alternative space of urban dwelling

*Esther Yeboah Danso-Wiredu, Jens Kaae Fisker, and Lee Pugalis*

### Introduction

Combating urban poverty has been a key priority of the United Nations (UN) for decades; a commitment recently affirmed by the Quito Declaration on a new urban agenda which was adopted as a UN resolution in December 2016. The resolution identifies "the persistence of multiple forms of poverty, growing inequalities and environmental degradation" as some of the "major obstacles to sustainable development worldwide, with social and economic exclusion and spatial segregation often an irrefutable reality in cities and human settlements" (UN, 2017: 2). More specifically, the declaration recognises that

> the rising number of slum and informal-settlement dwellers, are affecting both developed and developing countries, and that the spatial organisation, accessibility and design of urban space, as well as the infrastructure and basic services provision, together with development policies, can promote or hinder social cohesion, equality and inclusion.
>
> (UN, 2017: 7)

As a result, the new urban agenda reaffirms the commitment of the global community to improve the living conditions of slum-dwellers as part of a broader goal of eradicating poverty (Pugalis et al., 2014a). While concerted efforts have already been made to alleviate slum conditions, such as meeting the target of the Millennium Development Goals to significantly improve the lives of 100 million slum-dwellers well in advance of the 2020 milestone, "urbanization continues to outpace improvements in slum conditions" (UN, 2014: 50). In absolute terms, the number of slum-dwellers is increasing, with estimations suggesting that 863 million people resided in slum conditions in 2012 compared to only 650 million in 1990 (UN, 2014). The rapid pace of urbanisation is particularly acute in sub-Saharan Africa, which according to UN-Habitat (2004) statistics is the most rapidly urbanising region of the world: over the forty-year period to 2050, projections suggest that approximately 20% of the world's urbanised population will reside in Africa.

Slums in sub-Saharan Africa are growing as fast as the urban population in general and the region has the highest annual slum and urban growth rates – 4.53% and 4.58%, respectively – of any world region; nearly twice those of southern Asia, where rates are 2.2% and 2.89%, respectively (UN-Habitat, 2006). In 2001, the population of Ghana living in poor areas was estimated at 4,993,000 people, growing at a rate of 1.83% per annum; the figure had increased to 5.8 million by 2010 (Ministry of Water Resources, Works and Housing, 2012). Whereas the city of Accra has a population density of 250.73 persons per hectare, population density in poor areas within the city is 607.8 persons per hectare, with most living in poor and dangerous conditions along railway lines and banks of waterways (Accra Metropolitan Assembly, 2011). In Greater Accra alone, it is estimated that nearly one-third of the population lives in poor communities (Accra Metropolitan Assembly, 2011) and the number of deprived communities has been estimated at seventy-eight (Ghana Centre for Democratic Development, 2012).

The largest poor community in Ghana is the Old Fadama slum in Accra. The neighbourhood faces multiple problems and the Ghanaian state has adopted a policy of non-recognition that cuts off Old Fadama from public provision of everything from schools and roads to sanitation and electricity. Media and state officials continue to vilify the community and living conditions are poor and precarious. Nevertheless, inhabitants manage to produce – or obtain access to – basic services and infrastructures. Although Old Fadama is still not a place that anyone would choose to inhabit if given the choice, improvements to living conditions have been effected by its inhabitants in what would otherwise appear to be an intractable situation of complete state neglect. This prompts us to challenge the unfortunate habit of stigmatising the slum as a place defined purely on the basis of what it lacks and the associated tendency to strip slum-dwellers of their agency. We propose instead that slum-related urban issues need to be addressed with a point of departure being the slum itself and the agency of its inhabitants. As such we trace the footsteps of subaltern urbanists such as Ananya Roy and Alex Vasudevan by asking how the Old Fadama slum is being produced as an alternative urban space in the specific context of the Greater Accra urban region. We ask this question with the aim of highlighting how a view from the slum can engender innovative and workable solutions not just in Old Fadama but also in the wider urban region, where the ongoing housing crisis remains a top priority for policy development.

Only from such a vantage point is it possible to come up with meaningful ways to meet the urgent challenges that inhabitants are faced with on a daily basis. Fortunately, Old Fadama is a relatively well-studied case allowing us to build upon knowledge derived from previous studies on a wide range of topics. Empirically, the chapter draws on material from fieldwork conducted by the first author from 2012 to 2015 in four poor communities in Accra and Winneba. Qualitative fieldwork in Old Fadama included fifty-seven in-depth interviews with purposively selected respondents as well as various observational methods;

this has been documented in interview transcripts, field notes, and photographs. Additional documentation has been obtained from official sources such as the Accra Metropolitan Assembly. The chapter is organised into two main sections. In the first section we review pertinent international literature on slum-dwelling and informal urban governance to close in on a clearer conception of what it means to be an urban dweller on the blind side of the state. This allows for an initial conceptualisation of how slums are produced as alternative spaces of urban dwelling. In the second section we employ the conceptual and analytical framework thus sketched to investigate the Old Fadama slum in Accra as an alternative urban space of dwelling.

## Urban dwelling on the blind side of the state

### *Slum-dwellers as agents of urban change*

The term "slum" has pejorative origins and stigmatising connotations dating back to the nineteenth century, which characterise these variegated spatial formations as "abnormal" spaces of despair. As a result, this controversial term, evoking images of clandestine practices and urban ills, has often been neutralised by the adoption of associated notions, such as spontaneous or informal settlements (Dagdeviren and Robertson, 2009). Yet, as exemplified by organisations such as Slum/Shack Dwellers International (SDI) and the National Slum Dwellers Federation in India, the term "slum-dweller" also has emerged as a source of self-identification among those who live there (McFarlane, 2011; Hooper and Ortolano, 2012) and, therefore, has regained legitimacy. Indeed, slums can be spaces of hope, resilience, enterprise, and ingenuity (Pugalis et al., 2014b). Moreover, the UN continues to rely on the twin terms "slums and informal settlements" for quantitative data collection, definition of policy objectives, and implementation of development programmes in relation to dwelling and urban poverty.

Yet, the UN perspective on slums is not innocent. It defines a slum as "a contiguous settlement that lacks one or more of the following five conditions: access to clean water, access to improved sanitation, sufficient living area that is not overcrowded, durable housing and secure tenure" (UN-Habitat, 2016: 57). This is an entirely negative definition in which slums are defined simply by listing what they lack as part of a continuum from "less deprived" to "more deprived" (Pugalis et al., 2014b). Slums, perceived through a deficit lens, are a problem to be addressed and their formation (and, thus, existence) is scripted as a result of "failed policies, poor governance, corruption, inappropriate regulation, dysfunctional land markets, unresponsive financial systems, and a lack of political will" (UN-Habitat, 2016: 57). Hence, the policy remedy for these abnormal urban spaces is typically exogenous interventions, including physical rehabilitation and improvement programmes. Representation of slums as physically contained problems also conceals their relational attributes and neglects a fuller consideration of broader socioeconomic processes.

The negative definition of slums was propagated by the UN, but its popularisation owes much to Mike Davis and his *Planet of Slums* from 2006. Taking his cue from *Slums of the World* (UN-Habitat, 2003), Davis paints an apocalyptic picture of a future urban world that "squats in squalor, surrounded by pollution, excrement, and decay" (Davis, 2006: 19). Packed with a ceaseless string of examples from slums across the planet, the book is a *tour de force* of the worst the urban world has to offer. Davis makes little attempt to dig up even a morsel of hope along the way and ends up positioning the slum as "a fully franchised solution to the problem of warehousing this century's surplus humanity" (Davis, 2006: 200). While reaffirming many of the urban ills catalogued by Davis, Pieterse and van Donk (2008: 176) respond to this kind of dystopianism by encouraging researchers "to step beyond a narrow, reactive, interminably critical posture, to one where we take responsibility for letting the light shine through the darkness that engulfs our cities".

The main problem with the UN perspective, particularly its apocalyptic derivatives, is that it tends to strip slum-dwellers of agency. Subaltern urbanists have responded with pointed critiques that seek to revert this tendency without either romanticising slum-dwellers as revolutionary heroes or neglecting the various ailments that do characterise everyday life in the slums. In the words of Roy (2011: 224): "Writing against apocalyptic and dystopian narratives of the slum, subaltern urbanism provides accounts of the slum as a terrain of habitation, livelihood and politics". In contrast to the negative definition employed by the UN, subaltern urbanism shifts attention to what the slum is instead of what it is not. With Vasudevan (2015) the refurnishing of slum-dwellers with agency is achieved through the notion of squatting. He makes use of three interrelated frames in which this is alternately conceived of as (1) "an *informal* set of spatial practices and tactics"; (2) "a *makeshift* approach to housing and shelter"; and (3) "a *precarious* form of inhabiting the city" (Vasudevan, 2015: 340). With a nod to Pieterse, he deploys these frames to answer a question that also animates the current chapter: "to what extent can practices that were designed for the purposes of survival and the extension of often highly precarious forms of life offer a touchstone for other alternative imaginings of cityness?" (Vasudevan, 2015: 339).

### *Informality and urban governance*

There is an almost intuitive and taken-for-granted association between slum-dwelling and urban informality which needs to be problematised from the outset. With Roy (2011: 233) we can assert that "the splintering of urbanism does not take place at the fissure between formality and informality but rather, in fractal fashion, within the informalised production of space". This entails that urban informality "is as much the purview of wealthy urbanites as it is of slum-dwellers" (Roy, 2011: 233), although with the notable difference that the informalities of the affluent are not often vilified while those of slum-dwellers are. Still, urban informality is clearly an important aspect of life in the slum, but it cannot be confined to this bounded spatial unit, just as formality cannot be said to be completely absent. Likewise, the distinction between informal and formal is far from straightforward. In other words, some conceptual clarification is needed in order to begin to account for the kinds of governance arrangements that emerge and evolve in slums.

As a point of departure, Helmke and Levitsky (2004) offer a typology of informal institutions which can help shine a light on the relations that exist between formal and informal governance arrangements. They identify four types of relation: complementary, substitutive, accommodating, and competing (see Table 8.1). This perspective is sufficiently compatible with the subaltern urbanism of Roy in the sense that it does not envision that informality somehow exists outside of the formal structures of power, but rather as a significant constitutive moment within them. It has to be interjected, however, that the distinction between conjunctures with "effective" and "ineffective" formal institutions cannot be seen as pre-given settings but instead are situations that arise precisely from the co-constitutiveness between formal and informal institutions.

Complementary informal institutions are those that reinforce effective formal institutions by "filling in the gaps". They "may also serve as a foundation for formal institutions, creating or strengthening incentives to comply with formal rules that might otherwise exist only on paper" (Helmke and Levitsky, 2004: 728). Accommodating informal institutions belong to similar settings but their outcomes diverge from the aims of the formal institutions to which they relate. This means that they work subversively by "bending the rules": "they contradict the spirit, but not the letter, of the formal rules" (Helmke and Levitsky, 2004: 729). Whereas they do not reinforce the intentions behind formal institutional arrangements, they do tend to provide stability, because they afford actors accepted ways of reconciling their own interests with diverging formal rules without having to act in open revolt. By contrast, competing informal institutions are more openly opposed to their formal counterparts; they "are incompatible with the formal rules: to follow one rule, actors must violate another" (Helmke and Levitsky, 2004: 729). Finally, substitutive informal institutions emerge in situations where outcomes intended by formal institutions are attained in spite of their failure to be enforced, because informal institutions with convergent outcomes act as proxies.

*Table 8.1* Typology of formal-informal relations

| *Outcomes* | *Effective Formal Institutions* | *Ineffective Formal Institutions* |
|---|---|---|
| Convergent | Complementary | Substitutive |
| Divergent | Accommodating | Competing |

Source: Helmke and Levitsky (2004: 728)

## The production of Old Fadama as an alternative urban space

With reference to slum-dwelling we adopt the three frames introduced by Vasudevan (2015) to elucidate (1) which *informal* practices and tactics are employed by slum-dwellers; (2) how inhabitants come up with *makeshift* solutions in the provision of housing; and (3) in what ways slum-dwelling can be seen as a *precarious* form of urban life. Furthermore, in order to analyse the processes of urban governance associated with the provision of housing in the slum we also adopt the typology of relations between informal and formal institutions as introduced by Helmke and Levitsky (2004).

### *The urban context of Greater Accra, Ghana*

Rural-urban migration has characterised the Ghanaian urban system for decades, fuelling the growth of slums and urban sprawl, especially in Greater Accra (Tutu, 2014). In 2012, more than half of the Ghanaian population was urban, while in Accra 51% of inhabitants lived in informal settlements (UN-Habitat, 2012). Urban authorities have largely failed to provide the expansion and upgrading of housing, services, and facilities needed to accommodate the continuing influx of urban newcomers. Simultaneously, privatisation and marketisation of the housing sector have resulted in socio-spatial differentiation of housing in Accra to the extent that the urban poor are effectively cut off from accessing formal housing markets (Yeboah, 2000; Owusu et al., 2008; Agyei-Mensah and Owusu, 2012). Thus, neoliberal urban policies in combination with weak state capacities and improper implementation of planning regulations reinforce a situation in which the urban poor are forced to find other solutions for their housing needs (Konadu-Agyemang, 2001; Grant, 2009).

Following a global pattern (UN-Habitat, 2003, 2016), the urban poor in Accra have responded to their economic exclusion by appropriating vacant lands and public spaces as informal urban settlements. But they have not done so in a haphazard, chaotic, and anarchic fashion. Rather, according to Gillespie (2016), they have introduced a commoning feature to urban processes whereby informal practices, such as the renting of squatter structures and the unsanctioned use of public spaces as marketplaces, have been normalised. Informal-formal divides are furthermore blurred by the fact that "Ghana's land tenure system is governed by both customary and formal land administration systems" (UN-Habitat, 2012: 17), with customary land tenure accounting for about 75% of all land ownership (UN-Habitat, 2009: 16). But this does not mean that informal settlements are recognised as legitimate by state authorities, quite the contrary. Regulatory frameworks in Accra offer "no policy to guarantee access to land for the poor or protection from eviction" while "city-authority threatens eviction and discourages the provision of social facilities" (UN-Habitat, 2009: 15). As a result, "informal settlements have evolved into a sub-tenure system or 'squatter tenancy' as there is no housing provision for the urban poor" (UN-Habitat, 2009: 15).

Since the publication of these dire assessments, several policy initiatives have seen the light of day, but, as shown by Danso-Wiredu and Loopmans (2013), these have mostly consisted of promises and paper evidence with no practical measures.

### *Precarious urbanism in Old Fadama*

One of the tracts of urban land appropriated by rural migrants and the urban poor is situated on 31.3 hectares along the Odaw River and the Korle Lagoon (see Map 8.1). Known as Old Fadama, this community housed 79,684 people when the latest headcount was conducted in 2007. A community leader estimated a figure of more than 100,000 in 2013 (Old Fadama Development Association (OFADA) secretary, interview, 2013), making a population density of 2,424 people per hectare (Farouk and Owusu, 2012; see Danso-Wiredu, 2016 for more details). These figures are highly uncertain and difficult to confirm, but inconsistency is not out of the ordinary as demographic statistics in African slums are often fragmentary or completely absent (Arimah, 2010). Bordered on two sides by the river and the lagoon, the community is also squeezed in-between two scrap sites. On the remaining side, to the northeast, Old Fadama is bordered by the Abossey-Okai Road on the other side of which the Agbogbloshie market is located.

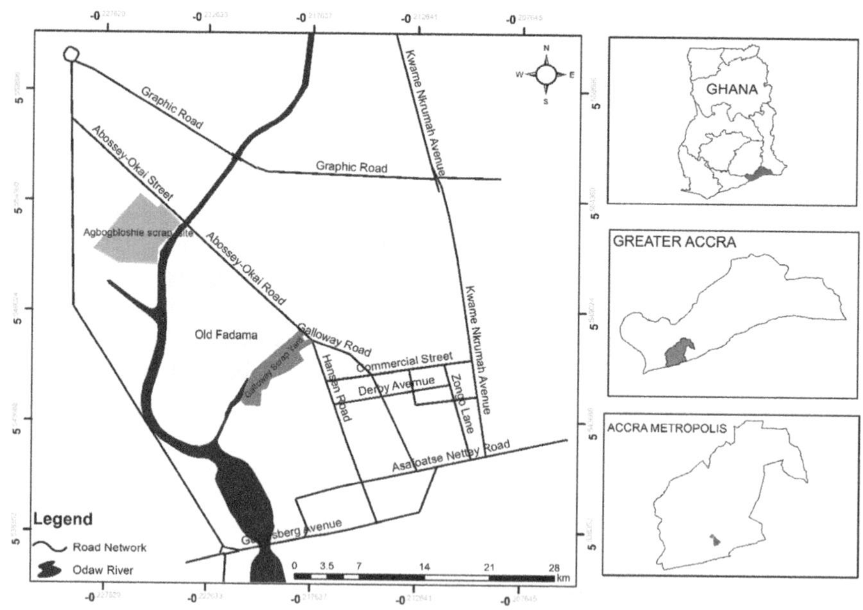


*Map 8.1* Map of Old Fadama relative to Accra Metropolis, Greater Accra, and Ghana
Source: map by Esther Yeboah Danso-Wiredu

Old Fadama sits on land that used to belong to the Ga people who founded Accra in the 1600s. It was acquired by the state in the 1960s with the intention of using it for the Korle Lagoon Ecological Restoration Project (KLERP). At this time the land was already settled by migrants who were then displaced to New Fadama, a few kilometres away, to make way for the lagoon project. This never materialised and the land was repopulated in the 1990s when ethnic conflicts in Northern Ghana accelerated migration from the rural north to the urban south. They joined economic migrants from within and beyond Ghana and now form the majority of Old Fadama inhabitants. The site provided inhabitants with a beneficial location in terms of access to work and commercial opportunities, not least because of the proximity to the Agbogbloshie and other markets (Afenah, 2012). The two neighbouring scrap sites also play a key role in the complex urban economies in which Old Fadama is embedded. These sites are at the receiving end of large amounts of electronic waste exported (often illegally) from Europe, and many Old Fadama inhabitants base their livelihoods on the precarious and environmentally hazardous work of salvaging metals and other valuables from this waste (Grant and Oteng-Ababio, 2012).

State authorities do not provide infrastructure or services for Old Fadama, but have adopted a policy of non-recognition (Grant, 2006: 2). Reminiscent of other slums, through the service planning and delivery eyes of the state "it is as if these neighbourhoods are invisible" (Pugalis et al., 2014b: 520). The official stance of the Accra Metropolitan Assembly (AMA) is that Old Fadama is a squatter community and therefore does not qualify for infrastructural development by the state. Largely supported by the Ghanaian media – in which the community is frequently referred to as "Sodom and Gomorrah" – state authorities portray Old Fadama as an unwanted community and a disgrace to the country (Grant, 2006; Afenah, 2012; Amoako, 2016). Eviction threats are routinely issued by new governments, but, even though a court ruling in May 2002 gave the AMA the authority to evict inhabitants (Du Plessis, 2005; Afenah, 2012), the threats have never been effectuated.

The long-standing neglect of the area by state authorities has left it in a deplorable condition. During the rainy season Old Fadama is waterlogged and the lack of drainage causes parts of the community to become impassable. Services such as public schools and healthcare facilities are also non-existent. On top of this, disastrous fires pay repeat visits to the community, which is left vulnerable from makeshift electrical installations and a dense urban fabric of mostly wooden structures. Figure 8.1 shows the aftermath of such a fire which levelled a whole section of the slum in 2012. The river and the lagoon have gradually been filled with waste (see Figure 8.2), causing environmental harm and the spread of diseases such as cholera. An outbreak in 2014 forced the AMA to close down over thirty food vendors in the community (Citifmonline, 2014) with the aim of curtailing the spread of the disease.

Dwelling in Old Fadama, then, is a precarious form of urban life. Livelihoods are difficult to sustain and often require participation in hazardous activities. Living conditions are unhealthy in general and also carry heightened

*Figure 8.1* Aftermath of a fire in Old Fadama with one of the community mosques in the background

Source: Esther Yeboah Danso-Wiredu, May 2012

risks in the form of lethal outbreaks of both disease and fire. Inhabitants live here mainly because their choices are limited. Yet, for all the neglect and vilification by state and media, the community has shown a certain resourcefulness to develop and retain informal governance arrangements and also to effect improvements in living conditions.

### *Makeshift urbanism and group room dwelling*

Building, sustaining, and governing an urban community of around 100,000 people on the blind side of the state in a congested and unfavourable location requires creativity, cooperation, and resilience. The first challenge was to make the waterlogged land habitable. Inhabitants have achieved this gradually by filling vacant plots with sawdust from a nearby timber market to absorb the water and allow the erection of structures. The second initial challenge was how to acquire the land. What appears to state eyes as illegal squatting on state land masks a more complex reality in which migrants bought the land plot by plot from its customary owners, the Ga. Rather than haphazard squatting the

*Figure 8.2* The lack of services such as waste removal causes health hazards in the community
Source: Esther Yeboah Danso-Wiredu, December 2013

repopulation of Old Fadama took place in a relatively orderly fashion that respected customary land entitlements. It follows that land in Old Fadama is largely commodified, with land prices ranging from GH₵100 to GH₵900 per plot (GH₵1 equalled US$3.3 in 2012). The price depends not only on the land or structure in question, but also on the relationship between seller and buyer (see also Danso-Wiredu, 2018). Sales of land and structures are invariably oral arrangements involving the use of witnesses in the payment process.

The majority of inhabitants (68.1%) of Old Fadama own the structures in which they reside, while less than one-third (28.9%) obtain shelter through various rental schemes (People's Dialogue on Human Settlements, 2010). Much the same pattern is found among the people interviewed for this study. Among tenants it has become a widespread practice to live in so-called group rooms with the purpose of lowering rents. Most tenants thus rent structures in groups of five to ten people, paying GH₵2–3 per week per person. Such an amount is insignificant, less than one-tenth of a day wage for an average *kayaoo* (female head porter) in Old Fadama. These structures range from 10 x 10 feet to 14 x 14 feet and consist of a single room used only as sleeping quarters (see also Ofosu-Kusi and Danso-Wiredu, 2014). While this is a new phenomenon in Ghana it is not unique to Old Fadama. Evidence from the study suggests that it is also practised in nearby communities such as Agbogbloshie.

Group room dwelling reflects a radical departure from urban rental arrangements and conventional Ghanaian understandings of what a home is, but the phenomenon can be traced to traditional housing arrangements in the countryside. The norm in rural and indigenous parts of towns in Ghana is the multiple family dwelling, where different families rent rooms in the same compound and share facilities (see also Danso-Wiredu, 2018). Group room dwelling, then, can be seen as an urban translation of rural traditions, which has had a profound influence on the informal rental system through which inhabitants obtain shelter. It also has implications for everyday urban life in the community. Cumulatively, rents paid on the structures are relatively expensive compared to their size, but individually, group rent is much cheaper and more convenient to pay. All the *kayayei* – female head porters (see Figure 8.3) – interviewed for the study lived in such group rooms and they all indicated cost as their motivation. According to their leader, most *kayayei* used to sleep in the streets, but the emergence of group rooms has encouraged some of them to pay for shelter.

Group rooms provide sleeping space only. All other aspects of domestic life have to take place elsewhere and, as a result, Old Fadama is full of communal

*Figure 8.3* *Kayayei* head porters at work
Source: Esther Yeboah Danso-Wiredu, July 2013

showers, shared toilet facilities, and other basic amenities. With no access to a kitchen, food is mainly obtained from the many street vendors and makeshift restaurants that also populate the community. While such communal living engenders a highly social form of urban life, it also fosters social blights such as stealing, violence, and unrest. Because domestic life is lived almost completely in public, Old Fadama is nothing if not lively, and there is a peculiar blurring of public and domestic space (see Figure 8.4). This also means that privacy is scarce; indeed, for group room dwellers it is virtually non-existent. Furthermore, the quality of the structures rented by groups is not always fit for human habitation. Kayayei Youth Association members, for example, have had to contend with leaking roofs under which residents sit with their head pans on anytime it rains (interview, Head of Kayayei Youth Association, January 2014). Thus, even if group room dwelling seems to reflect a convenient innovation for inhabitants, such arrangements also raise many unanswered questions, some of which are worrisome.

Structures available for rent are largely owned by slum landlords/ladies who are often opinion leaders and involved in various organisations in the community. Not all of them live in Old Fadama and their activities are not limited to housing. Many partake in the profitable business of providing access to

*Figure 8.4* A typical street in Old Fadama with a blurring of domestic and public life
Source: Esther Yeboah Danso-Wiredu, May 2012

facilities that dwelling structures in Old Fadama lack. They own communal showers, toilets, and other basic amenities which are charged for use on the spot. Water is sold at the communal showers for use in manual launderettes, and electricity is accessed illegally through residents with meters from the Electricity Company of Ghana (ECG). These operations also involve the hiring of various caretakers who manage the facilities and receive payments on behalf of owners, especially those who do not reside in Old Fadama.

Compared to the formal housing market in Accra, the informal market in Old Fadama is made accessible to the poor because of lower prices, weekly instead of monthly rent collection, and the absence of advance rent payment. The latter can be particularly prohibitive in the formal market, where two-to-three years of advance rent is typical (Arku et al., 2012). This is not strictly legal as the Ghanaian Rent Act 2009 allows for a maximum of six months' advance rent, but it has nevertheless become the norm (Arku et al., 2012), thus reflecting another blurring of the informal-formal divide. These were also the key reasons for renting in the informal housing market reported by respondents in this study.

Group room dwelling has entailed the introduction of new rental procedures. The informal nature of the arrangements does not translate into a lack of systematicity. On the contrary, practices are conducted according to well-defined but unwritten norms and procedures. In the case of group room renting, one person typically identifies a room, gets assurance from the slumlord/lady and then looks for people to share the rent with. This person continues to act as group leader and is the only one to liaise with the owner in all matters concerning the room. The leader collects the rent on a weekly basis and passes it on to the landlord/lady. The role thus requires a high degree of trust on the part of co-renters. Similar arrangements can be found in formal housing markets, where multi-occupant renting is also widespread. But in Old Fadama all the occupants have to share the same room and people therefore prefer to live with those that they can have intimate relationships with. It is common to find people in the same room who migrated from the same village or town or at least speak the same language.

### *Urban grassroots and ethnic leaders*

Designations such as "slum" or "informal settlement" belie the fact that urban life in Old Fadama is highly regulated with precise procedures, rules, and norms that govern the ways in which "things get done". The key actors in this complex system of urban governance across the informal-formal divide fall into three groups: ethnic leaders, urban grassroots organisations, and actors associated with the Ghanaian state. The latter are ostensibly absent but nevertheless turn out to play their own part, albeit often indirectly. Urban grassroots organisations are largely informal but many of them do have written or oral constitutions which guide them.

When the area was first repopulated, it was initially perceived to be a transit point for newcomers, a place where rural migrants stayed while gaining a foothold on urban life before taking up more permanent residence elsewhere in Accra. This was gradually exposed as an illusion and, according to the Ghana Federation of the Urban Poor (GHAFUP), it was from this recognition that urban grassroots organisations began to be created in the 1990s:

> The influx of many people into the community, coupled with lawlessness, made the community one of the most dangerous places to visit in Accra. Old Fadama became home to most of the country's criminals in the 1990s. This, together with the inhumane nature of the structures and the numerous environmental problems earned the community its popular name *Sodom and Gomorrah*. But things have changed since the residents decided to take their destiny into their own hands and changed things for the better by establishing associations to get things done at the community level.
>
> (GHAFUP representative, February 2014)

The key organisation has been OFADA, which spearheaded infrastructure provision in the community. Formed in 1997 (and formally registered in 2000) it functions as an umbrella for all organisations in Old Fadama, including the sixteen sub-chiefs, the imams, the "Alhajis", and highly respected community members. Apart from the general aim of community development, OFADA also works towards the specific objectives of ensuring security and cleanliness in the area. The provision and maintenance of infrastructure such as roads, sewerage, and drainage are at the heart of these concerns. In this work, OFADA has received support and help from GHAFUP, together with a collaboration established through the People's Dialogue on Human Settlements (from which GHAFUP is an offshoot), and SDI, both of which are also active in Old Fadama.

GHAFUP also works independently on its own projects in the community. In July 2013 it installed rubbish skips in some sections, where the *kayabola* – rubbish collectors – can deposit their rubbish and pay for the usage of the skip. It also rents out wheelbarrows to builders, operates communal showers, and has distributed rubbish bins among food vendors and shop owners (see Figure 8.5). Infrastructure, facilities, and services are also provided through the efforts of various community-based economic associations such as the Kayayei Youth Association, Scrap Dealers Association, and Konkomba Yam Market Association (KYMA). Pipes have been laid to channel liquid waste into the lagoon, a number of mini drainage systems have been built, and access roads that cut through the congested built environment have been established. Communal labour days are organised every three months where leaders of various groups in the community organise voluntary communal cleaning in their respective areas (see also Danso-Wiredu, 2018). The absence of services such as public schools – the commute by foot to nearby public schools is too

*Figure 8.5* Communal showers installed and managed by GHAFUP
Source: Esther Yeboah Danso-Wiredu, July 2013

long for young children – are substituted by private individuals as a business opportunity. There are fifteen privately owned schools in the community, one of which offers a junior high school, according to the Parent Teacher Association (PTA) Chairman. The schools are set up without permission from the Ghana Education Service, and proprietors/proprietresses usually rent structures which are used for other purposes in the night, such as cinemas. Congested classrooms and the absence of safety measures for pupils are the norm.

These practices of infrastructure and service provision reflect informal institutions that substitute for the district assemblies that are responsible for such provision in state-recognised neighbourhoods. The organisation of OFADA comes closest to that of a local state, but many other actors are involved in this complex ensemble where various community organisations mix with economic actors from the informal sector. What sets OFADA apart is the fact that it also plays a regulatory role. For instance, toilet and shower operators indicated that they sought permission from OFADA before installing new facilities. Similarly, traders and entrepreneurs sought permission before siting their businesses in the community. Moreover, structure owners and residents have been entreated by OFADA to gradually replace wooden structures with cement block structures in the interest of reducing the ubiquitous fire hazard. Most replacements, however, only materialise when structures are actually destroyed by fire. For instance, a blaze in May 2012 levelled a section of well over 100 structures (displacing 3,500 people), which were subsequently replaced by cement blocks with aluminium roofing (see Figure 8.6) (Owusu, 2013). These efforts also raise the profile of OFADA in the eyes of state authorities and the general public, which adds to the picture of OFADA substituting for a district assembly.

Yet, once again, OFADA is not alone in effecting this substitution. It has gained its legitimacy and authority by cooperating with, and incorporating in its way of organising, various elements of the traditional forms of rule that residents have been accustomed to in the rural areas from which they originate. OFADA has mimicked the traditional system, where hereditary chiefs command respect and hold power in their respective areas. Rather than governing a geographical area, in Old Fadama ethnic chiefs assume responsibility for their own ethnic group, wherever they may reside in the community. Residents report matters of concern to their own chief, who then attempts to find a resolution. According to the OFADA secretary, "it is the chiefs who rule the community at the moment; since the state's governance is absent, they devise means to govern the community" (interview,

*Figure 8.6* Older wooden structures (left, in the foreground) are gradually replaced by newer cement structures (right, in the background)

Source: Esther Yeboah Danso-Wiredu, July 2013

OFADA secretary, February 2014). A resident explained more precisely the role played by chiefs:

> Normally the chiefs are not involved in land or structure sales, but if the oral agreements are disrespected by one faction, the chiefs are invited to find solutions to the issue at stake . . . in the same way, if there are disputes regarding the settling of debts and if the debtor has any property, the chiefs will rule that the property should be sold to settle the debts. Judgment passed by the chiefs is accepted by the factions involved.
>
> (Interview, an opinion leader, January 2014)

This situation was confirmed by interviewed chiefs who also reported on the nature of matters in which their help was typically sought. Family matters and marriages were particularly common, but they also had been called upon to bail residents out of jail. A similar role was played by religious leaders, especially imams from the many mosques (over 100 according to OFADA). The leading imam thus explained:

> The people usually consult me, mainly to pray for their work and families. Apart from that the religious leaders also settle marital disputes as well as disputes between families and neighbours. Anytime a fellow Muslim needs urgent financial assistance, the Imam collects what we call "sadaqah" [charity] in aid of the person in need.
>
> (Interview with an imam, February 2014)

Apart from the continuous role of counsellor, informal judiciary, and welfare provider, ethnic and religious leaders also serve as leaders of the numerous organisations under the OFADA umbrella. Appointment to these posts was conducted in various ways and not always hereditary, as exemplified by the Konkomba ethnic group:

> Among the Konkombas, we elect our leaders unlike other groups who consider wealth or commandeering attitudes of a person before choosing him/her to lead. But with us, you have to go through the ballot box before you become the Chairman of the Konkomba Yam Market Association.
>
> (Interview, KYMA secretary, February 2014)

Yet other appointments were made pragmatically on the basis of qualifications. The OFADA secretary, for instance, indicated that he was "appointed to be the secretary when the leaders realised I have knowledge on sanitation management and because I work with the AMA" (interview, OFADA secretary, February 2014). This also shows how the formal absence of the state was belied by actual circumstances, where individual actors tended to "wear several hats" at once and whose personal networks indicated

*Table 8.2* Leadership criteria for some of the organisational leaders interviewed

| *Organisation* | *Core Objective* | *Position* | *Leadership Legitimacy* |
|---|---|---|---|
| Scrap Dealers Association | Economic | Chairman | By appointment |
| Moosi Ethnic Group | Socio-cultural | Chief | Royal lineage |
| Dagomba Ethnic Group | Socio-cultural | Chief | Royal lineage |
| GHAFUP | Community development | Organiser | Appointment |
| Kayayei Youth Association | Economic | Head Kayayei | Appointment |
| Konkomba Yam Market Association | Economic | Secretary | Election |
| Old Fadama Association | Community development | Secretary | Appointment |
| Naawuri Youth Association | Welfare | Assistant ladies' organiser | Appointment |

connectivities that could not be formally recognised. The appointment procedures for some of the most important organisations are indicated in Table 8.2. Common to all the leaders was that none of them was paid but all worked voluntarily.

## Concluding discussion

In this chapter we have explored the production of Old Fadama as an alternative space of urban dwelling in Accra. The alternative trajectory of urban development evidenced in this case has not been a matter of choice, but rather one of necessity. The influx of rural migrants from the north produced a housing scarcity in Accra, which has yet to be adequately addressed by state actors at either the urban or national levels. The newcomers needed shelter and when they found the formal housing market to be inaccessible they had to look elsewhere. The vacant, waterlogged tract of land now known as Old Fadama was just one of the places they went to. Deprived of even the most basic services and infrastructures, residents were not only neglected but also vilified as squatters and parasites by state authorities and media alike. Instead of sinking into complete chaos, however, the slum has gradually been transformed into a self-governing community existing and evolving in spite of formal neglect and vilification.

The preceding sections have applied the frames of *makeshift, informal*, and *precarious* to the case of Old Fadama. Here, urban life is *makeshift* in the sense that residents have innovated alternative dwelling arrangements in which old Ghanaian traditions of compound-dwelling are transposed to an urban setting in the form of group rooms. It is *informal* because it relies purely on oral agreements among community members for settling ownership and rental arrangements. Furthermore, the community boasts of a range of informal and semi-formal organisations which collaborate on resolving issues and disputes as well as initiating community development projects. Finally, it is *precarious* because it carries heightened risks for its inhabitants through fire hazards, disease outbreaks, and a generally unhealthy environment.

Urban governance arrangements in the community mainly comprise a combination of substitutive and competing informal institutions. Due to the policy of non-recognition on the part of the Ghanaian state in general and the AMA in particular, formal institutions are at best weak in Old Fadama. Residents and non-governmental organisations (NGOs) have taken it upon themselves to govern the community in the formal absence of state authorities, but they have done so in ways that are selectively divergent and convergent with state interests. Because initiatives were brought about as a response to an untenable situation in the 1990s – earning Old Fadama its pejorative nicknames – the informal governance arrangements are characterised by pragmatism rather than idealism. This accounts, for instance, for the eclectic ways in which community leaders are appointed to their posts.

To grasp the co-presence of substitutive and competing informal institutions it is necessary to acknowledge that the ostensible absence of the state is not complete. Rather, the role of the state is characterised simultaneously by a "convenient absence" and a "brutal presence" to borrow the words of Amoako (2016: 14). In Old Fadama non-recognition is convenient for the AMA, because it allows the local authorities to avert the costly responsibilities associated with the provision of infrastructure, healthcare, education, and other public services. But this does not prevent the authorities from being violently present through aggressive policing and the constant threat of eviction. In this situation it becomes difficult to disentangle substitutive and competing institutions. When community-based actors provide infrastructure and services the outcome is convergent with state interests, but as their legitimacy and authority in the community grow they become competing authorities that also weaken the power of the AMA. Furthermore, close informal links have been forged between the AMA and organisations such as OFADA and GHAFUP, which also make it untenable to separate formal and informal authorities and their interests. This serves as further confirmation of points made by Afenah (2012) and Amoako (2016) about the unfeasibility of simple dichotomies in this complex situation. It also serves to underpin and give further nuance to the catalogue of resistance tactics outlined by both Grant (2006) and Paller (2014, 2015).

The main attraction of Old Fadama for those who reside there is the accessibility of its housing market. Prices are affordable to the urban poor and rental arrangements match their needs: weekly instead of monthly rent collection and no advance rent to be paid. As such it is an alternative to the marketised and liberalised housing market that prevails in the recognised districts of Accra as investigated by Arku et al. (2012). This has amounted to a normalisation of informality in the housing sector of urban economies, thereby supporting Gillespie's (2016) argument about the role of informal economies. As shown by Obeng-Odoom (2012), the formal housing market in Accra bears the imprints of a neoliberalisation process that has affected Ghana since the 1980s. Old Fadama is thus also posed as an alternative to the housing systems produced by neoliberal urbanism, even if this is not directly articulated by grassroots actors. In this sense, residents share many of their struggles for shelter and livelihood with slum-dwellers around the world. More than a shared condition, this is also manifested by the active presence of SDI, which means that Old Fadama is directly embedded in what McFarlane (2009) has called a "translocal assemblage" that connects localised struggles across the globe.

To be sure, urban life in Old Fadama is highly precarious and problematic. Even with ongoing improvements, housing continues to be substandard in general, with some structures still unfit for human habitation due to congestion, leaks, and lack of ventilation. Fire hazards are a persistent threat to inhabitants as is the risk of disease from bad hygiene, untreated waste products, missing drainage, and the poisonous smoke from scrap metal salvaging that envelops the community. On top of these bodily hazards comes the mental strain that follows from living bereft of any possibility of domestic privacy, and with the ever-present threat of eviction. This, then, is not the story of a community to be copied, but it is nevertheless a story from which much can be learned.

First, group room dwelling illustrates that the provision of housing need not be thought of exclusively via imported understandings of housing as self-contained family units. The old Ghanaian tradition of compound-dwelling could be transposed to urban settings in the pursuit of affordable, high-quality housing in informal as well as formal housing markets. Pioneer projects such as Amui Djor Housing already exist (see Danso-Wiredu and Midheme, 2017), and such experiences may prove valuable, alongside those of slum-dwellers, for a broader push towards urban compound-housing estates. State institutions are well positioned to spearhead such efforts in collaboration with NGOs and urban residents.

Second, the case also indicates how simple adjustments such as weekly rent payments and the elimination of advance rent can significantly lower the barriers of entry to formal housing markets. Again, the state is in the best position to address this, beginning with the enforcement of existing provisions in the Rent Act.

Finally, the emergence and consolidation of relatively efficient informal governance arrangements confirm that slum-dwellers themselves are to be taken seriously as resourceful agents in resolving the often intractable issues in which they are embedded, and the effects of which they suffer. This should not be taken as an excuse for continued state neglect, but rather as an invitation for constructive cooperation, perhaps along the lines of what Seeliger and Turok (2013) have called adaptive governance. Residents have found efficient ways of getting things done, but they are woefully short of resources and would be spared immense hassles and hazards if Old Fadama was to be recognised as a regular urban district. This, however, would have to be a process of mutual integration rather than an assimilation or normalisation on the part of the community. A turn towards urban grassroots also requires state actors to come to terms with the fact that the current strategy of letting the private sector resolve the housing deficit through liberalisation and marketisation has largely failed and must be abandoned.

On these matters our findings point broadly in the same direction as the new urban agenda of the UN (2017: 19), which encourages "strategies that go beyond physical and environmental improvements to ensure that slums and informal settlements are integrated into the social, economic, cultural and political dimensions of cities". Again, integration does not mean assimilation. Rather, "a tractable and variable approach" is needed to "accommodate informal and interim solutions within more formal structures and systems" (Seeliger and Turok, 2013: 188). But this requires meticulously obtained in-depth knowledge about the informal, interim, and alternative solutions that already exist in the practices of urban governance, planning, and community development in slums across the globe. It is our hope that studies such as this one can contribute to the production of tailored efforts at mutually beneficial integration between formal and informal urban settlements in ways that are carefully attuned to the existing ensemble of local practices on both sides of this often blurred and fuzzy frontier.

## References

Accra Metropolitan Assembly (2011) *Participatory Slum Upgrading and Prevention, Millennium City of Accra, Ghana* (Slum Situation Analysis Report). Accra: UN-Habitat.

Afenah, A. (2012) Engineering a Millennium City in Accra, Ghana: The Old Fadama Intractable Issue. *Urban Forum*. 23. 527–540.

Agyei-Mensah, S., Owusu, G. (2012) Ethnic Residential Clusters in Nima, Ghana. *Urban Forum*. March. 23(1). 133–149.

Amoako, C. (2016) Brutal Presence or Convenient Absence: The Role of the State in the Politics of Flooding in Informal Accra, Ghana. *Geoforum*. 77. 5–16.

Arimah, B.C. (2010) *The Face of Urban Poverty: Explaining the Prevalence of Slums in Developing Countries*. Working Paper No. 2010/30. Helsinki: World Institute for Development Economics Research.

Arku, G., Luginaah, I., Mkandawire, P. (2012) "You Either Pay More Advance Rent or You Move Out": Landlords/Ladies' and Tenants' Dilemmas in the Low-Income Housing Market in Accra, Ghana. *Urban Studies*. 49(14). 3177–3193.

Citifmonline.com (2014) Cholera Outbreak, AMA to Shut Down More Chop Bars. 25 September. Available at: http://citifmonline.com/2014/09/25/cholera-outbreak-ama-to-shut-down-more-chop-bars.

Dagdeviren, H., Robertson, S.A. (2009) *Access to Water in the Slums of the Developing World*. Working Paper No. 57. Brasilia: International Policy Centre for Inclusive Growth.

Danso-Wiredu, E.Y. (2016) The Puzzles of Living in Urban Poor Communities: The Role of Informal Governance Structures in Housing Provision in Accra and Winneba, Ghana. Dissertation available from the author.

Danso-Wiredu, E.Y. (2018) Housing Strategies in Low Income Urban Communities in Accra, Ghana. *GeoJournal*. 83(4). 663–677.

Danso-Wiredu, E.Y., Loopmans, M. (2013) The Gap between Visions and Policies. Housing the Poor and Urban Planning in Ghana. *Planum*. 26(1). 2–11.

Danso-Wiredu, E.Y., Midheme, E. (2017) Slum Upgrading in Developing Countries: Lessons from Ghana and Kenya. *Ghana Journal of Geography*. 9(1). 88–108.

Davis, M. (2006) *Planet of Slums*. London: Verso.

Du Plessis, J. (2005) The Growing Problem of Forced Evictions and the Crucial Importance of Community-Based, Locally Appropriate Alternatives. *Environment and Urbanization*. 17(1). 123–134.

Farouk, B.R., and Owusu, M. (2012) "If in Doubt, Count": The Role of Community-Driven Enumerations in Blocking Eviction in Old Fadama, Accra. *Environment and Urbanization*. 24(1). 47–57.

Ghana Centre for Democratic Development (2012) National Policy on Slums Needed. *Daily Graphic*. 14.

Gillespie, T. (2016) Accumulation by Urban Dispossession: Struggles over Urban Space in Accra, Ghana. *Transactions of the Institute of British Geographers*. 41(1). 66–77.

Grant, R. (2006) Out of Place? Global Citizens in Local Places: A Study of the Informal Settlements in the Korle Lagoon Environs in Accra, Ghana. *Urban Forum*. 17(1). 1–24.

Grant, R. (2009) *Globalizing City: The Urban and Economic Transformation of Accra, Ghana*. Syracuse, NY: Syracuse University Press.

Grant, R., Oteng-Ababio, M. (2012) Mapping the Invisible and Real "African" Economy: Urban E-Waste Circuitry. *Urban Geography*. 33(1). 1–21.

Helmke, G., and Levitsky, S. (2004) Informal Institutions and Comparative Politics: A Research Agenda. *Perspectives on Politics*. 2(4). 725–740.

Hooper, M., Ortolano, L. (2012) Motivations for Slum Dweller Social Movement Participation in Urban Africa: A Study of Mobilization in Kurasini, Dar es Salaam. *Environment and Urbanization*. 24(1). 99–114.

Konadu-Agyemang, K. (2001) A Survey of Housing Conditions and Characteristics in Accra, an African City. *Habitat International*. 25(1). 15–34.

McFarlane, C. (2009) Translocal Assemblages: Space, Power and Social Movements. *Geoforum*. 40. 561–567.

McFarlane, C. (2011) Assemblage and Critical Urbanism. *City*. 15(2). 204–224.

Ministry of Water Resources, Works and Housing (2012) Draft National Housing Policy, 2012. Accra: Government of Ghana.

Obeng-Odoom, F. (2012) Neoliberalism and the Urban Economy in Ghana: Urban Employment, Inequality, and Poverty. *Growth and Change*. 43(1). 85–109.

Ofosu-Kusi, Y., Danso-Wiredu, E.Y. (2014) Neoliberalism and Housing Provision in Accra, Ghana: The Illogic of an Over-Liberalised Housing Market. In: Asuelime, L., Yaro, J., Francis, S. (eds) *Selected Themes in African Development Studies*. Cham: Springer. 95–109.

Owusu, M. (2013) Community-Managed Reconstruction after the 2012 Fire in Old Fadama, Ghana. *Environment and Urbanization*. 25(1). 243–248.

Owusu, G., Agyei-Mensah, S., Lund, R. (2008) Slums of Hope and Slums of Despair: Mobility and Livelihoods in Nima, Accra. *Norsk Geografisk Tidsskrift*. 62(3). 180–190.

Paller, J.W. (2014) Informal Institutions and Personal Rule in Urban Ghana. *African Studies Review*. 57(3). 123–142.

Paller, J.W. (2015) Informal Networks and Access to Power to Obtain Housing in Urban Slums in Ghana. *Africa Today*. 62(1). 31–55.

People's Dialogue on Human Settlements (2010) *Community-Led Enumeration of Old Fadama Community 2009, Accra – Ghana*. Accra: Housing the Masses. 33.

Pieterse, E., van Donk, M. (2008) *Developmental Local Government: Squaring the Circle between Policy. Consolidating Developmental Local Government: Lessons from the South African Experience.* Cape Town: UCT Press. 51.

Pugalis, L., Giddings, B., Anyigor, K. (2014a) Informal Settlements: The Prevalence of and Barriers to Entrepreneurial Synergies in Slum Communities. In: Pugalis, L., Liddle, J. (eds) *Enterprising Places: Leadership and Governance Networks.* London: Emerald.

Pugalis, L., Giddings, B., Anyigor, K. (2014b) Reappraising the World Bank Responses to Rapid Urbanisation: Slum Improvements in Nigeria. *Local Economy.* 29(4–5). 519–540.

Roy, A. (2011) Slumdog Cities: Rethinking Subaltern Urbanism. *International Journal of Urban and Regional Research.* 35(2). 223–238.

Seeliger, L., Turok, I. (2013) Averting a Downward Spiral: Building Resilience in Informal Urban Settlements through Adaptive Governance. *Environment and Urbanization.* 26(1). 184–199.

Tutu, R.A. (2014) Dilemmatic Experiences of Young Migrants in Accra, Ghana: The Merciless Hands of Pirate Urbanization and Landlordism. *Journal of Housing and the Built Environment.* 29. 637–656.

United Nations (UN) (2014) *World Urbanization Prospects: The 2014 Revision Highlights.* New York: UN.

United Nations (UN) (2017) *Resolution 71/256.* Resolution Adopted by the General Assembly on 23 December 2016. New York: UN.

UN-Habitat (2003) *Slums of the World: The Face of Urban Poverty in the New Millennium?* HS/692/03E. Nairobi, Kenya: UN-Habitat.

UN-Habitat (2004) *Urban Land for All.* Nairobi, Kenya: UN-Habitat.

UN-Habitat (2006) *The State of the World Cities 2006/7.* No. HS/814/06E. Nairobi, Kenya: UN-Habitat.

UN-Habitat (2009) *The Right to Adequate Housing.* Fact Sheet No. 21. Nairobi, Kenya: UN-Habitat.

UN-Habitat (2012) *Ghana Urban Profile.* Nairobi, Kenya: United Nations Human Settlements Programme (UN-Habitat).

UN-Habitat (2016) *Urbanization and Development. Emerging Futures.* Nairobi, Kenya: United Nations Human Settlements Programme (UN-Habitat).

Vasudevan, A. (2015) The Makeshift City: Towards a Global Geography of Squatting. *Progress in Human Geography.* 39(3). 338–359.

Yeboah, I.E. (2000) Structural Adjustment and Emerging Urban Form in Accra, Ghana. *Africa Today.* 61–89.

# 9 In-between the planned grid

## *Kothi* sexuality, domesticity, and urban interstitiality in Chandigarh, India

*Preetika Sharma*

### Introduction

Entering Kajheri, an urban village, one experiences a shift from the wide, smooth, and straight roads of the beautiful city of Chandigarh, to bumpy, narrow, and twisting streets. Everywhere in the village hoardings and advertisements promote "hotels", "rented rooms", "lounges", and so forth. Such big signs and banners stand in stark contrast to the sedate vistas of Chandigarh's garden homes. In mid-2015, I had the pleasure of visiting Kajheri many times, usually on the back of the scooter of my key informant, Vijay,[1] a queer activist and a self-identified transwoman. On one such occasion Vijay had come to visit her friends. We entered a street and approached a two-storey building with four rooms on each floor. This was the first time I had met with Suresh, a self-identified *kothi* (the Hindi term for an effeminate man). He was the first *kothi* to rent this building and over a period of time many of his *kothi* friends, who faced trouble finding a home in the city, came to this building to rent a room. At the time, Suresh shared the building with twelve other *kothi* men. They essentially lived as a family unit, splitting household tasks, taking care of each other, and sharing their meals. They earned a living by doing sex work.

The *kothis* of Kajheri represent an opportunity to rethink the mutually constitutive relation between sexuality and space. In this chapter, I illuminate the disrupted yet continuous relationship between the urban village and the surrounding city as well as the everyday life of the *kothi* men, bridging their livelihood and domesticity. This is achieved by looking through a theoretical lens of urban interstitiality, domesticity, and sexuality. I seek to answer these questions: how do *kothi* men manifest their queer identities through everyday practices and performances (Butler 1990) in the village? What negotiations are required for them to live in the village and what role does interstitiality play in bringing the back stage (i.e. the domestic) performance of *kothi* men to the forefront (Goffman 1990 [1959])? And, to what extent does this happen? As such, the chapter is concerned with the production of an interstitial urban space and with urban interstices as places of alternative urban becomings. This is achieved through an investigation of the concepts of sexuality and home in the urban interstice of Kajheri.

In the subsequent sections, I start by examining the literature on urban interstices as it relates to domesticity and sexuality. I also explain the term *kothi* and the position of *kothi* among the *hijra samaj* in India. I then present methodology and findings from my research, mainly drawing on a range of insights derived from interviews of *kothi* men. I focus primarily on the lived experiences of *kothi* men in the village, looking at their utilisation of various tactics by which they navigate and rework the village space and also make visible sexual differences. I also touch upon their domestic lives.

## Urban interstices: intersection of sexuality, domesticity, and urban interstitiality

There are contradictory views on the city as a space for queer identity. Urban space has been understood as a space for sexual freedom where homosexuals find escape from traditional life (Aldrich 2004) and create a sense of sexual possibilities (Bell 2001). From the Marxist view, on the other hand, the surveillance of sexual desires and expression is crucial for the social reproduction and constancy of capitalist society. This stability of urban life is dependent upon the perpetuation of the nuclear family (Hubbard 2012). Due to this contradiction, a constant game of hide and seek of sexual identities is inherent to urban space. Strong institutions of the state, like the police, the judiciary, planning and housing authorities, public hospitals, etc., discipline sexual practices to maintain a heteronormative moral order in the city. The law of the land and moral order qualify the legality of the sexual act in a particular space:

> Space and sexuality are particularly incendiary issues as they are linked to bodies: both the body of the city (to which entry is sought to be controlled) and the bodies of particularly women and those with transgressive sexuality (where access is sought to be regulated).
>
> (Phadke 2006: 14)

Hence, the city acts as an active agent in expression as well as suppression of sexualities (Hubbard 2012). Wright (1997: 69) has rightly argued that the juxtaposition of "sick" and "well" in the social imaginary leads to the "production of social-physical spaces by privileging urban spaces of surveillance, both self-surveillance and control over one's 'deviant' body, and the surveillance of those external bodies perceived as too fat, too dirty, too dark or too sexual".

A deeper layer of invisibility is added to the queer community at home. Home is a synonym for the heterosexual family that characteristically provides privacy, security, and strong "claims on people's time, resources and emotions" (Allan and Crow 1989). Most of the customs and traditions in an Indian patriarchal family do not accommodate homosexual identity and hence contribute to upholding the heterosexual social order. For Indian housing societies too,[2] "a family can only be a patriarchal, heterosexual family: a man, his wife, 'his' children" (Menon 2012).

For people with non-conforming gender identities living with heterosexual family members, home can prove to be a place of oppression and subversion (Johnston and Valentine 1995). A large number of *kothi* men in India have married women under societal pressure and fathered children. No one in their family or office, apart from a few men in the park, where *kothis* cruise to find partners, know about their sexuality (Seabrook 1999).

Gentrified gay neighbourhoods have long been the centre of attention in scholarship on sexuality and space (Sibalis 2004). Banerjea (2015) has been among the scholars who have pointed out the need for research on queer spaces in ordinary heteronormative neighbourhoods to understand queer organising in a better way. By researching the lives of *kothi* men in Kajheri, I attempt to heed this call by turning attention to the ways in which queer identities navigate and rework the interstitiality of urban spaces and negotiate with the heteronormative structures that dominate life in the village and the city. My understanding of interstitiality leans on the influential work of Andrea Mubi Brighenti (2013), which complicates previous notions of urban interstices. Brighenti moves beyond taken-for-granted dichotomies of periphery/core and city/suburb and examines interstices as "in-between-ness" due to the "fact of being surrounded by other spaces that are either more institutionalized, and therefore economically and legally powerful, or endowed with a stronger identity, and therefore more recognizable or typical" (Brighenti 2013: xvi). He approaches the interstice as an "active component" that can only be appreciated by considering the "dynamics of power and resistance, of fluidity and boundedness, of mobilities and moorings, of smoothness and striatedness" (Brighenti 2013: xvi). As such, Brighenti comes close to Bourriaud's (1998) anatomical view from which interstitial spaces may act as tissues that do the job of linking and connecting within the body of the city (quoted in Lévesque 2013).

Interstices, understood in this way, are composed of numerous interactions among actors that live together in a particular spatial setting (Brighenti 2013). The interstice has been studied as a space full of possibilities and "alternative discourses" (Lévesque 2013: 34), while others have elaborated on the meaning of interstices as "spaces of uncertainty" (Cupers and Miessen 2002), "ambivalent landscapes" (Jorgensen and Tylecote 2007), "terrain vague" (Barron and Mariani 2013), etc. In her research on Bachoura, a neglected neighbourhood in Beirut, Lévesque (2013) writes that improvisation of these spaces can "act as imaginative devices for differentiation and informal reinvention" leading to "unveiling marginalized potentials" (Lévesque 2013: 34) and "possible futures within the city" (Lévesque 2013: 45). In fact, urban interstices also have been understood as spaces which are institutionally created and whose marginal character restricts users and dwellers to be either "just passing" through or to be "out of frame" if their use or dwelling becomes less transitory (Tonnelat 2008). For the occupiers themselves the interstice may be of prime importance irrespective of its marginal or non-marginal status among citizens in surrounding areas. Nevertheless, it may require special strategies of everyday life to live among other subjects in interstitial spaces (Duncan 1978).

## *Kothi* identity

Broadly speaking, *kothi* is a term indicating a South Asian gender identity in which men express their feminine sense of self and are receptive partners in their relationships with other men (Gill 2016). The degree of their atypical gender role varies over a wide range from feminine to masculine expressions. *Kothis* refer to their husbands as *panthi* (Gayatri 2005) and to their boyfriends as *giriya*. A few *kothi* men whom I met also referred to *panthi* as their permanent sexual partner and *giriya* as a temporary sexual partner. Generally, in a relationship a *panthi* takes a masculine gender role whereas a *kothi* takes a feminine role (Stief 2017). *Kothi* and *panthi* have been compared to "sissy" and "butch" in American English (Stief 2017) and activo/pasivo in Latin culture (Carballo-Die´guez et al. 2004). *Kothi* identity has been studied across scholarly themes like gender studies (Stief 2017), violence (Chakrapani et al. 2007), sexual behaviour and HIV studies (Chakrapani et al. 2008; Woodford et al. 2012; Mayer et al. 2015), and mental health (Mimiaga et al. 2013), but there has been scant attention given to the domestic life of *kothi* men.

It is important to differentiate between the *kothi* and *hijra* communities due to comparisons between the two identities made by the respondents. The comparisons were due to the fact that the society does not accept anything beyond the conventional man/woman binary and only has conditional, i.e. institutional, acceptance for the third gender. *Hijra samaj* in India is a well-known and culturally-accepted community for the transgender population. The cultural institution of *hijra samaj* accommodates the third gender—transwoman or hermaphrodites. *Hijra* refers to a transwoman who is required to undergo castration to assimilate into the *hijra samaj*. *Kothi* men may be castrated only due to their personal desire for physical change. *Kothi* men are not acknowledged in a society where the *hijra* population is worshipped by many communities in India. It has been understood that many queer community members become assimilated within *hijra samaj* (Nanda 1999) for shelter, livelihood, and a chance to live as their sexual selves. But *kothi* men, mostly (there are exceptions), are not bound by the structures of *hijra samaj* (Stief 2017). They live outside the strict rules of this institution and lead independent lives.

## Methodology

This work is part of my doctoral research which began in August 2015. I interviewed many members of the queer community in Chandigarh to explore their experiences and understanding of queer spaces in a modern planned city. Initially, I reached out to the queer community through a non-governmental organisation (NGO) called the "Saksham Trust". The Saksham Trust works for the rights of sexual minorities in Chandigarh and towards sensitising people to gender issues. Many non-gender-conforming people in Chandigarh are connected to this NGO and they have a strong virtual and physical network.

This network helped me in getting acquainted with many members of the community and in carrying out my research.

This particular study about Kajheri began in mid-2015. It involved interviewing twelve *kothi* men who lived together in a rented building in the village. The interviews were in-depth, generally with a semi-structured format. They focused upon the relationships of the *kothi* men in the house and their experience of living in the village. Seven out of the twelve *kothi* men were from small towns in the state of Punjab and five were from the bordering state of Haryana. Eleven of the interviewees were aged between nineteen and twenty-five. One *kothi*, the first to live in this building, was thirty-eight at the beginning of the study. All the *kothis* did sex work for their livelihoods. I visited Kajheri many times, sometimes for interviews and at other times for lunches, birthday celebrations, and regular gatherings. I primarily employed the methods of participant observation and in-depth interviewing in this study.

## Kajheri: an urban interstice in Chandigarh

Kajheri pre-dates the present city of Chandigarh. Spatially, Kajheri is bounded by the administrative boundary called "*lal dora*", which can be translated as the Red Chord. In 1908, the British created boundaries around the residential land of rural villages in India to maintain revenue records. These areas, referred to as *lal dora* regions, fall outside the urban regulatory framework and are not allowed to be acquired for any developmental projects, even where the surrounding lands have been thoroughly urbanised. This was done primarily to guard against the rural developments of the villages. The concept of *lal dora* persisted even after the Partition of India in 1947, which of course halved the state of Punjab.

After 1947, Lahore—the then-capital of Punjab—went to Pakistan, which resulted in an Indian Punjab that lacked a capital city. The state recognised that there was an urgent need for infrastructure to handle the administrative needs of the area, especially the refugee problem in Punjab (Kalia 1999). Jawaharlal Nehru, the then-Prime Minister of India, decided to build a new capital for Punjab, which would have no connections with the dark past, but would instead help to develop faith in the future of the nation (Fitting 2002). Agricultural lands were acquired for building the new capital city of Punjab—Chandigarh— and 8,500 acres of fertile land were acquired at the foothills of the Shivalik Hills (Shaw 2009). The city grid was built on the agricultural areas of the acquired land from the villages that had existed prior to Chandigarh, but the residential areas of the villages were not demolished. Consequently, many *lal dora* areas, like Kajheri, are now surrounded by industries, housing apartments, extended cities, etc. and have themselves remained aloof from the urban infrastructural developments that other cities have undergone (Kumar 2015).

India's demographics are shifting from predominantly rural to urban at a very fast pace (Nagendra et al. 2013). Kajheri and many other interstitially located villages in Chandigarh's extensively-studied (Joshi et al. 1999; Kalia

1999; Perera 2006; Shaw 2009) grid structure exemplify this shift. These urban villages are host to various marginalised peoples who cannot find space in Chandigarh city. This includes many migrant labourers and minority groups that migrated to the city to avail themselves of economic opportunities. Villagers began to provide rental services, usually by converting their homes into rental structures, only after the completion of the planned grid of the city in the 1960s. Over time, this has made these villages fairly urban and lively sites. Urban villages, as they are surrounded by the city, offer proximity to most jobs, yet at the same time offer remoteness from urban policing and surveillance. The ongoing change in the livelihoods, population, and lifestyle of these villages is resulting in blurred borderlands between the developed city grid and the village.

With similar changes happening in many cities, there is a need to take up "more continuous approaches of urban representation" rather than following the urban-rural dichotomy (Nagendra et al. 2013: 15). Such transformation of urban villages in Chandigarh is not a phenomenon specific to this city; according to a study of Kotla Mubarkpur, an urban village and *lal dora* area in Delhi, it also has undergone a steep increase in its residential land and a sharp drop in the extent of its agricultural land. The major source of income in this village now comes from renting, due to the influx of migrants (Chattopadhay et al. 2014). Such visible changes involve complex processes that occur when the culture of the city migrates to the village and the village is included in the city (Shah 2012). Both citizens and villagers experience a new culture in this process. For instance, Shah (2012: 18) describes how villagers came to the gardens of the Delhi School of Economics, which was built on the former agricultural lands of the village of Chandrawal, to cut grass for their cattle and how they threatened to kill the watchman if he stopped them from entering the premises.

The rhetoric of the "planned city" misses out on life in these villages and what is invisible or invisibilised from the city. The link between optimism and technology shows that those who believe globalisation and the planned city comprise an inherently progressive force fail to examine the inherent power differentials exacerbated by globalisation. The "modern", "advanced", "smart", "fashionable", and "beautiful" outlook of Chandigarh does not accommodate the life in its interstitial spaces. This is where Kajheri village fits into what Lévesque has termed *vague urbain*:

> The terrain vague is not an empty lot we look at from a distance, behind the protection of the fence. With our two feet into the middle of it, the vague urbain forces us to accept and think of other ways of understanding how life in the city can be found and imagined . . . who might have something novel to offer, revealing itself incrementally as one uncovers its sense of being, its traces of past, present and future events.
>
> Lévesque (2013: 36)

Kajheri forms a similar case where its residents have built a life of their own in the interstitiality of the village, which provides them with space for alternative and illegitimate activities. It is significant that Chandigarh has been planned with a socialist ideal in mind, and an attempt has always been made to make the city inclusive and progressive. Urban villages in Chandigarh give us an opportunity to study if Chandigarh measures up to its initial ideals, or if it has eventually been shaped into something else entirely.

## Life in Kajheri village

Kajheri village is surrounded by developed sectors that are separated from the village by well-built roadways. Kajheri opens towards the road with a dumping site for construction materials, behind which buildings of all sizes are squeezed together. Villagers have constructed buildings beyond the permissible height, making the village area very congested. This has happened because *lal dora* villages are outside the urban regulatory framework of the city. Most city residents do not access Kajheri, which has a less-than-stellar reputation in the surrounding city. From a distant view the village appears unplanned and dirty, and generates suspicion. But that view hides the buzzing places inside it. If one walks into the village, it turns out to be full of life and busy throughout the day; auto-rickshaws and taxis keep the streets packed. Due to the small area of the village, however, villagers mostly commute on foot and keep the streets lively. Houses in the village open towards the streets, so one can see the balconies with plants, clothes hanging to dry, and people basking in the sun. The streets are also kept busy by passengers coming from the bus station in Sector 43 opposite Kajheri. This bus station is one of the major modes of commuting to neighbouring states. Most of the bus passengers in need of a hotel or customers for sex work conveniently commute to Kajheri. Certainly, this bus station has had a key role in raising the economy of the village and the blooming of its hotel business.

The village population is heterogeneous in composition: old village residents who are still engaged in dairy farming mix with micro-level service providers, people from the labour class who live on rent, and many others to form a wide spectrum of people from a lower to middle class background. One can always find elderly residents and shopkeepers on the streets of the village, sometimes sitting in groups or in the shops reading newspapers. During my regular visits to the village, I was able to build a rapport with some of them. I tried to sense some of the factors that made Kajheri an attractive place to live. I ascertained, first, that Chandigarh, being a highly bureaucratic and politically-important centre, has gained a special place in the region. It is a union territory and capital of two states—Punjab and Haryana—which makes it the administrative head of both these states and, being a union territory, independent administrator of itself. Hence, the city is dominated by high officials and upper-middle-class residents. This population, with its modern lifestyle, makes it one of the most expensive cities in the region. The prices of paying guest accommodation are very high in the city. Due to unaffordable housing, a significant part of the population therefore lives in the urban villages. Second, there is no surveillance and activities of hoarding, prostitution, etc. can only be managed in the absence of high levels of surveillance. The disorder in the village stands in contrast to the surrounding city, which is characterised by facade controls, a policeman stationed at every traffic junction, and building regulations. Hence the village acts as a safe haven for everyone who might feel vulnerable in the city proper, where their activities would be subject to an unwelcome disciplinary gaze.

For an outsider it is difficult to identify Kajheri as a dwelling place of the *kothi* community. Like all other places in India where queer communities dwell, Kajheri village is also a "heteronormative zone" (Banerjea 2015). But the villagers understand the sexual identity of *kothi* men and it is "an accepted way of living in the village" (Raju, thirty-five, Kajheri resident). *Kothi* men have been living in the village for only five years but there is a feeling of attachment to the village in their stories. Most of it comes from the way of life that has developed in the village over time. Anonymity and sex work as a source of livelihood are two points that play a key role in keeping *kothi* men in the village and bringing a sense of freedom. More than 50% of the houses of the village are being developed into hotels, many of which run an underground economy of prostitution and so do the *kothi* men at home. Therefore, a lot of stability in the village lies in keeping each other's secrets and keeping the issues limited to the village. As expressed by an elderly Kajheri resident: "People in the village are very intelligent. They prefer to solve small issues of fight or crime themselves. Coming of police is anyway not considered good for anyone". These sentiments were reaffirmed by Suresh, who stated that: "Everyone in the village knows who we are, and maybe they don't see us of any harm. Or they also have something to hide. We also know a few inside stories, but none of our business. We just do our work". To better understand the everyday life of *kothi* men in the hustle and bustle of the village, I spent my days together with them.

### *... in the house*

The *kothis* living with Suresh had all spent their childhoods with their families in a heteronormative setting and this was sometimes reflected in their mindset, aesthetics, and relationships. They lived together as a closely knit group and went through all kinds of emotions—anger, love, happiness, fear—together. All the *kothis* lived in different rooms in the building but they had a common household. Suresh lived on the second floor of the building; its facade had dirty corners, but his room was neat. Initially upon arrival in Chandigarh none of them had a place to live. Suresh was the first to rent a room in Kajheri on a low budget, and then everyone else followed. When Suresh came to Chandigarh in 2007, it was the first time that he had met people with similar sexual choices and also the first time that he had come across the term *kothi*. Initially, Suresh did not like others calling him *kothi*. He translated *kothi* as "bitch". He related a story told to him by a friend that made him hate the term even more: "there was a *kutiya* [bitch] that reached Lahore following a dog. It is from the word *kutiya* that the *kothi* word is derived on the similar understanding that *kothi* can go anywhere to meet his *giriya* [lover]".

Most encounters that he described took place in the toilets and at the bus station in Sector 43. Here he observed men checking out, touching, and approaching other men. It took time for him to become part of the group and, in the process, he became acquainted with other *kothi* men at the bus station who had problems in finding living space, and he asked them to rent a room in the same building. Most of them decided to move to the village due to a lack of choice. They primarily moved due to discrimination at home and in the workplace, and in search of a safe space where nobody would identify them and they could have sexual freedom. Twenty-one-year-old Lolo, for instance, stated that:

> Nobody in my house or in the city will like if I keep long hair and big breasts. In my village the villagers will know what I was earlier and what I have become. Here (in Kajheri) I am amongst my friends who are like me.

Although they could now somehow afford to live in the city that had left them jobless and vulnerable, as Lolo explained:

> We wear women dresses at night. This is not allowed in the sectors. We can afford a flat in the sectors but then there will be no work. I have many friends in the sectors that live in PG [paying guest accommodation] but then they do regular jobs not sex work.

The interstitiality of Kajheri village therefore served as a space of dwelling for *kothi* men, something which was otherwise absent in the city.

As its first occupant, Suresh was considered head of the household and, for instance, had assigned the work of washing utensils to Deepika, aged twenty-two. He washed all the utensils once a day in the morning. Tamanna, aged twenty-five, was considered to be the best cook in the house. He cooked brunch for everyone: "I like to live in a family more. I like to do household chores—washing clothes, utensils, cooking food, cleaning house". Other *kothis* sometimes assisted him in the kitchen and everyone referred to Tamanna as "*ma*" (the Hindi term for mother) because he cooked food for everyone. Suresh divided the household work between all the *kothis* and scolded them if there was any brawl over work.

A few *kothis* had pasted pictures of their *giriyas* and families on the walls of their rooms. Rooms had no material display of queer identity, as could be seen in representations of queer homes elsewhere. Many times Suresh had thought about getting more electronic items like a washing machine for the house. He was very particular about how the house looked, especially if someone from the outside visited his place: "These people [other *kothis*] have no tension of making a house. They spend all the money in shopping. But there should be everything in the house. I am saving money to buy a washing machine. It will decrease our workload".

Unity among everyone was another highlight in the house. Almost everyone referred to each other as "*pakki saheli*" (Hindi term for strong girlfriend). Sakhi, aged twenty-four, and Paro, aged twenty-three, mentioned their strong friendship with each other many times. Unlike the others, they had visited each other's houses in the state of Haryana. They had told their parents that they worked together in a company in Chandigarh and their families did not know about their sexuality. They boasted about keeping each other's secrets. This unity was clearly reflected when there was a tussle with a client:

> We all are one if there is any fight with the client. Once when the client asked for more time from Deepika and started arguing, we all came together and charged him ten times more and asked him to leave.

Hence, home for *kothi* men was an assortment of various emotions as well as physical activities. It provided private space for discussing and expressing sexual identity. Spaces like the kitchen, Suresh's room etc. and material things resulted in a shared identity among *kothi* men. Although all the *kothi* men paid separate rents for their rooms, a sense of unacceptability in their society bound them and contributed to the home-making process as they lived together.

### ... *on the streets*

When I asked Suresh why he did not rent a house in the city he explained that:

> [the other *kothis*] do not like to go outside this circle. Because if they will leave this building there will be no income. The world outside this circle is very bad. Actually, the world is not bad, we are bad. If we will stay in the city and do wrong stuff, people will not let us stay. If I walk like a girl, people will tease me. People [in Kajheri] know what we do. That is it! If dirty water flows towards the city then everyone will stop it. If clean water will flow, everybody will welcome it.

Suresh had lived in the village for the longest time, so he held a sense of authority in directing the behaviour of the *kothi* men in the village. All the *kothis* were cross-dressers but strictly no one went out in the village cross-dressed during the daytime. *Kothis* were expected to have some measure of control over their self-expression even in the village. Also at home, I rarely saw them cross-dressed, but they often expressed their desire for wearing women's clothes. They dressed up in women's clothes only in the evening when they had to go for sex work. At five in the evening, all the *kothis* started getting ready and were done by seven. They wore heavy make-up to hide their facial hair and took pride in the fact that they were able to pass as women.

After sunset, they all left the village on foot and went to the bus station. They walked the streets of the village very confidently. It was all part of a normal routine for the villagers. They generally gave a slight greeting to their neighbours, a few shopkeepers from whom they bought stuff, and others who equally reciprocated greetings to them. Suresh mentioned that they sometimes felt strangers, generally boys on the street, looking at them but they did not make eye contact to avoid any kind of argument or comments. In public, they talked to each other in their exclusive language. Suresh told me that this language was common among all the *kothis* in North India. By creating the language barrier they tended to create a private space for themselves in an otherwise domestic milieu. At home they used this language to decide a price in front of a client or to have any other secret discussion.

Upon reaching the bus station they spread out and waited for clients to approach them. They made gestures and facial expressions to make men aware of their presence. If any client came, they went with them to a dark place behind the bus station or took them to their rooms in Kajheri, for which they charged INR400 over the normal price. Two *kothis* sometimes shared a room with their clients. Police at the bus station did not interfere in the work of the *kothis* in the night time. Suresh explained that:

> We are not afraid of the police. Few of them ask for favours at times and that's ok. The police have many soft targets other than us on the bus stand to make money. They sometimes warn us to not disturb the public and do our business quietly.

All the *kothis* stayed close to each other at the bus station in fear of a fight. They had faced several incidents of arguments and violence at work. So they always remained alert to face any such situation. At around one o'clock in the morning they called each other to get together to go back home. They got their takeaway dinner while coming back. They all ate together and then went to sleep. Next day they started their day around nine o'clock in the morning and did all the household chores, watched television, did personal stuff, made food, etc.

In the daytime, the *kothis* mostly remained confined to the village because they feared teasing and physical violence. They believed that boys were able to make out their queer identity from the way they walked and now it was very difficult to walk "straight". Deepika explained the desire and fear associated with leaving Kajheri to visit the city:

> Everybody wants to go out in the city. We all are sitting in this room. Don't you think we also wish to go out? We also wish to go out for a walk in the rose garden or *shanti kunj*. We all have vehicles. But why don't we go? Because we think boys will meet us in the garden and pass cheap comments.

They bought household goods from the village market. If required, Suresh also went to the market in Chandigarh to buy things. Once I went along with Suresh to the Sector 22 market in Chandigarh. He pointed at a man and told me that he was his client. The man seemed shocked to see Suresh in the market and quickly disappeared from the scene. Clients rarely met the *kothis* outside the village that functioned as the "peripheral location of their friendship" (Hart 1995) or professional relationship. None of the *kothis* had any social relationship with their clients and did not want any romantic or sexual relationship with the villagers as it would expose them to risk. Only Lolo stated that he had many male friends with whom he went out in Chandigarh. He was considered the most beautiful in the group and always shared his beauty tips with the others; mostly, he was busy getting himself groomed. Bebo, aged twenty-two, explained that "He [Lolo] does not go out alone. He is very beautiful, that's why. Boys will eat her if he goes out".

## Conclusion

In this chapter, I have conducted an ethnographically informed analysis at the intersection of sexuality, domesticity, and urban interstitiality. For this I have focused upon the *kothi* men who live in Kajheri village, a largely unregulated and unplanned "island" within the confines of the rigidly planned grid of Chandigarh city. I see interstitially located Kajheri village as a vital site for the production of alternative dwelling and economic spaces for the sexual minority of *kothi* men. Having migrated from various parts of the surrounding regions, these young individuals have left conventional family life behind and now live in the village in a commune. Residence in the village provides anonymity to the *kothis* that is fundamental for their living, livelihood, and everyday outlook in the city. As gathered from the interviews, *kothi* men find the "rustic", "rural", "illiterate", and "messed-up structure" of the village a secure place for living.

Over time, the advantages of interstitiality have attracted various illegal activities that have become part of village life along with the presence of this sexual minority group of *kothi* men. The urban interstice, in other words, has become a shared space for marginalised groups and those in need of anonymity and protection from the policing gaze of the planned city. The stability of interstitial space thus lies in its disorder and the mutual silence, or disattention towards this disorder, of the subjects who inhabit it. Therefore, alternative spaces are successfully built within it; however, interstitiality does not ensure free self-expression because of the dominance of heteronormative ideology which also can be detected among the *kothi* men. Gender expression by *kothi* men occurs under the constant influence of a spectre of illegitimacy of self-identity. Along with remaining silent about their sexuality and escaping from their families and society, the *kothis* also tried to keep their sexuality understated in the village.

Whereas they have been able to produce an alternative space of urban dwelling that allows them to pursue their own way of life to some extent, and with some measure of safety in an otherwise hostile environment, their efforts in this regard are utterly defensive. Therefore, the transformative potential in terms of generating alternative trajectories of urban development in

Chandigarh and beyond is limited. Yet, by showing how urban interstices such as Kajheri become hotbeds for the marginalised and clandestine undercurrents of urban life, this chapter contributes to identify and locate the kinds of places where advantageous conditions exist for the production of alternative urban spaces. It is in this sense that the urban interstice, embodied in India by the *lal dora* areas, holds a transformative potential that may play a role in enacting alternative urban futures.

## Notes

1 I have kept the identity of the respondents confidential and used pseudonyms.
2 The term "housing societies" is popularly used in India to encompass residential buildings that have been divided into flats. These societies have a set of framed rules for their functioning and they are registered with the regi.

## References


Aldrich, R. (2004) Homosexuality and the City: An Historical Overview. *Urban Studies*. 41(9). 1719–1737.

Allan, G., Crow, G. (1989) *Home and Family: Creating the Domestic Sphere*. Basingstoke: Macmillan.

Banerjea, N. (2015) Critical Urban Collaborative Ethnographies: Articulating Community with Sappho for Equality in Kolkata, India. *Gender, Place & Culture*. 22(8). 1058–1072.

Barron, P., Mariani, M. (eds) (2013) *Terrain Vague: Interstices at the Edge of the Pale*. New York: Routledge.

Bell, D. (2001) Fragments for a Queer City. In: Bell, D., Binnie, J., Holliday, R., Longhurst, R., Peace, R. (eds) *Pleasure Zones: Bodies, Cities, Spaces*. Syracuse, NY: Syracuse University Press. 84–102.

Bourriaud, N. (1998) *Esthetique relationnelle* [*Relational Aesthetics*]. Dijon: Les presses du reel.

Brighenti, A.M. (2013) The Urban Fringe as a Territorial Interstice: On Alpine Suburbs. In: Brighenti, A.M. (ed) *Urban Interstices: The Aesthetics and the Politics of the In-Between*. New York: Routledge.

Butler, J. (1990) *Gender Trouble: Feminism and the Subversion of Gender*. New York and Abingdon: Routledge.

Carballo-Die´guez, A., Dolezal, C., Nieves, L., Dı´Az, F., Decena, C., Balan, I. (2004) Looking for a Tall, Dark, Macho Man. Sexual-Role Behaviour Variations in Latino Gay and Bisexual Men. *Culture, Health & Sexuality*. 6(2). 159–171.

Chakrapani, V., Newman, P.A., Shunmugam, M., McLuckie, A., Melwin, F. (2007) Structural Violence against Kothi-Identified Men Who Have Sex with Men in Chennai, India: A Qualitative Investigation. *AIDS Education & Prevention*. 19(4). 346–364.

Chakrapani, V., Newman, P.A., Shunmugam, M. (2008) Secondary HIV Prevention among Kothi Identified MSM in Chennai, India. *Culture, Health & Sexuality*. 10(4). 313–327.

Chattopadhay, S., Dey, P., Michael, J. (2014) Dynamics and Growth Dichotomy of Urban Villages: Case Study Delhi. *International Journal for Housing Science & Its Applications*. 38(2). 81–94.

Cupers, K., Miessen, M. (2002) *Spaces of Uncertainty*. Wuppertal: Müller und Busmann.

Duncan, J. (1978) Men without Property: The Tramp's Classification and Use of Urban Space. *Antipode*. 10(1). 24–34.

Fitting, P. (2002) Urban Planning/Utopian Dreaming: Le Corbusier's Chandigarh Today. *Utopian Studies*. 13(1). 69–93.

Gayatri, R. (2005) *With Respect to Sex: Negotiating Hijra Identity in South India*. Chicago, IL: University of Chicago Press.

Gill, H. (2016) Kothi. In: Wong, A., Wickramasinghe, M., Hoogland, R., Naples, N.A. (eds) *The Wiley Blackwell Encyclopedia of Gender and Sexuality Studies*. Chicester: Wiley. DOI: 10.1002/9781118663219.wbegss059.

Goffman, E. (1990 [1959]) *The Presentation of Self in Everyday Life*. London: Penguin Books.

Hart, A. (1995) (Re)Constructing a Spanish Redlight District: Prostitution, Space and Power. In: Bell, D., Valentine, G. (eds) *Mapping Desire: Geographies of Sexualities*. London: Routledge. 195–207.

Hubbard, P. (2012) *Cities and Sexuality*. New York: Routledge.

Johnston, L., Valentine, G. (1995) Wherever I Lay My Girlfriend, That's My Home. In: Bell, D., Valentine, G. (eds) *Mapping Desire: Geographies of Sexualities*. London: Routledge. 99–113.

Jorgensen, A., Tylecote, M. (2007) Ambivalent Landscapes—Wilderness in the Urban Interstices. *Landscape Research*. 32(4). 443–462.

Joshi, K., Jeanneret, P., Fry, E.M., Drew, J.B. (1999) *Documenting Chandigarh: The Indian Architecture of Pierre Jeanneret, Edwin Maxwell Fry, Jane Beverly Drew*. Ahmedabad, India: Mapin.

Kalia, R. (1999) *Chandigarh: The Making of an Indian City*. New York: Oxford University Press.

Kumar, M. (2015) Erstwhile Villages in Urban India. *Development in Practice*. 25(1). 124–132

Lévesque, C. (2013) Welcome to Bachoura, or the Found City as Interstice. In: Barron, P., Mariani, M. (eds) *Terrain Vague: Interstices at the Edge of the Pale*. London: Routledge. 47–61.

Mayer, K.H., Gangakhedkar, R., Sivasubramanian, M., Biello, K.B., Abuelezam, N., Mane, S., Risbud, A., Anand, V., Safren, S., Mimiaga, M.J. (2015) Differing Identities, but Comparably High HIV and Bacterial Sexually Transmitted Disease Burdens, among Married and Unmarried Men Who Have Sex with Men in Mumbai, India. *Sexually Transmitted Diseases*. 42(11). 629–633.

Menon, N. (2012) *Seeing Like a Feminist*. New Delhi: Zubaan and Penguin Books India.

Mimiaga, M.J., Biello, K.B., Sivasubramanian, M., Mayer, K.H., Anand, V.R., Safren, S.A. (2013) Psychosocial Risk Factors for HIV Sexual Risk among Indian Men Who Have Sex with Men. *AIDS Care*. 25(9). 1109–1113.

Nagendra, H., Unnikrishnan, H., Sen, S. (2013) Villages in the City: Spatial and Temporal Heterogeneity in Rurality and Urbanity in Bangalore, India. *Land*. 3(1). 1–18.

Nanda, S. (1999) *Neither Man nor Woman: The Hijras of India*. Belmont, CA: Wadsworth Publishing Co.

Perera, N. (2006) Chandigarh: India's Modernist Experiment. In: Gordon, D.L.A. (ed) *Planning Twentieth Century Capital Cities*. London: Routledge. 226–236.

Phadke, S. (2006) Sexuality & Space: Thinking through Some Issues. *Inplainspeak*. January. 10–14.

Seabrook, J. (1999) *Love in a Different Climate: Men Who Have Sex with Men in India.* London and New York: Verso.

Shah, A.M. (2012) The Village in the City, the City in the Village. *Economic and Political Weekly.* XLVII(52). 17–19.

Shaw, A. (2009) Town Planning in Postcolonial India, 1947–1965: Chandigarh Re-examined. *Urban Geography.* 30(8). 857–878.

Sibalis, M. (2004) Urban Space and Homosexuality: The Example of the Marais, Paris' "Gay Ghetto". *Urban Studies.* 41(9). 1739–1758.

Stief, M. (2017) The Sexual Orientation and Gender Presentation of Hijra, Kothi, and Panthi in Mumbai, India. *Archives of Sexual Behaviour.* 46(1). 73–85.

Tonnelat, S. (2008) Out of Frame. The (In)Visible Life of Urban Interstices—A Case Study in Charenton-le-Pont, Paris, France. *Ethnography.* 9(3). 291–324.

Woodford, M.R., Newman, P.A., Chakrapani, V., Shunmugam, M., Kakinami, L. (2012) Correlates of HIV Testing Uptake among *Kothi*-Identified Men Who Have Sex with Men in Public Sex Environments in Chennai, India. *AIDS and Behavior.* 16(1). 53–62.

Wright, T. (1997) *Out of Place: Homeless Mobilizations, Subcities, and Contested Landscapes.* Albany, NY: SUNY Press.

# Part 3

# Alternative urban spaces of public life

# 10 Reclaiming democratic (public) spaces through music

## The case of Viaduto Santa Tereza in Belo Horizonte, Brazil

*Fausto Di Quarto*

### Introduction

This chapter explores how cultural and artistic interventions in urban space can shape collective identities and create momentum for the political activism of social movements. In particular, it is claimed how sound and its effects on space can act as a medium for social transformation (Cox, 2011; Labelle, 2010), thereby engendering the power to reconfigure and repoliticise urban relations (Connor, 2004; Deleuze and Guattari, 1987). The role of emotions created in collective actions through artistic and cultural productions (like music and dance) are inaccurately underestimated, since they represent important means to reinforce a sense of solidarity with the group and shape a "collective identity" in common struggles (Brown, 2016). The chapter shows how music and sound operate in (re)creating space and place-making, not only as a dissenting voice in the urban landscape, but also by producing momentum for political activism, which is obtained together through contestation and the proposal of alternative ways of (re)creating new spaces. To this end I investigate artistic and cultural productions that are set in motion in order to challenge the status quo of institutional power. Music, in this context, is conceived as a universal vector allowing full sensory reappropriation propagating through space, boundless and undisciplined, disclosing the city's invisible "power borders" and producing change by bringing forth problems and opportunities that feed the need for discussion and comparison between different subjects (Dayrell, 2005; Lamotte, 2014; Leite, 2004).

In Brazilian cities, because of the structural processes imposed by institutional power during the dictatorship (1964–1984), a centralised and technocratic urban planning regime has emerged. In this context, public spaces represented for a long time sites for potential revolutionary dissent and conspiracy to be contrasted by instituted power (Duhau, 2001; Isenburg, 2002; Tonucci, 2009). In this chapter such a site under a bridge called Viaduto Santa Tereza (VST) in Belo Horizonte (BH) is analysed as an interstitial space (Bhabha, 2001 [1994]; Johnston, 2000).[1] I discuss how this area has become a hot spot for the musical, cultural, and political life of BH. Thanks to the artistic movement Familia de Rua (FdR), which started in 2008 to use this empty space for the Duelo de MCs (rap freestyle "battle"), the site has become one of the most notable examples of cultural experimentation and political commitment in the city and in Brazil (Jayme and Trevisan, 2012; Rena et al., 2013). Evidence showed a negotiation of power relations and an ongoing struggle for democratic politics in the city council during which the VST came to embody the right to the city for groups calling for transparency and participation in the political arena of BH. This represents an example of how urban social movements use public spaces as the locus of political struggle and appropriate it to counteract contemporary urban neoliberalism (Fani, 2007; Harvey, 2002 [2000]; Lefebvre, 2014 [1968]).

Fieldwork research on the VST took place between July 2008 and June 2009 during a visit to the Universidade Federal de Minas Gerais in BH. The research was carried out as an active participant and spectator, and much of the data are based on interviews (open and semi-structured) for the most part carried out during the days of the official events. Part of the research was carried out in order to make a documentary film,[2] which also constitutes part of the results of the research. The people surveyed range from participants in the events to city council officials who have overseen the restructuring of the area. Part of the research was also based on city council documents, newspaper articles, blogs, internet sources, and information relating to events coordinated by FdR.

## Sound, music, and the production of (political) spaces

Throughout history, geography, as the art of description, has produced images and representations of the world, often through the particular techniques of cartography. In this sense the world "out there" could only be known through its visual representation. In recent decades the social sciences have attempted to frame new approaches to space, place, and territories through a non-visual take (at least in part) leading to a greater understanding of the social, cultural, and economic phenomena, which could encompass multiple senses embedded in places (see also Chapters 2 and 3 in this book). The acoustic dimension has been one of these: "For twenty-five centuries Western knowledge has tried to look upon the world. It has failed to understand that the world is not for beholding. It is for hearing" (Attali cited in Back and Bull, 2008 [2003]: 9).

Back and Bull (2008 [2003]: 18) talk about the power of soundscapes – the acoustic environment that can be perceived by humans – as fluid surfaces that change through different sounds, instead of a static topography to be represented in maps. Deleuze and Guattari (1987: 8, 11–12) treat this dimension as a territorial articulation, or better said, the result of an act or a strategy that defines a spatial identity that creates a protected, but permeable, circle. In their words, if an acoustic emission exists – as a strategy of territorialisation – then listening constitutes the strategy of individuation and the acoustic environment reveals the presence or the activity of a subject. These sonic events constitute a horizon, a soundscape. Murray Schafer, in his *The Tuning of the World* (1977), talks about the acoustic space as an invisible space, a world of invisible fluidities; a certain type of space where the typical dualism inside/outside makes no sense (see also Back and Bull, 2008 [2003]: 16–18, 318). In fact, one can be inside and outside at the same time, contrary to the visual space that is made out of surfaces, sound is surface and depth at the same time. In this sense acoustic space is ubiquitous and eliminates the distinction between "here" and "there".

In other words, sounds territorialise space where they act, while at the same time sound itself is not constrained by it. Acoustic space has no borders, it only ceases to exist when sound particles do not oscillate anymore. Its limits in this sense are not so much geographical as they are temporal. But every subject that is listening gives different meanings to sound. The sonic fact (Back and Bull, 2008 [2003]) can evoke emotions, thoughts, and reflections in different ways, according to the various functions or meanings they are embedded into, valorising, contextualising, or contesting different social practices, rituals, and human actions. Sound contributes to provide specific senses of place rather than an abstract idea of space. In this sense acoustic spaces are the antithesis of non-places (Auge, 2003 [1993]), since they are imbued with human actions and social practices. This means that, contrary to Cartesian conceptions of space, sound gives an active, multiple, and relational meaning to space. Ultimately, "as sound, music fills and structures spaces within us and around us, inside and outside. Hence, much like our concept of place, music can appear to envelop us, but it can also appear to express our innermost feelings" (Kruse, 2003: 154). Organised sounds, i.e. music, as a form of social communication, require communality of practice in the performance as well as in the audience; music in this sense becomes an experienced practice. Thus, "the analysis of music within the social sciences raises inherently geographical questions, particularly around how musical practice carves spaces of performance, expression and culture, and how it shapes social spaces of identity, belonging and community" (Jazeel, 2005: 233).

Lefebvre (1991 [1974]) talks about homogeneous, planned, abstract space as counterposed to lived and relational space, where identities are born, also from alterity, throughout territoriality. Spatialised identities are aimed at creating similarity and otherness, confirmed and challenged at the same time. Social relations are produced and continually redefined in a process that is real and imagined at the same time (Soja, 1996: 6). Any spatial form that acquires sense, according to the meanings and functions society gives to it in its action, becomes a relevant geographical object of study in this sense (Santos, 2008 [1996]: 109). Public spaces are the most representative type of relational places of contemporary cities where otherness and sameness are articulated in a process of spatial appropriation through symbolic and hierarchical practices (Harvey, 2002 [2000]; Lefebvre, 2014 [1968]). In public spaces, most of the time, consumption patterns are key elements in shaping social identities; here we encounter global economic networks where access to parts of the city are restricted according to socio-spatial inequalities, and where identity and appropriation are peculiar to different levels of economic consumption (Harvey, 2002 [2000]). Places, subordinated to the logics of consumption, confer different social statuses according to how dwellers make use of them; different modes of consuming space create different urban identities.

David Harvey uses the Lefebvrian concept of heterotopia (different from its Foucauldian counterpart) and redefines it as a liminal social space of possibility where "something different" is not only possible, but fundamental for the defining of revolutionary trajectories (2012: XVII). These spaces are not embedded in revolutionary moments of history, on the contrary, they are spontaneously part of irruptive moments when diverse groups see, even for a moment, the possibility of collective action that can create something radically different. The body, as the locus of political resistance, can be seen as a medium through which political emancipation becomes possible (Harvey, 2002 [2000]: 130, 2012: 161–162).

In this study, music and bodies reveal a different way to do politics, inscribed in everyday spaces. Through music an alternative narrative shows encounters and confrontations that find great resonance (physically and discursively) thanks to the spoken word and the act of performing.[3] Through music it is possible to recognise tactics and strategies that address the transformation of urban lives; this public action reveals a contestation that can be considered a political action. The production of space itself is deeply political, always in process, and reveals relations of power and dominance but also keeps open the possibility for imagining and realising alternative modes of spatial production (see Chapter 1 in this book). Dikeç (2005: 181), echoing Rancière, reminds us that politics takes a place, i.e. it is spatialised: "Spatialization becomes the very condition of politics precisely because it constitutes an integral element of the disruption of the natural order of domination".

In this research the importance of a particular type of space is furthermore underlined: interstitial spaces. These are framed as low-prestige and non-dominated spaces that permit an easier negotiation and more flexibility to be used by dwellers. For Bhabha (2001 [1994]: 15) these spaces open up "the possibility of a cultural hybridity that entertains difference without an assumed or imposed hierarchy". Johnston (2000: 74) defines them as "sites of resistance, complicity, trans-culturation and scattered hegemonies", which, as spaces of difference, are open to new identity appropriation and put together (potentially) as interaction actors that are usually distant. The VST in BH is conceived as one of these types of places (see Chapter 9 in this book for a detailed theoretical discussion on interstitial spaces) in which sound and music are the primary driving forces in the differential production of an urban space for public life.

## Belo Horizonte: from segregated city to the crisis of public spaces

BH was the first planned city in Brazil, conceived in 1895 according to European positivist ideology. The proclamation of the Republic in 1889 occurred within the spirit of *ordem e progreso* (order and progress); BH was conceived in fact as a symbol and maximum aspiration of these ideals, embodying the perfect modern and functional city (Tonucci, 2009). The conveyance of the old political power in the state of Minas Gerais from Ouro Preto, the previous capital, to BH meant the negation of the old imperial order – the chaotic city shielded in the mountains – and the consequent affirmation of modernity and progress in an a priori planned city that promised unlimited urban growth: "It synthesizes as no other city in Brazil, the trust in the utopian ideal city, elaborated starting from the most advanced know-how of that time" (Tonucci, 2009: 3). The engineer Aarão Reis was motivated for his plan by rationality, functionality, and social hygienism, inspired by the urban plans of Hausmann and L'Enfant (planners of Paris and Washington). From the former he inherited the wide and monumental avenues and from the latter the orthogonal and symmetric plan. The main goals were to have a good circulation of traffic, cleanliness, ventilation, aesthetics in geometrically traced streets, space control, and functional segregation (Bahia, 2007).

As a matter of fact, the creation of BH can only be fully understood if placed within the political context of Brazil at that time, which encompassed the establishment of the Republic and the abolition of slavery (Lemos, 2010). In fact, the Republican ruling classes believed that poverty and misery were the characteristics of an archaic country, being the legacy of the empire-colony duality, and that the material and moral progress achieved by liberal-bourgeois society would be sufficient to improve society while also ending social "disorder" (Mendonça, 2003). The plan of the new state capital was therefore a reflection of the ideology of the ruling class that had no interest in the housing problems of "disadvantaged" social groups and their relative segregation (Leme and Fernandes, 1999).

As Map 10.1 clearly shows, the spatial segregation was already present in the designed plan. The urban area had a regular and orthogonal layout with wide, symmetrical streets and dwelling blocks of the same size; regulations and planning were set up exclusively for the central area while almost no plan was conceived for the informal occupation in the outskirts of the city. This plan resulted in the

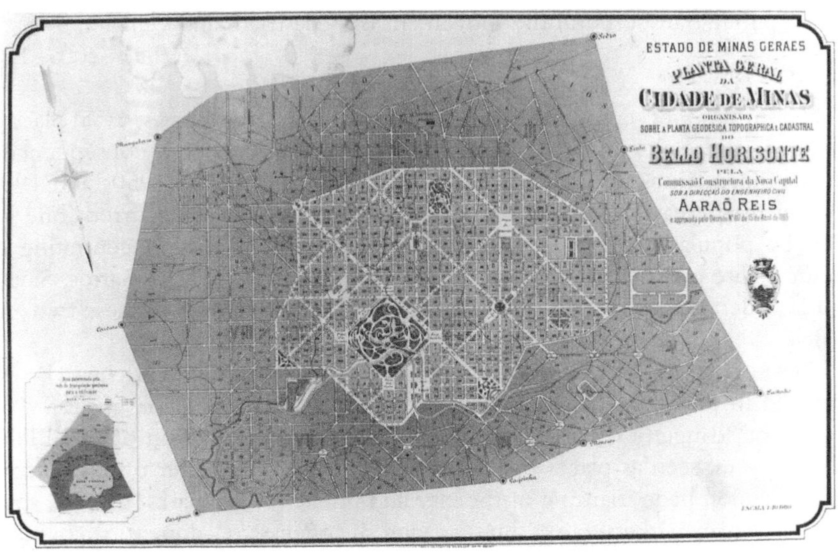


*Map 10.1* General plan of Belo Horizonte in 1889

Source: Comissão Construtora de Belo Horizonte (1895), available at: https://commons.wikimedia.org/wiki/File:Planta_BH.jpg

expulsion of popular classes from the centre, which, unable to pay for the privileged location, were still forced to depend on it, being the cornerstone of the city's economic, logistical, and political functions (Tonucci, 2009). Since the 1900s, the population to the north of the centre had exceeded that of the core: "favelas and neoclassical wooden houses, monumental public buildings of functionalism, lanes and great avenues, suburb and center, all come simultaneously in this city of contrasts, planned for being a model" (Costa, 1994: 54). New self-segregated areas for the elites as well as an urban expansion out of the city centre took place, new satellite cities (workers' suburbs) and a process of favelisation in the centre and in the peripheries shaped the new BH (Villaça, 1998).

The expansion of non-planned areas continued for the whole century, resulting in the growth of favelas (which doubled), an increase in crime rates, and emptying of the city centre (Tonucci, 2009). As a result of these processes, the urban space began to be produced through a succession of private real estate investments. Public spaces in particular are considered marginal by the municipality and therefore represent the smallest amount of the space developed. In the last twenty years the municipality has planned a renovation of the city centre, which was considered to be in a state of environmental, social, and economic degradation. Solutions were sought:

> to make improvements in the physical and environmental quality of the area, with emphasis on the recovery of cultural and architectural heritage, the expansion of green areas, the reduction of noise, atmospheric and visual pollution, as well as the dynamism of spaces and improvement of conditions in public transport and the movement of pedestrians and vehicles.
>
> (Vilela, 2009: 107)[4]

The process of emptying the centre of the upper classes as a place of residence and (subsequently) commerce and work has been a consequence of the transformations that have taken place in BH during the 1950s and 1960s. During these years a spatial subdivision of the city centre occurred: one part used by popular classes for street trades and another one concentrating the political elite and the new bourgeoisie in the districts of Funcionarios, Savassi, and Lourdes; the street Rua da Bahia still represents a divisor of these two areas (Vilela, 2009).

The new forms of consumption, the spatial segregation of richer classes – enclaved in protected dwellings by fences and guards – and the exclusion and control of "dangerous social classes" have led to a stigmatisation of social life in public spaces, seen as places of danger and distrust. The better off also increasingly abandon pedestrian use of the city and public spaces (parks, squares, streets of the popular markets, etc.), thus carrying out their extra-domestic activities in specialised reserved spaces (Duhau, 2001; Serpa, 2007). This mechanism has triggered a process of greater perception of insecurity and a relative desertification of such areas. In this way, spaces now "emptied" become actually riskier because they are less frequented. BH, as a car city, conceived and built for public power, has created urban forms reduced to mere spaces of circulation, preventing the use of public spaces and therefore expelling bodies (Tonucci, 2009; Vilela, 2009).

In this context a polarisation has emerged regarding the practices related to the use of public spaces. On one hand the popular classes tend to make dominant use of the streets and of public spaces; while, on the other, the middle classes use these spaces only as a transit point for their cars, between specialised and socially homogeneous enclaves.

## The Viaduto Santa Tereza

In the beginning of the 1920s, BH lived through an era of great transformations, from an administrative and bureaucratic hub it became an industrial and commercial city. The construction of a viaduct linking the city centre to the first new neighbourhoods of Floresta and Santa Tereza was one of the great projects of the decade. Inaugurated in 1929, it represented the most important civil engineering construction in the whole state of Minas Gerais; the viaduct synthesises pioneering work and momentum towards the future (modernist, positivist, and functional), symbolised by its reinforced concrete work (an absolute novelty for those times) and its aesthetic plasticity.

The VST began to have a first-order function in the local and regional road system. It allowed (and still does) an intense circulation of pedestrians and vehicles from the neighbourhood of Praça da Estacao (a public space hub) to the eastern region, composed of the "traditional neighbourhoods" (*bairros tradicionais*) of Floresta and Santa Tereza. This has served to intensify trade (which until then consisted of street vendors in the residential neighbourhoods) and access to public life, as it facilitated access to the city centre. In addition, the bridge became part of the imaginary of local artists, becoming an urban reference point from which to draw inspiration for their work. Structural problems appeared over the years but were ignored until the 1980s. In 1988, the whole structure and area were definitively protected and declared a cultural heritage site. The area underneath the bridge had become a storage area for municipal road equipment, served as an occasional parking lot, and provided extemporaneous accommodation for beggars and drug dealers. This space, however, had great potential, given its privileged location in the centre of the city, its articulation with the local road system, and the proximity to other spaces for cultural activities nearby (Praça da Estaçao, the municipal park, and the literary cafés). Considering these peculiarities, the municipality of BH planned to recover the site for differentiated uses, proposing it as a place for recreational and cultural activities, believing that material recovery of the bridge alone, without any actual reframing for the practices under the bridge, would have been useless. The idea of the intervention aimed at the revalorisation of the cultural heritage of the viaduct and its rehabilitation in the urban context, also transforming the space under the bridge by imagining different uses for it and a full appropriation by different types of dwellers.

The entire area was restored and remodelled in two years. In the area under the bridge – which was completely cleared – the restyling provided an amphitheatre, a bar, an area for shows and fairs, as well as a public bath and a police station. The inauguration of the area, after delays and bureaucratic slowdowns, took place in 1999; however, despite all the good intentions, the entire area lost public interest and became an obsolete and dangerous place, again at risk of degradation. Ultimately, despite the attempt to reshape its historical-cultural identity within the urban context, the results obtained were quite different from those imagined in plans, revealing the limits of the project. The whole area lost interest in dwellers' mental geographies as well as in planners' expectations. As a matter of fact, a virtuous cycle of embedded practices related to the new area and its renovated look never took place; as a result, the whole area returned to a state of abandonment and neglect, becoming a shelter for the homeless and a hiding place for drug dealers and junkies.

## Through music: claiming space, creating new places

In BH, hip-hop culture took hold at the beginning of the 1980s. Breakdance became the main rhythm danced in the suburbs of BH, becoming a real fashion in places of great visibility.[5] This meant a reappropriation of the spaces by young people who were previously excluded from these parts of the city. The intention to bring forms of entertainment to the population that did not have access to them was often dampened by the police authorities that did not tolerate the unauthorised meeting of many people in public spaces (Dayrell, 2005; Machado, 2003). As a result, the movement was stopped and forced to appear less explicitly and continuously. At the beginning of the 1990s, however, a popularisation of this cultural movement through the media resulted in a growth of the phenomenon. The events and groups grew large in numbers and returned to be visible in the streets, dislocated in various parts of the city, mainly the suburbs (Santa Tereza) or favelas:

> People from lower classes are interested in hip hop not only because they are from the suburbs, but also because they cannot go to a bar or anything like that. You are born and all you have around is that. ... We are born near the favela; therefore we express what we feel. ... The periphery is a conglomeration of people forgotten by politicians and everyone. As it happens here, they often waste a lot of money on the police and we do not even have a square to play football for free.
>
> (Interview cited in Machado, 2003: 127)

Furthermore, the proliferation of community radios (like Radio Favela) and clubs specialising in more underground musical styles brought together people from middle and lower classes. New followers gradually joined and groups of skaters also increasingly embraced this new culture, giving rise to spontaneous encounters in public places in the city centre (especially Praça

Sete and Praça da Estação). These groups slowly migrated to the areas below the VST.

Appropriation of the area under the bridge started in July 2007, when the group FdR decided to do rap music "battles" in Praça da Estaçao, a few metres away from the VST. Because of the rain, the group decided to move a few hundred metres below the bridge of Santa Tereza. The FdR ("street's family") is a cultural collective that was active in the local hip-hop movement from the early 2000s.

> I've been skating for 15 years; together with these people at some point we started to meet [August 2007] in Praça da Estação to do the free-style battle. At some point we felt the need and we wondered "who is going to do it?" The name *familia de rua* has been used as a reference: at the end of the day everything started in the streets ... This event has become so successful for being able to aggregate an ever-growing number of people living in these urban environments, that is, the streets. These parts of the city are the ones that create people's ties.
>
> (Leo, FdR)

Gradually, the movement gained strength and, as a member of the municipal council supported it, it managed to obtain electricity, public baths, and police service during the events. The important effect of appropriating the VST has certainly been the change in perception of the area, which was considered to be risky by many dwellers (see Figures 10.1 and 10.2). Luciana, in this regard, underlined the fact that now

> people come and see the space in a different way, and maybe they start to think of that space in a different way. ... I've heard several times about assaults, thefts, even though nothing has ever happened to me. During the events it is clear that it is very secure, also because people today see this space differently. I'm here today and I feel secure because there is this event going on. Here it has improved a lot, yes. Not only music, but any artistic intervention contributes to decrease a lot the problem of violence.

The fact that the events take place outdoors is very important considering that in BH (and in Brazil more broadly) social classes are segregated in different territorial enclaves according to levels of consumption and ethnic background (Fani, 2007; Jayme and Trevisan, 2012; Serpa, 2007; Tonucci, 2009). Leisure activities are highly lucrative and tend to be concentrated in socially homogeneous places, i.e. "safe" spaces that traditional public spaces do not offer. The increase in privatisation and marketing of cultural activities generates social asymmetries, producing unconventional, marginal, and peripheral cultures, based on economic exclusion that generates marginalised movements (like hip-hop in the peripheries or baile funk in favelas) (Bastos et al., 2017). In this regard, the Duelo de MCs creates a radically different space (Rena et al., 2013) since it:

*Figure 10.1* The contemporary appearance of Viaduto Santa Tereza
Source: Barnabé (April 2012), available at: www.flickr.com/photos/casaforadoeixominas/7122186195

*Figure 10.2* Duelo de MCs under the VST
Source: author's archive, July 2009

> brings together beggars and fancy girls, going through all kinds of underground movements, and I find it interesting to use the public space . . . that is ours! Thank God I have the option to do other things in the evening, but for many people the only form of fun is here, that's enough.
>
> (Aline, follower)

The hip-hop imaginary is linked, at least spatially, to the context of the suburbs of large urban centres and to a feeling of exclusion (Black, 2014; Jeffries, 2014; Lamotte, 2014); in this case, it is a type of structural, informative, and ethnic exclusion. It derives from precarious education and jobs as well as from spatial distance from the city centre, which generates an inability for dwellers to fit into the prevailing urban socio-economic dynamics. Exclusion is also linked to the absence of the subjects of peripheries in a socio-political sphere of public opinion and mass media. In fact, the periphery is treated either according to negative stereotypes, or superficially by political agents or the media, which stigmatise it as the space of poverty, unhappiness, or crime. Another type of exclusion is ethnic, or rather racial, as most of the Brazilian suburbs are in fact inhabited by African descendants (Cunha and Ramos, 2007).[6] In this scenario, hip-hop allows young people of these areas to project their daily experiences in the city through artistic creation. Through hip-hop new individuals acquire visibility, coming out of the stigmatised territories of the city and arriving at the media scene bringing "new" discourses, hidden by traditional politics. In line with Johnston and Bhabha, I consider the VST as an interstitial urban space that opens up new potentials for hybrid cultures and identities, without imposing a top-down use of it, putting together in interaction actors that are usually geographically and socially distant. This is expressed in the words of Daniel and Camilla:

> Since there is a lack of diversion in BH whereby people who do not have their own space, then everybody comes here . . . They all fit together, I've never seen a fight or anything like that. . . . I like the movement more than hip-hop: I find it nice to be able to bring BH into a small space, many people of different cultures, different tastes . . . all kinds of people from various cultural groups . . . And then being for free, people of every income. If you come on a Friday night here you see it is a puzzle, there is a meeting of tribes.

Through music and especially through the presence of people performing it, the relationship between sound and physical interaction can be further stressed. During the events, in fact, the space under the viaduct becomes an acoustic space where performing music embodies a political act, i.e. a strategy to overcome invisibility and claim presence and visibility in the streets. Ana Fani (2007) – echoing Lefebvre – makes clear that the right to the city can only be fully realised by accentuating the search for "self-management". Through the clash/encounter between authorities and social actors, the "rules" of living collective spaces are defined, even through violent or repressive actions.

> The fact that we are here every Friday is already a way to assert our right to occupy a public space. Like the first time we came nearby to Praça da Estaçao ... we gathered less than thirty people and the police had already arrived to repress us, saying that we could not use the square. How can't we use a space that belongs to us? So here we are trying to exercise this right to occupy the space. We did not lose this space because we knew as we arrived, we fought face to face and said "No, this is a public space, we have the right to use it! Why don't you let us use the space? Won't you let us do that? Okay, we'll do it anyway!" And then they said: "Shit! Let's release it or we will have problems ..." And I believe that's the way things can change: if people claim, if they assert their rights and take to the streets and protest.
>
> (Leo, FdR)

One of the policemen working during the events made clear how space negotiation clashed with state priority, e.g. public order:

> When there is no show here it's all normal and quiet, as you can see. But when the event takes place at night, unfortunately ... there are people who use the space for drug use, scribbling on the walls, drinking alcohol ... you know there are many vendors. ... the organisers should tell people to use more consciously the space, because if you leave everything in the hands of the police ... the police will do its job, and it is repressive! I cannot dissuade people saying "don't do this, do not do that ..." I have to get there and show a cop attitude.

After the start of the rap battles in Praça da Estação, the police intervened several times to limit events due to the volume of the sound, as well as to stop the shows for patrolling. In some cases the organisers of the events have actually protested, defining themselves in mourning against the participants because of "the neglect and degradation for drugs use, space integrity, and lack of respect with the hip-hop movement".[7] The public administration though, in recent years, has been using the space for cultural events, officially recognising the potential of the area, giving new centrality for this type of event. The last event was the commemoration of BH's 120 years through a festival and most of the musical events took place in the VST.[8]

The negotiation of the use of public spaces between authorities and young dwellers of peripheral areas in BH has been an issue in current times. As Rena et al. (2013) and Jayme and Trevisan (2012) show, the main political effect of the use of this space has been the recognition of great political significance of the area, becoming the space for new political subjectivities (Assembleia Horizontal Popular, Grupos Tematicos) that claim the counter-hegemonic use of the city as a common. In December 2009, the mayor of BH decreed a ban on the use of Praça da Estaçao (next to VST), announcing the introduction of fees for using public spaces. This provoked an immediate reaction, which gathered around the movement "Praia da Estação – the square is ours".[9] A similar thing happened in 2014 when the VST was occupied by movements claiming transparency and popular participation.[10] This shows how the area spatially embodied the starting point for a new type of political contestation that has gathered momentum against new processes of urban sanitation, in line with the contemporary trends of speculative use of the city and discouragement of the free use of public spaces in the name of renovation for touristic use and infrastructural improvements (CMI – Centro de Media Independente Brasil,2010).[11]

In BH there are also other types of appropriation of public space through music. The two most significant are the Quarteirão do Soul and the Rood Boss Sound System. The first refers to an event of soul music dances open to all and taking place in the street. It is aimed at reviving the American black dance and culture of the 1970s based on pride and enhancement of black identity as a fundamental theme, allowing people to affirm their value, their importance, and their identity in the streets, reappropriating it through total sensory control.[12] The other is related to Jamaican music, mainly reggae and ska, in line with the tradition of sound systems outdoors; it has no fixed place but, rather, moves from time to time between various places in the city. If music has the power to unite people, the sound system incorporates different musical genres, mixes and merges them. As Henriques suggests (cited in Back and Bull, 2008 [2003]: 318), it generates a noisy, excessive, chaotic situation, breaking pre-established social rules, and being subversive of the harmony and peace of the social (and political) body. Hence, the story of the VST has to be seen in the broader context of urban politics in BH, where music, artistic expression, and multisensuous bodily appropriation of public spaces has come to play an increasingly important role in enacting political change from below.

## Concluding remarks

In Brazil, music has contributed – especially in the last fifty years – by developing a form of oral expression that would give vent to the concerns, pleasures, and sufferings of communities, offering the possibility of transcending the harsh conditions of life, first, from the dictatorship and, later, from structural inequalities. This study has explored how political processes can develop simultaneously with concrete collective artistic proposals in the urban environment. It is a direct example of how, through dissent, a common space was claimed, generating artistic intervention as both the means and goal, in a process of conflict and participation, giving also momentum for new political actions. The area underneath the viaduct represents today a key point in the local musical scene of BH where events of different natures are performed (including screenings of documentaries, shows, dances, and the usual MCs' battle); working as a new meeting point for people of different social classes, disparate cultural taste, and different cultural levels, as evidenced by the field research. People in the most diverse places of the city (the suburbs and favelas) participate as active actors (as well as users) of the event.

A reappropriation of a public space, therefore, which is extraneous to the dominant capitalist system, thanks to its universal "musical" nature, also succeeds in giving a new meaning (a new identity) to an urban place that had become obsolete in the mental cartography of dwellers. What gains relevance here is the effect that music has on the urban space and the power relations it generates. The appropriation of this space acts as a mode of negotiating citizenship, mainly through:

- affirming a place and a presence in the city through a struggle for public space and a claim for street presence, where bodies represent a political act, to publicly manifest themselves, performing emancipation and resistance;
- managing conflict with the authorities (generated when citizens actively take over the streets) and putting on the public agenda the right to rediscuss the use of public space and, more generally, to what extent urban dwellers have the right to use and produce the city;
- the interaction of disparate actors of the city who confront themselves within a cultural event corroborated by music, bringing to the forefront different socio-cultural imaginaries, tensions, and expectations.

The concept of centrality reframes the idea that the city centre holds a power of attraction; centrality has the ability to concentrate wealth, power, information, knowledge, and traffic: in a nutshell, everything (Lefebvre, 2014 [1968]). The appropriation of the space under the viaduct serves to restructure public space and democratic agonism, redefining and renegotiating a shared living space within the city. As explained before, the city of BH has striven over the years to recover and reinsert this (residual) space in the urban area without succeeding because it never opened a space for political confrontation and participation over the use of (that) public space. One of the most important effects of appropriation (even if symbolic and temporary) has been to transform the area into a centre of interest for other groups that now use the space for different types of events. For this reason I believe that, as Casaglia (cited in Lefebvre, 2014 [1968]) suggests, it is not through the intervention of specialists but rather through participation and agitation that urban life can recover its capacity for integration and participation. According to this view, generalised self-management is the basis of the "right to the city" (Lefebvre, 2014 [1968]). This necessarily involves a movement from below. The voices that sing reveal social and political proposals, especially in a context like Brazil, where growing socio-economic polarisation limits the chances to influence public decisions (Castro, 2006; Fani, 2007). In BH, the VST embodies – metaphorically and metonymically – the effects of planning the city from above and a reappropriation – both symbolic and material – from below.

## Notes

1 Interstitial spaces are framed here as low-prestige and non-dominated spaces that permit an easier negotiation and more flexibility to be used by dwellers.

2 https://youtu.be/oiccUUmflG4.
3 In this research we refer to the experienced musical practice known as *hip-hop* and its cultural practice. Founded in 1973 by DJ Africa Bambaata as a strategy to soothe ongoing clashes between young gangs in the Bronx, it was aimed at replacing conflicts with musical (rap), dance (breakdancing), and artistic (graffiti) competitions. Youngsters who attended the local dances represented and "defended" in this way the respective neighbourhoods of belonging, confronting each other, and celebrating for the first time a personal expression through rhythmic poetry and frenetic dances. Hip-hop was born as a new socio-cultural stage that can be seen as part of a process of socio-political demand inspired by the ideas of Martin Luther King, Malcolm X, and the Black Panthers. It promoted black identity and territorial pride, designed to subvert negative stereotypes related to African descendants. It slowly started to be understood also as a social movement, claiming urban improvements for rappers' neighbourhoods, trying to fight the police violence, and proposing the recognition and insertion of the black community management and administration processes. Having undergone a strong media exposure, hip-hop crossed the United States borders and expanded all over the world; it has been adopted as a cultural manifestation globally, always relying on the urban universe as its background.
4 Other urban redevelopment plans were carried out in the last twenty years aiming at restructuring transport and transit in the central areas (1995); stimulating use of public spaces in order to increase life quality (1999); steering socio-economic and cultural inclusion through environmental plans and social security (2004); and (again) revitalising public spaces and degraded areas in the name of sustainable socio-economic and environmental development (2007).
5 In Brazil at the beginning of the 1980s hip-hop had already mobilised a substantial segment of the youth of the favelas and the suburbs of the cities. Starting from a moment of racial conscience and black pride, disclosed in the soul music by local artists (Jorge Ben Jor, Tim Maia, Cassiano, etc.), what gained importance and media relevance was the breakdance. Little by little during the 1980s the other hip-hop practices (graffiti and rap) spread out – especially in São Paulo, Brasilia and BH – encompassing fashion, gestures, and language, to build a set of new codes and signs that are collectively codified and articulated (Dayrell, 2005).
6 With the urban reforms of the last century, public spaces were increasingly forbidden to the black population. Brazilian elites did not introduce new social concepts and practices with regard to the fate of African descendants that would allow socio-economic integration; the concern of the elites was to find a solution that would maintain the power and maintenance of the same power geometries. The expulsion of this part of the population from urban centres meant that these people headed to the hills (where favelas were born) and to the suburbs, thus distancing themselves from the pulsing centres of the city. Politically this strategy represented a way to relegate "black territories" from public policies, so as to weaken the political consciousness of inhabitants in the struggle for the right to urban space and its socially built territories.
7 See: Familia de Rua (2009).
8 See: SouBH (2017).
9 The movement stated a clear message on the internet: "The decree N° 13,798 OF DECEMBER 09, 2009 of our mayor of BH, Marcio Lacerda, prohibits any type of event from happening in Praça da Estação. The question remains: who is interested in the fact that public spaces are merely areas of passage and consumption? If we are denied the right to remain in any public space in the city, we will occupy these spaces in a fun, playful and seemingly unpretentious way. Bring your bathing suit (shorts, shorts, bikini, swimsuit, underwear), chairs, towels, umbrellas, farofa . . . Bring drums and guitars! Bring food to a collective banquet! Where? Praça da Estaçao of BH.

When? Saturday, 16/01/2010, 09h30min. How much? For free!" Source: CMI – Centro de Media Independente Brasil (2010).

10 See: PosTV (2014).

11 This was also related to the forthcoming events of the international soccer World Cup in 2014.

12 It has occurred every Saturday from 2pm in the centre of BH in *Goitacazes* street (centre district) since 2002.

## References

Auge, M. (2003 [1993]). *Nonluoghi: Introduzione a un'antropologia della surmodernità* [Non-Places: An Introduction to Supermodernity]. Milan: Eleuthera.

Back, L. and Bull, M. (eds) (2008 [2003]). *Paesaggi sonori. Musica, voci, rumori: L'universo dell'ascolto* [The Auditory Culture Reader]. Milan: il Saggiatore.

Bahia, C.L.M. (2007). Metamorfoses da metrópole [Metamorphoses of the Metropolis]. *Revista do Arquivo Público Mineiro*. XLIII(2), July–December. Available at: www.siaapm.cultura.mg.gov.br/modules/rapm/brtacervo.php?cid=966andop=1.

Bastos, C.D., Magalhães, F.N.C., Miranda, G.M., Silva, H., Tonucci Filho J.B.M., Cruz, M. de. M. and Velloso, R. de C.L. (2017). Entre o espaço abstrato e o espaço diferencial: ocupações urbanas em Belo Horizonte [Between Abstract Space and Differential Space: Urban Occupations in Belo Horizonte]. *Revista Brasileira de Estudos Urbanos E Regionais*, 19(2), 251–266. http://doi.org/10.22296/2317-1529.2017v19n2p251.

Bhabha, K.H. (2001 [1994]). *I luoghi della cultura* [*The Location of Culture*]. Rome: Meltemi.

Black, S. (2014). "Street Music", Urban Ethnography and Ghettoized Communities. *International Journal of Urban and Regional Research*, 38(March), 700–705. DOI: 10.1111/1468-2427.12098.

Brown, A.J. (2016). Above and Below the Streets: A Musical Geography of Anti-Nuclear Protest in Tokyo. *Emotion, Space and Society*, 20, 82–89. DOI: 10.1016/j.emospa.2016.01.005.

Castro, M.C.P.S. (2006). Dilemas para a construção do espaço publico brasileiro [Dilemmas for the Construction of Brazilian Public Space]. In: Rousiley, M. and Castro, M.C.P.S. (eds) *Mídia, Esfera publica e identidades coletiva* [Media, Public Sphere and Collective Identities]. Belo Horizonte: ED. UFMG, 139–152.

Connor, S. (2004). Sound and Self. In: Smith, M.M. (ed) *Hearing History: A Reader*. Athens: University of Georgia Press, 54–66.

Costa, H.S.M. (1994). Habitação e produção do espaço em Belo Horizonte [Housing and the Production of Space in Belo Horizonte]. In: Monte-Mor, R.L. (ed) *Belo Horizonte: espaços e tempos em construção* [Belo Horizonte: Spaces and Times under Construction]. Belo Horizonte: CEDEPLAR/PBH, 51–77.

Cox, C. (2011). Beyond Representation and Signification: Toward a Sonic Materialism. *Journal of Visual Culture*, 10(2), 145–161. DOI: 10.1177/1470412911402880.

Cunha, H. and Ramos, M.E.R. (eds) (2007). *Espaço urbano e afrodescendência* [Urban Space and Afrodescendence]. Fortaleza: UFC Edições.

Dayrell, J. (2005). A musica entra em cena: o rap e o funk na socializaçao da juventude em Belo Horizonte [Music Comes onto the Scene: Rap and Funk in the Socialisation of Youth in Belo Horizonte]. Doctoral dissertation. Universidade de São Paulo. Available at: http://bdae.org.br/bitstream/123456789/1591/1/tese.pdf.

Deleuze, G. and Guattari, F. (1987). *A Thousand Plateaus: Capitalism and Schizophrenia*. Minneapolis: University of Minnesota Press.
Dikeç, M. (2005). Space, Politics and the Political. *Environment and Planning D: Society and Space*, 23(2), 171–188. DOI: 10.1068/d364t.
Duhau, E. (2001). La megaciudad en el siglo XXI: De la modernidad inconclusa a la crisis del espacio público [The Megacity in the 21st Century: From Unfinished Modernity to the Crisis of Public Space]. *Papeles de Población*. Available at: www.scielo.org.mx/scielo.php?script=sci_arttextandpid=S1405-74252001000400006.
Fani, A.C. (2007). *O Espaço Urbano: Novos escritos sobre a cidade* [Urban Space: New Writings about the City]. São Paulo: Labur ediçoes.
Harvey, D. (2002 [2000]). *Spaces of Hope*. Edinburgh: Edinburgh University Press.
Harvey, D. (2012). *Rebel Cities. From the Right to the City to the Urban Revolution*. London: Verso.
Isenburg, T. (2002). *Brasile: una geografia política* [Brazil: A Political Geography]. Rome: Carocci.
Jayme, J.G. and Trevisan, E. (2012). Intervenções urbanas, usos e ocupações de espaços na região central de Belo Horizonte [Urban Interventions, Uses and Occupations of Spaces in the Central Region of Belo Horizonte]. *Civitas – Revista de Ciências Sociais*, 12(2), 359–377.
Jazeel, T. (2005). The World is Sound? Geography, Musicology and British-Asian Soundscapes. *Area*, 37(3), 233–241. Available at: www.jstor.org/stable/20004456.
Jeffries, M.P. (2014). Hip-Hop Urbanism Old and New. *International Journal of Urban and Regional Research*, 38(March), 706–715. DOI: 10.1111/1468-2427.12106.
Johnston, R.J. (2000). *Dictionary of Human Geography*. 4th edn. Oxford: Blackwell.
Kruse, R.J. (2003). Imagining Strawberry Fields as a Place of Pilgrimage. *Area*, 35(2), 154–162. Available at: www.jstor.org/stable/20004305.
Labelle, B. (2010). *Acoustic Territories: Sound Culture and Everyday Life*. London: Bloomsbury.
Lamotte, M. (2014). Rebels without a Pause: Hip-Hop and Resistance in the City. *International Journal of Urban and Regional Research*, 38(July), 686–694. DOI: 10.1111/1468-2427.12087.
Lefebvre, H. (2014 [1968]). *Il diritto alla città* [The Right to the City]. Verona: Ombre Corte.
Lefebvre, H. (1991 [1974]) *The Production of Space*. Oxford: Blackwell.
Leite, R.P. (2004). *Contra-usos da cidade: Lugares e espaços publicos na experiencia urbana contemporanea* [*Counter-Using the City: Public Places and Spaces in Contemporary Urban Experience*]. Campinas (SP): UNICAMP.
Leme, M.C.S. and Fernandes, A. (1999). Urbanismo no Brasil: 1895–1965 [Urbanism in Brazil: 1895–1965]. Available at: https://archive.org/stream/urbanismo-gs/urbanismo-gs_djvu.txt.
Lemos, C.B. (2010). *Antigas e novas centralidades: a experiência da cultura do consumo no centro tradicional de Belo Horizonte* [Old and New Centralities: The Experience of the Consumerist Culture in the Traditional Centre of Belo Horizonte]. Belo Horizonte: Editora da Escola de Arquitetura da UFMG.
Machado, D.A.D. (2003). A reconstrução da promessa: as narrativas do hip hop e as identidades em contextos pós-tradicionais [The Rebuilding of the Promise: Hip-Hop Narratives and Identities in Post-Traditional Contexts]. Unpublished master's thesis. Belo Horizonte: UFMG.

Mendonça, J.G. (2003). Belo Horizonte: a metrópole segregada [Belo Horizonte: The Segregated Metropolis]. In: de Mendonça, J.G. Godinho, M.H. (eds) *População, espaço e gestão na metrópole: novas configurações, velhas desigualdades* [Population, Space and Management in the Metropolis: New Configurations, Old Inequalities]. Belo Horizonte: PUC Minas, 119–158.

Rena, N., Berquó, P., and Chagas, F. (2013). Biopolíticas espaciais gentrificadoras e as resistências estéticas biopotentes [Gentrifying Spatial Biopolitics and Biopotent Aesthetic Resistances]. *Lugar Comum*, (41), 71–88

Ribeiro, D. (2006 [1995]). *O povo Brasileiro* [The Brazilian People]. São Paulo: Companhia das Letras.

Santos, M. (2008 [1996]). *A natureza do espaço* [The Nature of Space]. São Paulo: Edusp.

Schafer, R.M. (1977) *The Tuning of the World*. Toronto and New York: McClelland and Stewart.

Serpa, A. (2007). *O espaço publico na cidade contemporânea* [Public Space in the Contemporary City]. São Paulo: Ed. Contexto.

Soja, E. (1996). *Thirdspace. Journeys to Los Angeles and Other Real-and-Imagined Places*. Oxford: Blackwell.

Tonucci, J.B.M. (2009). *Belo Horizonte: da cidade planejada à metrópole segregada* [Belo Horizonte: From Planned City to Segregated Metropolis]. In: Anais do XIII ENANPUR – Encontro Nacional da ANPUR (Florianópolis). Available at: http://unuhospedagem.com.br/revista/rbeur/index.php/anais/article/view/3022.

Vilela, N.M. (2009). Hipercentro de Belo Horizonte: movimentos e transformações espaciais recentes [Hypercentre of Belo Horizonte: Recent Spatial Movements and Transformations]. Master's thesis. Available at: www.bibliotecadigital.ufmg.br/dspace/handle/1843/MPBB-6XRKL9.

Villaça, F. (1998). *Espaço intra-urbano no Brasil* [Intra-Urban Space in Brazil]. São Paulo: FAPESP.

## Online sources

CMI – Centro de Media Independente Brasil (2010). Praia na Praça da Estação de Belo Horizonte contra o decreto do prefeito Marcio Lacerda [blog post]. 13 January. Available at: https://midiaindependente.org/pt/blue/2010/01/462799.shtml.

Familia de Rua (2009). Protesto e luto – Duelo de MCs (2009–2012) [blog post]. 15 April. Available at: https://duelodemcs.blogspot.it/2009/04/protesto-e-luto.html.

PosTV (2014). Viaduto Santa Tereza é ocupado por movimentos que reinvidiam transparência e participação popular [video file]. 9 February. Available at: www.youtube.com/watch?v=IQ_61bPbdX4.

SouBH (2017). 120 Anos BH – Viaduto Santa Tereza – Entrada Franca – Sou BH [blog post]. Available at: www.soubh.com.br/entrada-franca/120-bh-viaduto-santa-tereza.

# 11 Alternative spaces emerging from the Gezi protests

## From resistance to alternatives

*Basak Tanulku and Jens Kaae Fisker*

### Introduction

Protest events such as those associated with Occupy Wall Street, the 15M across a number of Spanish cities, and Gezi Park in Istanbul are some of the outward manifestations of a wave of urban social movements either emerging or picking up new momentum in the wake of the 2008 financial crisis. A flurry of studies have already analysed these and similar protests elsewhere from a host of different perspectives (e.g. Della Porta and Mattoni, 2014). What this chapter aims to do instead is to trace some of the ripple effects that continue to traverse the cities in which such protests are staged, even after the last activist has left the occupied site. In Istanbul the Gezi Park occupation – which took place during the summer of 2013 – has subsequently inspired the creation of a number of alternative urban spaces in a variety of Istanbul neighbourhoods. The chapter takes a closer look at two of these – a social centre and a guerrilla garden – to begin building an understanding of the radical afterlives engendered by the outbursts of radical energies that Gezi reflects.

The chapter begins by sketching the hegemonic urban forces that protesters came together in Gezi Park to oppose. This is necessary in order to get a clear picture of what the alternative spaces in question are posed as alternatives to. As it turns out, the specific alliance of neoliberal and conservative forces in operation here also made its particular mark on the make-up and priorities of protesters. Having thus gained a better contextual foothold, the chapter continues to outline its analytical approach and empirical methods, before proceeding to consider in turn the two case studies. Finally, a comparative discussion of the findings connects the chapter to the broader literature and sets up the conclusion.

### Struggle against neoliberal urbanism and national conservatism

The hegemonic forces against which the Gezi protests and subsequent alternative spaces have been directed are characterised ideologically by a peculiar mix of neoliberal urbanism and social conservatism of a nationalist bend. This reflects the particular brand of populist politics pursued by the ruling AKP party (see also

Tanulku, 2012). Founded in 2001, the party came to national power in 2002 and has since established itself as the governing party in most large cities, including Istanbul and Ankara. Described by Göksel (2015: 289) as "based on a hybrid identity formed out of two different ideologies, namely globalist/neoliberal ideals and conservative/nationalist sentiments", AKP politics may come across as a contradiction in terms. This has to be seen, however, in light of the populist nature of this political project in which AKP has "attempted to 'walk a tight rope' between neoliberalism and conservative nationalism in order to attract the largest possible number of voters" (Göksel, 2015: 289). As we shall see, it has also attracted a peculiar mix of opponents, driven to counter-hegemonic action by grievances directed against different components of this hybrid politics.

Honing in on the specificity of the situation leading to the Gezi Park protests exemplifies well how these disparate ideological components have been aligned in urban development projects. The transformation of Beyoglu and Taksim Square, where Gezi Park is located, thus can be read as a micro-example of the urban ideals promoted by the AKP. While paving the way for a more consumerist site of the kind favoured by neoliberal urbanism, the redevelopment was based strongly on Islamic and Ottoman values, particularly those associated with Sunni Islam (Eraydın and Tasan Kok, 2014). Regarding specific urban outcomes of the ideological entanglements encountered here, then, it is clear that an adequate explanation of what is going on would need to reach deep into the historical roots of modern Turkey and far across the transnational diffusion of neoliberal urbanism. Such an undertaking is beyond the scope of this chapter, but a few issues do prompt further elucidation.

First, it is important to understand, from a broader perspective, that urban processes are closely intertwined with those of global capitalism and that aggressive neoliberal urbanisation policies have played a key role in attenuating the mutually dependent character of such relations over the last thirty years (Harvey, 2008). This has resulted, for instance, in large-scale dispossessions and increasing polarisation between social classes. Many large cities have been transformed through various regeneration, or gentrification, projects leading to the generation of massive profits, accompanied by evictions and other forms of displacement resulting in dramatic changes in urban demographics. Cities have thus increasingly become highly influential sites in a global economy where urban land rent has become a significant source of profit. While this means that capitalism depends on urban processes, the post-2008 crisis has forcibly illustrated that the reverse is also true, as it reflects how the financial sector has impacted on urbanisation on a global scale (Harvey, 2008). Adverse effects of these processes are invariably felt by urban inhabitants, in particular, those who are already economically and socially marginalised. It should thus not be surprising that alongside the individualism and consumerism promoted by neoliberal urbanism, a widening array of oppositional urban social movements has also emerged (Harvey, 2008). The Gezi Park protests and the case studies presented in this chapter have to be understood as part and parcel of this much broader context.

Second, the peculiar alliance between neoliberalism and national, social, and religious conservatism meant that the oppositional forces that emerged in Istanbul and came together in the Gezi Park protests were as hybrid a gathering as the ideological jigsaw they joined to oppose. During its occupation the park thus brought together a curious cross-section of urban society: environmentalists; urban cultural heritage protectionists; youth and students; women; secular middle classes; nationalists; white and blue-collar workers; leftists from different standpoints; the LGBT community; human and animal rights activists; Alevis (people who adhere to a non-Sunni Islamic belief); Kurdish and Turkish people; the urban proletariat, precariat, and the homeless; anti-capitalist Muslims; pets and stray animals; and artists, actors, and TV personalities (see Yörük and Yüksel (2014) for a discussion of the demographic profile of protesters). We cannot, therefore, simplistically group them all with anti-capitalist urban social movements that struggle unequivocally for "the right to the city", even if such sentiments have clearly played a key and primary role among activists. Rather, it is important to recognise that what many activists reacted against was not capitalist and neoliberal urbanism per se, but its specific coupling with AKP conservatism and the increasingly authoritarian style of government experienced in recent years.

During the occupation, this broad array of protesters co-produced the park as an alternative urban space, bringing tents, books, food, and furniture to decorate the area. The park had sites reserved for a variety of activities, and tents used for sleeping and resting. Except for private sections such as tents, most of the park was accessible to all protesters. They held forums to discuss issues emerging within the park (Benlisoy, 2013), shared duties such as waste collection and cleaning collectively, and avoided monetary exchange as much as possible (see Günerbüyük (2013) for a detailed analysis of the socio-material production of Gezi). The occupation also presented itself as an opportunity for many opposition political parties, associations, platforms, and initiatives to advertise themselves, both through physical (streets, walls, banners, and posters) and virtual (social media, such as Facebook, Twitter, and YouTube) realms.

## Investigating the radical afterlives of Gezi

After the protests ebbed out towards the autumn of 2013, inhabitants in Istanbul, and elsewhere in Turkey, have continually lived under conditions of economic uncertainty and political oppression; however, the former occupants of Gezi Park were far from inactive. In addition to activity on social media and a number of smaller Gezi-inspired protests around the country, two initiatives deserve special attention. First, in the immediate aftermath, the atmosphere and spirit of Gezi were utilised to arrange open forums in several neighbourhoods, where participants would discuss how urban activism could proceed. Second, and often as a direct result of these forums, various alternative spaces were initiated in inner-city neighbourhoods where buildings or vacant land plots were squatted as social centres and guerrilla gardens for the benefit of urban inhabitants. As indicated in the introduction, the chapter takes an empirical interest in two of these. This section establishes an analytical framework for the empirical investigation, first, by outlining the particular understanding of "alternative spaces" employed, and second, by conceptualising the temporal dimension of and between such spaces.

### *Alternative spaces and the right to the city*

It should be clear that the activist sentiments that went into the occupation of Gezi Park comprised a heterogeneous ensemble of oppositional currents. Nevertheless, a simple set of shared principles did evolve to guide the organisation of everyday routines in the park: (1) collectivism, in the sense of sharing duties; (2) equality in terms of sharing resources and space; and (3) non-hierarchical management, understood as equal participation in decision-making processes. These are principles that can be seen to work against the socio-economic rationales associated with capitalism, while at the same time pursuing radical forms of democracy. By considering alternative urban spaces initiated and developed with these principles as their point of departure, the chapter draws attention specifically to spaces harbouring these specific values, while acknowledging that this reflects a narrow conception of "alternative spaces".

First, this conception implies a distinction between these spaces and other subcultural or countercultural initiatives based on the presence or absence of clear collective visions and preparedness to change society. As pointed out by Yates (2015: 19), subcultural and countercultural groups "normally do not try to consolidate, proliferate and diffuse their perspectives and collective conducts". Second, the conception also makes a distinction between these spaces and other non-capitalist practices such as bartering and unpaid domestic labour as seen in rural Anatolia or the slum housing on squatted lands instigated by the urban poor across Turkey. Again, the difference lies in the aims of activities. The squatters considered here act ideologically and aim strategically for societal change in a broad sense, whereas those other practices are primarily engaged in due to necessity and with a view to securing certain benefits for a particular group. Finally, the conception makes a distinction between the bottom-up nature of the Gezi-inspired alternative spaces and the top-down style of instigation associated with the many cooperatives that emerged as part of the modernist republican political project in the early decades of modern Turkey. These include everything from housing to agriculture and were enacted and subsidised by the state.

Another way of understanding the alternative spaces in focus here is by reference to the pursuit of a right to the city, which may include such diverse elements as the right to occupy and reclaim public spaces, the right to housing, transportation, and natural resources, as well as the right to struggle against various forms of urban revanchism (Vasudevan, 2015). While the conception of a right to the city originates with Henri Lefebvre's (1996) coining and development of the term, as a right to be struggled for it remains elusive and fuzzy, which goes a long way towards explaining its remarkable capacity for adaptation and appropriation by a diverse array of urban social movements operating in heterogeneous settings. Its relevance for counter-hegemonic urban struggle in Istanbul lies precisely in this amenability; although originally conceived of in anti-capitalist terms its oppositional sentiment is much broader in the sense that it simply establishes that the right to the city is specifically a right of urban dwellers to inhabit, appropriate, and produce urban space (Vasudevan, 2015). This makes Lefebvre's formulation as relevant in Istanbul today as it was in Paris in the 1960s.

A further reason for stressing the right to the city is that, by invoking active and productive habitation, it points beyond the defensive mode of struggle often associated with rights-based activism. In recent literature this productive form of urban struggle has perhaps been captured most fully by authors emphasising the production of urban commons; a theme that also permeates the political practices associated with Occupy-style protests such as those in Gezi Park. A focus on commons problematises any dichotomous separation of public and private spaces by challenging and subverting both. In short, the assertion of common spaces separates property rights from the right to use and access that property; just because some public or private actor owns a building or a piece of land they are not automatically entitled to decide who should be allowed to use or access their property, nor indeed to decide the manner of that use. The political act of squatting or occupation is a claim to such rights and an attempt to assertively designate the land or building as an urban commons (Huron, 2017; Williams, 2017). To summarise, the conception of alternative spaces applied in this chapter can be delineated in two complementary ways: (1) through a negative definition specifying that it does *not* include (a) conventional sub- and countercultural activities, (b) non-capitalist practices without a vision of broad societal change, and (c) top-down, state enacted cooperatives; and (2) through a positive definition that aligns alternative spaces with (a) the right to the city as a broadly conceived right to active and productive habitation, and (b) the production of urban commons as a challenge to existing property regimes based on a public-private dichotomy.

### *The lacuna of intra-urban social movement diffusion*

The specific research aim of this chapter is to elucidate some of the temporal dimensions involved in the production of alternative urban space. To this end, the Gezi Park protests are conceived of as a substantial disruption to prevailing urban trajectories. The ultimate question is how and to what extent this disruption has been forceful enough to bend trajectories or provoke the enactment of entirely new directions for urban processes. Tracing the ripple effect through the various Gezi spin-offs is one way of getting closer to an answer to this question. Obviously, the two case studies presented here can only provide indications and tentative answers, but they are just as important in terms of establishing productive directions for future research into these radical afterlives of urban protest. In terms of an analytical framework enabling research with such an orientation it is necessary to conceptualise the spatio-temporal ripple effect produced by protest events. As a start, we can quickly ascertain that this has little to do with the concentric circles produced by a stone thrown into a pond as such a metaphor might otherwise suggest.

From a global perspective, Agustin (2017) has suggested that what connects the recent wave of protest activities around the globe is a mixture of cosmopolitan dialogue and dialogism:

> Whilst dialogue is found in the politics of presence, expressed clearly in the squares and other public spaces, and in the communication through social networks, the dialogic element in the appropriation and imaginary conversation becomes essential. The identification of similar conditions of rupture for deepening democracy allows for emphatic imagining to have other struggles imaginatively present.
>
> (Agustin, 2017: 702)

Clearly, it would be too simplistic to downscale this approach as a conceptualisation of the intra-urban ripple effects in question here, but it does provide a productive entry point. First, it underlines that while Gezi may be seen as a very large stone thrown in the Turkish pond, it is also dialogically connected with other stones, producing their own ripples elsewhere. Hence, it is not coincidental that the Gezi principles outlined earlier have much in common with the principles guiding Occupy-style activism elsewhere. Second, it suggests that the ripple effect is not necessarily limited to initiatives that can be directly traced from Gezi through, for instance, an overlap in participants. This is attested to by the fact that Gezi was "imaginatively present" in subsequent protests elsewhere in Turkey.

The diffusion of protest and social movements has been a long-standing theme in the field of social movement studies. Like Agustin quoted above, what has characterised most of the diffusion-oriented literature on the current global wave of movements, however, has been the transnational dimension (the edited volume by Della Porta and Mattoni (2014) is a good case in point); that is, a ripple effect on a completely different scale than what we are dealing with here. Arguably, the scholarly infatuation with mapping transnational dynamics and relations has produced a significant blind spot where local diffusion is concerned. This means that the influence of major protest events is more likely to be evaluated by their capacity to affect transnational protest ripples, while their capacity to influence urban processes locally is ignored or glossed over as less important. Viewed from the position of those directly involved in protests this can only come across as an odd way of prioritising effects. Of course, many other studies employ a local perspective, focusing on specific protests in particular places, but these have tended instead to limit their attention to the occupied site or protest camp itself (e.g. Risager, 2016). In either case, the intra-urban scale is largely overlooked empirically and remains under theorised. The case studies in this chapter are meant to set up empirical and conceptual pointers that may help to rectify this situation.

### *Introducing cases and methods*

The two case studies that inform the chapter empirically were chosen due to their direct links to the Gezi protests. As such, they reflect two of the specific routes through the urban processes of Istanbul that ripples from Gezi have taken. In both cases the link to Gezi was comprised of the neighbourhood forums held in the immediate aftermath of the protests, when activists discussed where to direct their radical energies. The cases are differentiated from one another, on the one hand, by the nature of the site and activities, and on the other, by the neighbourhoods in which they were located. The Don Quixote Social Centre was located in a squatted building in the neighbourhood of Kadıkoy, while the guerrilla garden now known as Imrahor Garden was located on a squatted piece of land in Uskudar. Both neighbourhoods are in the Asian part of Istanbul but do not share many other characteristics. Data were collected during site visits in Kadıkoy between October 2016 and October 2017 and in Uskudar between August and November 2017. Qualitative interviews were conducted among activists participating in activities associated with the two alternative spaces, with local residents, and with public representatives at the neighbourhood level. Participation in workshops pertaining to collectivism, cooperatives, and urban gardens also informed the study along with various documentaries and short films about the two cases. Informants have been anonymised and are simply referred to with a "P" followed by a number.

## A squat in Kadıkoy: Don Quixote Social Centre

The neighbourhood of Rasimpasa, known locally as Yeldegirmeni, is located in the inner-city district of Kadıkoy, which is broadly characterised by its secular and liberal atmosphere and demography dominated by the middle classes. It is also an electoral stronghold for the Republican People's Party, the main opposition party in the National Assembly. As such, Yeldegirmeni was a logical place to go for Gezi participants who wanted to sustain their activism in a less hostile environment. This is confirmed by an activist from the Don Quixote Social Centre who related that opening a squat in Kadıkoy seemed reasonable since the local mayor was known to be tolerant towards squats and alternative spaces (P1). The social centre was opened in the autumn of 2013 in a squatted building. The timing of this move was not coincidental; as argued by Doğanay (2016), the Gezi protests and subsequent forums had been held in the open air, but as temperatures dropped towards the end of the year activists needed indoor venues to continue their activities.

"Yeldegirmeni" means windmill in Turkish and refers to the mills that once produced flour during the eighteenth century. The neighbourhood has a multicultural atmosphere seen in its churches, mosques, and synagogue as well as well-established schools and various amenities nearby. It has a building stock remaining from the non-Muslim minorities of the Ottoman Empire, which were among the first examples of high-rises in the Empire. According to the local governor, most of the building stock in Yeldegirmeni is under protection, while the area has seen significant population increases over the last fifty years (P2). The reputation for tolerance and a liberal atmosphere thus predates the protests, but the heightened political tensions of post-Gezi Istanbul have attenuated the perceived attractiveness of the neighbourhood. While making it a hotbed for activism, this has also contributed to a more problematic development. An informant from the Don Quixote Bicycle Collective remembers how pre-Gezi Yeldegirmeni was quiet and very cheap; there were several art studios and students could rent flats at meagre prices. After the protests, however, the area "boomed and experienced a dramatic increase in rent" (P3).

Most of the activists who squatted in the building that became the Don Quixote Social Centre were "veterans" from Gezi. During the early days of the centre in December 2013 they explained the main rationale in a YouTube video: "the domination of money and rent in daily life; all common areas are destroyed. In the city, there is not any space left to us, to take a breath" (various squatters, Capul TV, 2013). An activist additionally explained that they were brought together by the fact that "some people experienced certain kinds of abuse or exclusion in society" (P1). Along the same lines, a local artist described the centre as an "emotional place, which was formed to bring people together. We did not come together for a financial or another benefit. We came together to make something good. Because of that, we did not have much trouble" (P4).

The Don Quixote Social Centre was named in reference to Yeldegirmeni, the colloquial name for the neighbourhood, which means windmill. The building chosen by activists was multi-storey and lacked windows and a proper roof (see Figure 11.1). Ownership disputes meant that it had been vacant for almost twenty years. The squatters fixed the roof, installed windows and a door, and gradually converted the building into a multifunctional social centre. Several artists were involved in this process: the ground floor facade was covered with photographs of local people, and the interior walls were decorated with stencils commemorating the people who died during the Gezi protests. The interior also featured artwork depicting protests and occupations from other places and times (P4). Environmental concerns were prioritised during the restoration and photovoltaic equipment was installed on the roof along with a garden (P1, P5). In addition to the rooms designated for workshops and seminars, Don Quixote also included a kitchen, toilets, library, and rooms for children. The money needed to fix and decorate the building was collected through aid provided by volunteers and income from concerts and other events.

*Figure 11.1* Don Quixote Social Centre in 2014
Source: Basak Tanulku

The Gezi legacy was not only visible through commemorative artwork but confronted visitors as soon as they entered the building. On a board at the entrance was a list of "principles of common space", highly reminiscent of the Gezi Park principles presented earlier. The list prohibited all kinds of authoritarian ideas, segregation, sexism, homophobia and transphobia, racism, nationalism and hate discourse, and paedophilia, while also specifying that this was a place without alcohol and drugs. A non-capitalist credo was also carried over from Gezi and found its way into routine practices such as procuring fruit and vegetables through "dumpster diving" at the weekly markets in the neighbourhood (P1, P5), with the explicit aim of "avoiding money in everyday life as much as possible" (P1). Workshops and seminars held in the centre primarily served to discuss neighbourhood problems and various broader environmental and urban issues.

Initially, the squatters established friendly relations with neighbourhood residents. Locals joined their activities and activists did not report negative reactions in the early stages. Yet, as already indicated, Yeldegirmeni entered a period of rapid change in the following months, marked especially by an influx of new inhabitants and visitors to the area. International students, often part of the Erasmus Exchange Programme sponsored by the European Union, settled in the neighbourhood, which also became a magnet for visitors from other parts of the city. Businesses catering to the new inhabitants and users, including cafés, restaurants, art galleries, and artisan shops opened in quick succession. The centre itself certainly played some part in this process, although it is difficult to ascertain how important a factor it actually was. In any case, demand for rental apartments increased rapidly with rising rents becoming a lucrative source of income for homeowners. At the same time, Yeldegirmeni also became a recipient of refugees from the civil war in Syria, many of whom stayed in the social centre as temporary accommodation.

In the midst of these changes, tensions began to emerge between Don Quixote and neighbourhood residents. The local governor explained the situation from his point of view:

> There were held activities, such as conferences, music performances. However, they did not embrace the neighbourhood, since they were seen as political by the locals. … They are not locals. There were complaints, because of alcohol and inappropriate behaviour. People started to stay at the Centre. There are no shutters. Inappropriate. Also, the interest diminished.
>
> (P2)

These tensions were largely confirmed by activists who explained that hesitation and prejudice towards the centre grew because of problems with noise in the middle of the night and the introduction of lifestyles not appreciated by everyone. The difference in lifestyles was highlighted by activists as the main issue, but the tensions never erupted in major disputes, and one of the activists explained that "the Centre brought us together when we fed the stray cats, and it separated us when we made noise" (P1). This deterioration of external relations was accompanied by the emergence of internal strife as well. Whereas issues associated with the internal division of labour were handled through consensus and never resulted in serious disputes, more serious lines of conflict emerged as certain activist groups and political parties attempted to dominate the centre and demanded their own designated spaces inside it: "some groups wanted to have their own room, while the Centre had to be open to all. This created problems" (P4).

The internal disputes provoked some activists to leave and start a new squat in a different building in Kadıkoy. To signpost the connection to Don Quixote, the new squat was named Mr Samsa after the Franz Kafka character (Kühnert and Patscheider, 2018). A third squat called the Caferaga Solidarity Centre also emerged from the Gezi protests. This aptly characterises the perceived role of the social centre as the prime importer of squatting as a form of urban activism in the neighbourhood; as expressed by a worker at one of the local cafés: "There are squats all over Europe. Before the squatting started in Kadıkoy, the squats were in Bulgaria and Greece. Now there are squats also in Turkey" (P5). Eventually, all three squats were closed, and the original building of Don Quixote Social Centre was demolished (see Figure 11.2).

Various other sites have taken over the roles performed by the squats, most notably the Komsu Café Collective and the Kadıkoy Cooperative, which develop and promote non-capitalist economic practices. A proliferation of sub- and counterculturally oriented cafés catering to a variety of specific audiences also has come to play a part in this more complex radical landscape. Whereas the confrontational edge of activism in the neighbourhood has been blunted with the abandonment of squatting, this more variegated landscape seems capable of attaining a more permanent presence that could inspire the promotion of alternative lifestyles and non-capitalist economic practices.

## A guerrilla garden in Uskudar: Imrahor Garden

In Turkey, the history of urban gardens reaches back millennia as exemplified in Istanbul by the Kuzguncuk and Yedikule Gardens (Baser and Tuncay, 2010; Kaldjian, 2004). Additionally, the urban poor has long used both privately and publicly owned lands in the city for urban agriculture such as beekeeping and crop growing for personal consumption. These activities have also been linked with rural-urban migration as a way of continuing rural ways of life. The new surge of interest in urban gardens that followed Gezi has to be understood in the context of these historical traditions even if the current wave is inspired more by global environmentalist trends (Doyduk et al., 2015; Durusoy and Cihanger, 2016). In the Gezi-induced renaissance of urban garden activism, existing traditions and practices thus intermingle with imported ideas about guerrilla gardening, referring to the unsolicited conversion by activists of urban plots of land into new gardens and green spaces (Caputo et al., 2016). Several gardens were established, in post-Gezi Istanbul, including a community garden

*Figure 11.2* The same site in October 2017; a new building is under construction
Source: Basak Tanulku

in Kücük Armutlu (Doyduk et al., 2015), the Roma Garden in Cihangir (Yetişkul and Demirel, 2018), and the Imrahor Garden in Uskudar considered in this section. The commonality among these initiatives has been their appropriation of urban land that was either vacant or full of waste. Beyond guerrilla gardening, schools and municipalities have also showed renewed interest in establishing gardens for hobby and educational use, while actors in the private sector have initiated food production in cities in the form of home and roof gardening, permaculture, and hydroponic systems.

Imrahor Garden was one of the first in Turkey to be established by employing the specific kind of urban activism associated with guerrilla gardening. Again, the post-Gezi neighbourhood forums played a pivotal role. The Dogancılar Forum in Uskudar, however, stands out among the forums because it was held in a neighbourhood characterised by a strong Sunni-Islam tradition and identity, accompanied by electoral support for the ruling AKP party. Most other forums, such as that in Yeldegirmeni, were held in areas harbouring a more widespread critical attitude towards the AKP. Uskudar is a historic district that is home to many important buildings and landmarks, including mosques, cemeteries, covered bazaars, and hammams built during the Ottoman Empire. It is also known for its vibrant market and the Salacak shore with its mansions facing the historic peninsula and the Topkapı Palace. The Maiden Tower, situated on a rock in the sea, completes the picturesque vista. Typical residents are well educated and over middle age, yet, the local governor also notes that changes in demographics have occurred with upper classes, young couples, and singles moving in (P6). This transformation, however, seems not to have been as significant as has been seen in other areas of the city. A local educator-journalist relates that local identity is actively protected and that residents are generally interested in its protection and maintenance (P7).

The land squatted to create Imrahor Garden is located next to an old mosque and a cemetery. It belonged to a state charity and had been used by different businesses. The last tenant was a timber company that vacated the lot in 2012. It was then vacant until its occupation by activists from the Dogancılar Forum in 2014. In a YouTube video activists explained their rationale and intentions:

> We noticed this land in June. To be honest, we already knew this land. A timber company used it. ... We noticed that this land is full of a pile of debris. A vacant land. We were searching for a place to use as a green space. We thought why this land is not used as a green area, instead of being full of a pile of debris? We need green areas, in a city which is full of concrete. ... After the success of Kuzguncuk Garden, we thought this land could become an urban garden.
>
> (Yesil Bulten, 2014)

While the impetus for activism came from Gezi through the neighbourhood forum, this also makes it clear that their inspiration was also drawn from the deeper activist history in Istanbul around the protection of urban gardens and green spaces, exemplified here by the struggles over Kuzguncuk Garden, which date back to the 1980s (Mills, 2006). Practically, the squatters in Uskudar broadly followed the principles of guerrilla gardening and DIY urbanism by designing the garden without professional assistance or intervention. They cleared the debris and installed furniture such as tables and chairs. An open well, once providing water for the neighbourhood, was closed and circled with stones (see Figure 11.3). They utilised the walls surrounding the land as physical message boards to announce their meetings while also coordinating the work through social media. In this way, the primary activists were joined by local residents and activists from other neighbourhood forums to realise the intentions expressed by one activist: "We would like to clean this space and then give it back to local people. This land belongs to the locals. We are only mediators in this process" (Yesil Bulten, 2014).

The location of a guerrilla garden in a conservative neighbourhood was bound to create problems. Upon completion of the initial intervention of transforming the vacant, waste-infected plot into an urban garden, disputes between squatters and local residents quickly led squatters to abandon the site and the authorities to close the garden. Local residents, however, appropriated the land by continuing to use the garden independently of political organisations. What authorities and residents took issue with, then, was not the creation of new green space in their neighbourhood but their perception that this was a political act demonstrating

*Figure 11.3* Imrahor Garden in 2016. The land was cleaned up by squatters and local people
Source: Basak Tanulku

opposition to the prevailing regime. This makes for a peculiar case because ostensibly the garden shared many similarities with long-standing practices in Istanbul of using squatted land for gardening related to hobby use, personal consumption, and small-scale trade. These do not, in general, attract the attention of the authorities who often turn a blind eye to such activities when performed by the urban poor. The attitude towards guerrilla gardening was different because this was regarded as a political act and a potential threat to the authorities due to the close links with the neighbourhood forums and thus to Gezi.

But the story of Imrahor does not end there. As already indicated, the garden was preserved after the departure of squatters. Tended at first by local residents, eventually Uskudar Municipality moved in to take control and to institutionalise the garden as a municipal green space. The local governor explained the rationale:

> People from the Gezi (protests) gave the garden a name, while I embraced it. After the squatters left, the garden became a site for addicts or people who fed birds which created discomfort in the neighbourhood. They were also not locals. Instead, they came from outside. Once the municipality made it a garden, the land became secured. Now it becomes ours.
>
> (P6)

Institutionalisation involved a second round of transformation in which the garden was redesigned by the municipality and reopened in October 2017 (see Figure 11.4). Plots and pots were installed for the growing of flowers, vegetables, and spices. The arrangement of chairs and tables has been augmented by the addition of shading, and the old trees and well have been secured. Trees have been preserved while a small fence has been installed to separate the garden from the old cemetery next door. More significantly, a larger fence that is locked at night now surrounds the whole garden. Use of the garden is free but organised by the municipality; residents need to register and draw a lot, according to which small plots of land are distributed. Some plots have been reserved for municipal use by schools, mosques, and orphanages (P6). Regarding the original intentions of activists, this development has to be seen as somewhat ambivalent. Their aim to create new green spaces in a city they claim to be made of concrete clearly has been fulfilled, but their desire for the creation of urban commons has come up a bit short as their garden has ended up as a public space managed and controlled by the municipality, but freely accessible for use by local residents.

## Discussion: tracing the routes of Gezi ripples

As alternative spaces spinning off directly from the Gezi Park protests, the Don Quixote Social Centre and the Imrahor Garden provide two disparate windows through which to observe the ripple effects emanating from the disruption posed by the protests. In Yeldegirmeni we saw how the social centre, itself

*Figure 11.4* Imrahor Garden from the same viewpoint in November 2017
Source: Basak Tanulku

established as a continuation of the neighbourhood forums, clearly carried on the Gezi spirit. Activists visually commemorated the protests and embodied their continuation through squatting. Similarly, the guerrilla gardeners in Uskudar were directly inspired by Gezi and organised through the Dogancılar Forum when they went to search for sites to appropriate as green urban commons, and again Gezi-style squatting became their modus operandi. In both cases the original ripples eventually faded away as squatting was abandoned, but not without lasting effects on the respective neighbourhoods; effects that have to be seen as part and parcel of the radical afterlives of Gezi. Importantly, both cases demonstrate an active and deliberate pursuit of urban commons and a solid focus on claiming inhabitants' right to the city.

In Yeldegirmeni, the three squats (Don Quixote, Mr Samsa, and Caferaga), along with the Komsu Café Collective, all played instrumental roles in the development of what has become a variegated radical ecosystem, described by Kühnert and Patscheider (2018) as a "squatter scene". Whereas the original alternative space has been demolished, the production of other alternative spaces has diffused throughout the neighbourhood. Arguably, this process indicates a shift from a phase of activism focused on oppositional protest to a matured phase in which activists increasingly focus on the positive creation of alternatives; that is, a move from making confrontational claims that overtly challenge existing hegemonies to more subtle efforts aimed at showing, through the nitty-gritty of everyday life, that other urban worlds are possible. The emerging alternative milieu in Yeldegirmeni has provided important new spaces for groups that are either marginalised or neglected in mainstream Turkish politics, where conventional political parties and institutions are marked by elitist tendencies and a disconnection from the everyday lives of citizens. Instead, as noted by Doğanay (2016), these alternative initiatives produce everyday spaces taking an interest in the problems that touch people directly, including the rights of excluded groups (e.g. women, the LGBT community, and animals), food security, and specific urban and neighbourhood issues. As political spaces, they fill the gap left by mainstream politics and thus become permanent fixtures in the lives of urban inhabitants.

The focus on alternative economic practices embodied by the most notable initiatives still active today – the Komsu Café Collective and the Kadıkoy Cooperative – points specifically to the development of diverse economies as conceived of by Gibson-Graham (2006, 2008). Against capitalocentric perspectives they have promoted an imaginary in which capital is not assumed a priori to dominate economies; rather, they see a diverse economic landscape in which capitalist practices co-exist in mutual interdependence with other economic practices. Beyond the co-existence of capitalist and non-capitalist enterprises this logic extends to highlight that many enterprises are in themselves hybrid economic entities, just as individual urban inhabitants may engage in a wealth of different economic practices during the course of their daily lives. The urban economy of Yeldegirmeni embodies such hybridity. For some activists this has been seen as a problem of not being radical enough – a sentiment reported by Kühnert andand Patscheider to have played a motivational role in the Mr Samsa squat:

> One of the founding members of the Samsa Squat told us he wanted to live his life as far as possible outside of the "system". To him, this meant resistance in everyday life: not being part of consumerism at all.
>
> (Kühnert and Patscheider, 2018: 10f)

Rather than being a question of capitalist cooptation, Gibson-Graham's approach instead allows us to see the transformative potential of a proliferation of hybrid economic enterprises that could enact a wider hybridisation, or diversification, of economic urban life. The more problematic economic development in Yeldegirmeni pertains to gentrification. Whether alternative initiatives have acted as a driver in this process is impossible to ascertain, but in any case they do not seem to have impeded it. In the long run this may become a serious issue because displacement may cancel out the current possibilities for productive political encounters between a diverse mix of inhabitants from different socio-economic classes, educational backgrounds, religious affinities, and so forth.

In Uskudar the ripples followed a different route as Imrahor Garden was taken over by the municipality and institutionalised as an urban green space. While it is debatable whether activists succeeded in establishing urban commons, they certainly succeeded in their aim to create new green spaces for neighbourhood inhabitants. They also managed to forward their Gezi-induced ripples to the municipal government in a conservative area of Istanbul. Whereas this is not likely to lead to significant shifts in urban policy it does indicate that the influence of disruptive events such as Gezi is not confined to radical circles. The municipal takeover was clearly intended to control a perceived threat by depoliticising the garden but the local governor did acknowledge that Gezi activists had brought something of value into her neighbourhood (see Colomb (2012) for a discussion of similar ploys elsewhere). To be sure, Uskudar has not become a hotbed for urban activism, nor is this likely to happen in the near future. But Imrahor Garden is nevertheless living proof that even in the most hostile environment activist efforts to produce alternative urban spaces can have lasting effects. As a lesson for future activism, this suggests that, while it may be tempting to confine operations within more welcoming neighbourhoods such as Yeldegirmeni – to stay on home turf so to speak – urban change *is* possible, and therefore should be pursued, even under more difficult circumstances in places like Uskudar.

## Conclusion

By tracing two of the particular routes followed by ripples from the Gezi Park protests in Istanbul, this chapter contributes to a blind spot in recent social movement literature: the intra-urban diffusion of protest and activism in the aftermath of major, Occupy-style protest events. Conceiving of such events as disruptions to prevailing urban trajectories – metaphorical stones in urban ponds – entails an extended imaginary in which diffusion is seen as a ripple effect that traverses urban space, refracting along the way as it is transmitted through activists and their opponents, the specific sites they activate, the material urban fabric, and a diversity of neighbourhoods. Rather than creating an understanding in which all that is traced from the original disruption is taken to be its direct effects, this imaginary conceives of Gezi and similar events only as a new impetus introduced into an already dynamic and complex context.

Contrasts between the two case studies clearly show how refraction of the wave emitted by the radical potency of the Gezi disruption was differentiated already as it entered the neighbourhood forums. The specific circumstances engendered by disparate neighbourhoods altered the transmission of ripples by enforcing differentiated limits on activism regarding what was possible. The same point of departure, therefore, resulted in very different specificities. In both cases, what is notable at this early stage is that activists mixed the Gezi impetus with both imported ideas and local traditions; while they were able to draw on the long-standing Turkish practices of squatting and urban gardening, they also deliberately imported related ideas from international activist circles, specifically the southern European style of social-centre squatting and the fashionable notion of guerrilla gardening. This would seem to confirm the presence of a significant cosmopolitan outlook as theorised recently by Agustin (2017) and empirically evidenced in Istanbul by Kühnert and Patscheider (2018). The latter also substantiate, first, that a broader orientation towards claiming a right to the city and producing urban commons has actually taken hold in Istanbul's alternative milieus and, second, that this orientation is directly inspired by international intellectuals such as David Harvey, Antonio Negri, and Michael Hardt.

From the initial refractions introduced in the transmission through neighbourhood forums, the Gezi ripples begin to live their own lives in and with the neighbourhoods. In Uskudar the radical energies submitted by activists seem to have been partly repulsed and partly absorbed, in the sense that the material content introduced by activists (i.e. the garden) was welcomed and since appropriated in a gradual process of absorption, whereas the activists themselves and the political agendas they carried with them were opposed and repulsed. It is of course not surprising that a relatively small and isolated act of guerrilla gardening did not bring about substantial change in one of Istanbul's conservative strongholds, but activists can take heart from the fact that they did leave a permanent mark embodied and symbolised by Imrahor Garden. Similarly, it is also not surprising that radical energies fared better in Yeldegirmeni, where the ripples from Gezi were multiple and also resonated well with pre-existing attitudes in the neighbourhood. What is significant regarding intra-urban diffusion is that the disruptive energies from Gezi seem to have found a more permanent home in Yeldegirmeni, where activism can be sustained and developed over a longer timeframe, even if specific sites are not always long-lived. For all their concentration and amplification of radical energy in time and space, this is something that spectacular occupations and their protest camps cannot hope to achieve in and by themselves. If they are to matter as generators of real urban change, it is therefore vital that they diffuse into sustained, productive activism in and beyond the cities in which they are staged and with the communities they encounter. From a scholarly point of view, this once again underlines the need for producing theoretically sound and empirically informed knowledge about how processes of intra-urban diffusion actually work.

## Acknowledgements

We are indebted to the squatters, activists, and locals who provided valuable information on both cases, and on the neighbourhoods of Yeldegirmeni and Imrahor. This chapter could not have been written without their kind help and cooperation.

## References

Agustin, O.G. (2017) Dialogic Cosmopolitanism and the New Wave of Movements: From Local Rupture to Global Openness. *Globalizations*. 14(5). 700–713.

Baser, B., Tuncay, H.E. (2010) Understanding the Spatial and Historical Characteristics of Agricultural Landscapes in Istanbul. *A|Z ITU Journal of the Faculty of Architecture*. 7(2). 106–120.

Benlisoy, F. (2013) Gezi ve Forumlar: Başka bir Demokrasi Mümkün mü? [Gezi and Forums: Is Another Democracy Possible?] In: Sancar, N. (ed) *Sıcak Haziran: Sonraki Direnişe Mektup* [Hot June: Letter to the Next Protest]. Istanbul: Evrensel Kültür Kitaplığı.

Caputo, S., Schwab, E., Tsiambos, K. (2016) Emergent Approaches to Urban Gardening. In: Bell, S., Fox-Kamper, R., Keshavarz, N., Benson, M., Caputo, S., Noori, S., Voigt, A. (eds) *Urban Allotment Gardens in Europe*. Abingdon: Routledge.

Colomb, C. (2012) Pushing the Urban Frontier: Temporary Uses of Space, City Marketing, and the Creative City Discourse in 2000s Berlin. *Journal of Urban Affairs*. 34(2). 131–152.

Della Porta, D., Mattoni, A. (2014) Patterns of Diffusion and the Transnational Dimension of Protest in the Movements of the Crisis: An Introduction. In: Della Porta, D., Mattoni, A. (eds) *Spreading Protest. Social Movements in Times of Crisis*. Colchester: ECPR. 1–18.

Doğanay, G. (2016) Avrupa'da İsgal Hareketlerinin Kapsamı ve Turkiye Ornegi: Don Kisot Sosyal Merkezi [The Range of Occupy Movements in Europe and the case of Turkey: Don Quixote Social Centre]. *Marmara Universitesi Siyasal Bilimler Dergisi*. 4(2). 91–111.

Doyduk, S., Orbey, B., Gurel, N. (2015) A Rural Intervention in the Urban Context: An Urban-Poor Neighbourhood Agricultural Project in Küçük Armutlu, Istanbul. In: Brebbia, C.A., Florez-Escobar, W.F. (eds) *Sustainable City X*. Southampton: WIT Press.

Durusoy, E., Cihanger, D. (2016) Historic Landscape vs. Urban Commodity?: The Case of Yedikule Urban Gardens, Istanbul. *Megaron*. 11(1). 125–136.

Eraydın, A., Tasan Kok, T. (2014) State Response to Contemporary Urban Movements in Turkey: A Critical Overview of State Entrepreneurialism and Authoritarian Interventions. *Antipode*. 46(1). 110–129.

Gibson-Graham, J.K. (2006) *The End of Capitalism (As We Knew It). A Feminist Critique of Political Economy*. Minneapolis: University of Minnesota Press.

Gibson-Graham, J.K. (2008) Diverse Economies: Performative Practices for "Other Worlds". *Progress in Human Geography*. 32(5). 613–632.

Göksel, O. (2015) From Progress to Order: The "Kurdish Openings" and the Limits to Contentious Politics in Turkey. In: Gerges, F.A. (ed) *Contentious Politics in the Middle East. Popular Resistance and Marginalized Activism beyond the Arab Uprisings*. New York: Palgrave Macmillan.

Günerbüyük, C. (2013) Biz Buraya Oturmaya Gelmedik [We Did Not Come Here to Sit]. In: Sancar, N. (ed) *Sıcak Haziran: Sonraki Direnişe Mektup* [Hot June: Letter to the Next Protest]. Istanbul: Evrensel Kültür Kitaplığı.

Harvey, D. (2008) The Right to the City. *New Left Review*. 53(September–October). 23–40.

Huron, A. (2017) Theorising the Urban Commons: New Thoughts, Tensions and Paths Forward. *Urban Studies*. 54(4). 1062–1069.

Kaldjian, P. (2004) Istanbul's Bostans: A Millennium of Market Gardens. *Geographical Review*. 94(3). 284–304.

Kühnert, N., Patscheider, A. (2018) Gregor Samsa and Don Kişot Fighting against Windmills: Squatting in Istanbul as an Attempt to Resist Neo-Liberal Urban Politics. In: *Mapping Global City Istanbul*. Available at: http://www.kaee.uni-goettingen.de/mapping-istanbul/wp-content/uploads/2015/06/SQUATTING.pdf.

Lefebvre, H. (1996) *Writings on Cities*. Translated by E. Kofman and E. Lebas (eds). Oxford: Blackwell.

Mills, A. (2006) Boundaries of the Nation in the Space of the Urban: Landscape and Social Memory in Istanbul. *Cultural Geographies*. 13. 367–394.

Risager, B.S. (2016) The Eventful Places of Occupy Wall Street and Tahrir Square: Cosmopolitan Imagination and Social Movements. *Globalizations*. DOI: 10.1080/14747731.2016.1217623.

Tanulku, B. (2012) Gated Communities: From "Self-Sufficient Towns" to "Active Urban Agents". *Geoforum*. 43(3). 518–528.

Vasudevan, A. (2015) The Autonomous City: Towards a Critical Geography of Occupation. *Progress in Human Geography*. 39(3). 316–337.

Williams, M.J. (2017) Urban Commons are More-than-Property. *Geographical Research*. 56(1). 16–25.

Yates, L. (2015) Rethinking Prefiguration: Alternatives, Micropolitics and Goals in Social Movements. *Journal of Social Movements*. 14(1). 1–21.

Yetişkul, E., Demirel, S. (2018) Assembling Gentrification in Istanbul: The Cihangir Neighbourhood of Beyoğlu. *Urban Studies*. DOI: 10.1177/0042098017746623.

Yörük, E., Yüksel, M. (2014) Class and Politics in Turkey's Gezi Protests. *New Left Review*. 89(September–October). 103–123.

## Videos

Capul TV. (2013) Türkiye'deki ilk işgal evi – Yeldegirmeni Kadıkoy Donkisot Sosyal Merkezi [The First Squat House of Turkey: Yeldegirmeni Kadıkoy Don Quixote Social Centre]. 3 December. Available at: www.youtube.com/watch?v=ERBR0-WpY6Qand.

Yesil Bulten. (2014) Uskudar'da Bir Bostan: Imrahor [An Urban Garden in Uskudar: Imrahor]. 10 March. Available at: www.youtube.com/watch?v=KHZcP6NJK24and.

# 12 Citizen-led micro-regeneration

## Case studies of civic crowdfunding in London and Milan

*Silvia Gullino, Cristina Cerulli, Heidi Seetzen, and Carolina Pacchi*

### Introduction

The making of future cities involves the challenging of existing models of urban development while promoting alternative processes, practices, and digital technologies to make urban areas more socially sustainable and liveable, and more environmentally resilient. But who takes part in defining and designing the cities of the future? What roles do citizens play? How can their imagination, enthusiasm, and energy be mobilised for new modes of collaborative city-making? And, crucially, how can public assets be used to support such initiatives in a way that is effective and fair?

This chapter interrogates alternative forms of participation, urban development, and governance, generated through collaborative actions and interactions between a range of local community groups, with the support of local government agencies. This study draws on qualitative research carried out in London and Milan from 2015 to 2017 to investigate the growing phenomenon of civic crowdfunding projects in contributing to the making of future cities. The project involved fieldwork activities conducted in London and Milan consisting of semi-structured interviews with policy makers, walking interviews with local grassroots organisations, and workshops with civic crowdfunding platforms (based in the Netherlands, the United Kingdom and Italy) and local authorities (from London and Milan). While reflecting on the specificities of the case studies and their associated constellations of actors through translocal and transdisciplinary dialogues, this chapter also seeks to pose questions that need answering. What are the affordances of urban spaces produced in alternative ways and with the endorsement and support of local governments? What are the openings created by the shifting roles played by all the actors involved, working together in an oscillating dance that bypasses the conventional dichotomies of bottom-up/top-down, public/private, and individual/collective to create a third space of alternative urban life?

This chapter is structured in eight subsequent sections. In the first, we explore the origins of civic crowdfunding and the role of digital platforms in enabling citizens to promote and/or support civic initiatives. In the second and third sections we discuss the conceptual frames of the chapter by using actor-network theory (ANT) and diverse economies. After discussing civic crowdfunding in the United Kingdom and Italy in the fourth section, in the fifth and sixth sections we then explore a series of case studies in London and Milan as a starting point for a discussion on understanding civic crowdfunding projects and their ability to generate alternative urban spaces, before drawing our conclusions in the last section.

## Civic crowdfunding: a brief history

Crowdfunding is a model of financing projects generally through contributions from large groups of individuals and organisations (the crowd) (Belleflamme et al., 2013; NESTA, 2013) that can be used to support a wide range of projects. The term crowdfunding was first used in 2006, on the now-defunct 'fundavlog', an experimental site for producing video blogs, and became popular from 2008 with the establishment of global reward-based crowdfunding platforms like Indiegogo (2008) and Kickstarter (2009), and later with the emergence of dedicated civic crowdfunding platforms 'ioby' (2009), Spacehive (2011), Neighbor.ly, and Citizinvestor (Stiver et al, 2015).

Crowdfunders offer financial support to projects that they feel an affiliation with or that offer desirable returns. Projects can vary hugely, ranging from cultural production like commissioning artwork or producing movies or music, through the development of high-tech products, to socio-spatial projects concerning specific localities, for instance, such as connecting communities through food or events.

This way of fundraising, which has recently gained popularity for a wide range of purposes, takes place online through digital platforms, for example, Kickstarter and Crowdcube, where ideas for projects become visible to potential funders. Fundraisers set up the project, with its target funding, in one of the platforms and invite pledges from a wide range of supporters. Most platforms operate on an 'all or nothing' basis by which pledged sums are collected only if a funding target is achieved. In order to help reach their financial target, fundraisers generally also develop a suite of online tools (websites, social media channels, etc.), which are complementary to the crowdfunding platforms and, occasionally, are an alternative to them. Money is raised through different networks of peers (including family and friends), but mainly through social media (Twitter, Facebook, blogs, Instagram, etc.) in order to secure a larger base of support. Depending on what specific platform is used, supporters can receive different forms of benefits that are unique to that project: they can pledge money as a form of lending with financial returns (in exchange for equity, as a loan or as a pre-order of the product produced); however, supporters can also choose to donate because they believe in a particular cause, without expecting anything in return.

By supporting a great variety of goals like spatial interventions, community and artistic activities, and small start-up businesses, fundraising through crowdfunding has also found application in the built environment, often with a particular 'civic' angle. 'Civic' crowdfunding, as a sub-type of crowdfunding, shares its donation-based fundraising model, but has distinctly civic, and often spatial, aims. While Davies (2014) frames civic crowdfunding as aiming to fund public assets without rewards in return, in this chapter we adopt a broader definition of civic as benefitting the broader community, often within specific localities.

Raising funds from citizens to support civic, urban-regeneration projects, however, is not a new mechanism. Practices of public fundraising for civic projects, either through bonds or donations, have a long history and examples include the Statue of Liberty, the University of Sheffield, and the High Line Park to name just a few (Davies, 2013). The key innovation of civic crowdfunding is in the recently developed digital dimension of the platforms, which increases the potential and enhances communication to raise funds from relevant communities, both local and translocal. The use of digital platforms, such as the UK-based Spacehive and the Italian PlanBee or Eppela, allows citizens who have an internet connection to become either funders on projects of interest (e.g. a local park or a new high-street market) or promoters of new initiatives: from improving or designing new green spaces to creating art hubs, reusing derelict buildings and underused spaces, or creating shared community food growing spaces.

Through the mechanisms of civic crowdfunding, citizens acting as initiators can proactively design a project proposal, publish it on an online platform, attract supporters (funders), reach the funding target, and develop the project (Belleflamme et al., 2013). Although projects can vary in scale and type of financial support received – from a large number of people giving small donations to a small number of supporters giving larger donations – in general they tend to be locally-driven, capturing the imagination, enthusiasm, and energy of local people and contributing to local changes that go beyond the boundaries of the actual physical changes. By channelling efforts into specific outputs, civic crowdfunding projects have the ability to encourage community building and bottom-up place-making, and the potential to create new, alternative, forms of public participation and governance through citizen-led actions.

Crowdfunding, as an emerging and rapidly evolving field of practices and fundraising models, is constantly adjusting to changing technology and policy contexts and experimenting with hybrid models; this chapter aims to contribute to the development of critical understandings of the emerging field of civic crowdfunding and it might contribute to the production of alternative urban space, through altering local power dynamics, forging unexpected partnerships, and prototyping new governance and financial models.

## Crowdfunding through the lens of actor-network theory

In this section we aim to set out civic crowdfunding projects as part of a shifting set of actor networks, as initially described by Bruno Latour in his outline of actor-network theory (ANT) (Latour, 1993), which despite its name has been described not so much as a theory, but as a methodology or a means of conceptualising and describing the different elements of agency that make up social phenomena (Law, 2009). As such, ANT has been used by different researchers and in conjunction with a range of theoretical perspectives (Sheehan and Vadjunec, 2012). In the context of our research on civic crowdfunding, using an ANT perspective allows us to draw out three particular characteristics of crowdfunding projects. These are: (1) their socially horizontal organisation (both online and offline); (2) their flexibility; and (3) the underlying constellations of the symbolic and the material. In particular, the first two seem to constitute civic crowdfunding as an exciting, potentially inclusive, and more dynamic alternative to more traditional means of participation. At the same time, however, they also make crowdfunding projects harder to describe as well as to organise or even control, given that the direction of horizontally inscribed relationships can be multi-directional and more ambiguous than vertical (hierarchical) ones and they are more frequently subject to change.

With regards to the first of these characteristics – socially horizontal organisation – ANT develops a topographically, rather than vertically, organised model of social and material relations. It emphasises the way in which social practices, connections, processes of inclusion and exclusion, and instances of power are not simply the effect of social structures and hierarchies, but are complexly inscribed, negotiated, and shaped through different networks that operate through both micro and macro settings. Similarly, civic crowdfunding projects have no evident hierarchies or pre-inscribed structures. They link ideas, individuals and groups of people (crowds), resources, and spaces through malleable networks and shifting connections. Despite their topographical arrangement, however, these networks are not inherently inclusive and certain elements (people, spaces, organisations, etc.) may form more or less powerful or more or less successful connections than others. In order to understand these connections we need to look beyond common notions of social organisation and power, investigating how, often at the micro level, networks and connections are formed, shaped, and reshaped.

The second characteristic – flexibility – is at the very heart of the appeal of civic crowdfunding. The fact that crowdfunding projects are not rigid or formal structures, but are shaped and reshaped through the input of individuals, groups, crowds or organisations, means that they have the potential to allow for the spontaneity and immediacy, as well as the specificity of locality, often associated with high levels of engagement and activism. Within ANT, social structures such as *communities* do not exist as 'things' or 'glue', but, instead, the *social* is assembled by constantly changing relations between heterogeneous elements (Sheehan and Vadjunec, 2012: 919). On this understanding, social phenomena cannot be easily captured by referring to a more-or-less stable structure as they are messy, inchoate, and constantly developing; however, the flexible landscape of networks is also characterised by moments of stabilisation and entrenchment, which Sheehan and Vadjunec (2012) identify as instances of community. These temporary crystallisations and coalescences are contributing factors to the success of civic crowdfunding projects, and finding out how they develop over time is one of the challenges of our research.

Finally, one of the more intriguing aspects of ANT is that the elements of agency ('actants') in a given actor network are not necessarily human or indeed social, but combine the human and the non-human, materials, ideas, meanings or even emotions (Sheehan, 2011). The crowdfunding projects analysed below are very much assembled as a set of simultaneously meaningful and material relationships between people and identities; material objects and built spaces; images of community, emotional attachments, and social concepts; and social practices and ideals of collaboration. Intended as a theoretical backdrop and initial frame of reference, the three ANT features provide a starting point for how we might begin to theorise their social shape, helping us to understand the way in which they might, or might not, be helpful in developing citizen-led approaches to regeneration.

## Political economies of civic crowdfunding

Another starting point in understanding and categorising civic crowdfunding projects is to look into their political economies. Situated within a spectrum of initiatives trying to reconfigure citizen involvement in local state planning – from participatory budgeting to fora for citizen planning – civic crowdfunding makes use of digital platforms to raise money and fund assets and services for the public, sometimes with support from local government. Many of these projects explicitly frame themselves as alternatives to neoliberal modes of production of the city, putting forward their collective endeavour as a pragmatic, viable, alternative.

This broadly citizen-led nature of crowdfunding and the fact that, through backing, a mandate is given to projects, has been read as a mechanism for strengthening non-parliamentary democratic structures and practices, crucial for civic integration (Hollow, 2013). From a political economy perspective, however, crowdfunding also has been framed as a form of platform capitalism (Langley, 2016). Criticisms of crowdfunding refer to the challenge of its suitability as a replacement for public services, to the fact that, through narratives of project success, it regularly masks unpaid labour associated with projects, and that it monetises networks of social relations. Gibson-Graham's (2008) conceptualisation of diverse economies and their intentionally 'weak', loose, theory might offer another fruitful lens for looking at the spectrum of civic crowdfunding projects, describing them in terms of enterprise, labour, property, transactions, and finance and as to whether they are considered capitalist, alternative capitalist or non-capitalist. This could offer the foundations for a developing framework for articulating specific characteristics of crowdfunding projects in relation to economic understandings.

Many civic crowdfunding projects create and occupy precarious, shifting spaces that could be described as what Pickerill and Chatterton (2006) call 'autonomous geographies': spaces produced through a blend of resistance and creation, fuelled by a desire to explore non-capitalist models of citizenship. The social and physical spaces resulting from civic crowdfunding initiatives, therefore, potentially can emerge as alternatives to neo-liberal city production.

## The civic crowdfunding context in the United Kingdom and Italy

Current understandings of urban regeneration evade easy definitions and remain ambiguous in relation to scope, approaches, actors, and goals. Policies and practices vary significantly across different European regions, but in the United Kingdom and Italy, the geographical focus of our study, top-down approaches traditionally have prevailed, alongside local, specific, pioneering initiatives at the margins (Evans and Jones, 2013).

In the United Kingdom since the post-war period, urban regeneration meant reconstruction redevelopment and renewal of bombed sites and slum housing. In the 1980s Thatcher era, regeneration became synonymous with market-led redevelopment and flagship projects like shopping, leisure and sports centres, redeveloping central urban areas as catalysts, and attracting new financial capital. After the Urban Renaissance of the 2000s and its dominant design-led approach (Urban Task Force, 1999), more recently, urban regeneration has come to present strategies to change the urban environment in order to stimulate economic growth through, for example, infrastructure and residential-led development often for the global market (Imrie et al., 2009; Evans and Jones, 2013). These approaches have left little space for locally led initiatives, which, in the specific London case, are not harnessed in state-led policy initiatives (see e.g. Bailey and Pill (2015) for a discussion on empowering local communities through the Localism Act 2011).

In Italy, urban regeneration broadly refers to an approach to planning within existing cities that first emerged around the mid-1990s, aimed at an integrated and comprehensive intervention, able to work simultaneously on the physical, spatial, economic, and social aspects. The presence of a large number of brownfield sites, as well as the need to improve the quality of public space and to intervene in a comprehensive way on the (physically and socially) decaying public housing estates, brought about a wave of experimentation on urban projects. These were co-funded by European Union programmes, as in the case of the URBAN projects (Palermo, 2002), and by national ones, like Neighbourhood Contracts, launched in the early 2000s, to improve the spatial and economic qualities and social liveability of public housing estates. In the last decade, urban regeneration initially has been associated, at least in the public debate, with more sustainable urban planning models and with urban resilience (Sbetti et al., 2013), with a focus on urban 'peripheries' through an integrated policy approach – through national funding programmes and local area-based regeneration project proposals (Presidenza del Consiglio dei Ministri, 2016).

Crowdfunding projects, by promoting bottom-up processes and encouraging new forms of partnerships, raise questions for dominant processes of 'urban regeneration' that are harnessed to achieve goals such as economic growth and infrastructural developments, driven by political agendas and often controversial residential developments glossed as regeneration. What implications have hundreds of civic crowdfunding projects envisioned by local groups for redefining urban regeneration practices? Also, how are civic crowdfunding projects affected by being partially funded by local authorities and what are the characteristics of these spaces of temporary convergence and alignment between bottom-up and top-down, mainstream and countering, 'us' and 'them'?

This chapter attempts to explore potential answers to these questions by looking at case studies in London and Milan, where local authorities developed match-funding programmes to support civic crowdfunding initiatives. In London, projects that specifically aim at improving local areas have the opportunity to receive additional match funding through Crowdfund London from the Greater London Authority (GLA) (formerly the London Mayor's High Street Fund) (GLA, 2016). At the time of writing and since the London Mayor's High Street Fund initiative was launched in 2013, the GLA has provided support to fifty-nine projects, by pledging £800K and attracting over 5,500 backers.

All civic crowdfunding projects backed by the GLA are funded through Spacehive, a UK crowdfunding platform for civic projects varying hugely in terms of dimension, financial target (from a few hundred pounds for a music performance in a park, to over a hundred thousand pounds for a sculpture walk in East London), pledge size (from a few but large pledges for a project on community art to almost a thousand small pledges for a new green space), and promoters (from local community groups with a large and capillary support basis to a few local businesses investing locally). The GLA currently pledges funds at multiple points of the fundraising campaign for selected projects that meet the GLA priorities. This is different from the Municipality of Milano, which matches funds at one specific moment: when 50% of the fundraising target is reached. GLA provides match funding to projects that 1) show an impact on the high street; and 2) are innovative and show potential for achieving the final target.[1] By pledging while still fundraising, the GLA has taken the conscious decision of endorsing some projects and this helps to attract further pledges from supporters

In Milan, concurrently with the GLA in London, the Municipality started engaging with civic crowdfunding initiatives in 2014, with a programme that match funds civic initiatives once they reach 50% of their final target (Comune di Milano, 2014). Unlike the case of London, where Spacehive appeared as an official partner, the Municipality of Milano identified a suitable platform through a public tender, through which Eppela, a large reward-based Italian crowdfunder, was selected. Through a public call, proposals for civic crowdfunding projects were selected and eighteen effectively launched their campaign. Projects were hosted, in turn, on the Eppela platform for fifty days, giving each project some visibility. If within this timeframe they were able to collect pledges for half of their target, then the Municipality would contribute the other half (up to a total of

€50K for each project). The underlying approach of Comune di Milano is that, within a pool of promising grassroots projects, the Municipality prefers to support those that are the expression of community interest and engagement, and considers the quantity and quality of pledges as a good proxy of the latter.

The projects that took part in subsequent rounds of crowdfunding ranged from local welfare networks for disadvantaged social groups, through local food systems and the reuse of abandoned buildings, to innovative forms of neighbourhood welfare provision (Pacchi and Pais, 2017).

## Stories of micro-regeneration from London

This section focuses on two London projects that made use of the digital platform Spacehive to raise funds to implement innovative ideas: 'Peckham Coal Line', a proposal to transform an old railway line in South London into an urban park; and 'Global Garden, Global Kitchen', a project to transform unused space in Tottenham, North London, into a new community food garden and kitchen where local people can learn to grow and cook a mix of produce.

### *Peckham Coal Line*

The 'Peckham Coal Line' project is a London-based civic crowdfunding project that received match funding from the Mayor of London in the form of a pledge on a chosen crowdfunding platform, Spacehive. The Peckham Coal Line is an elevated 1km-long park, designed to run on disused railway coal sidings and to create a green link between two neighbouring high streets in Queen's Road Peckham and Peckham Rye. The park has been envisioned to run along the railway line, across underused sites, and behind residential developments.[2]

At a local level, this project has already attracted funds (over £75,000 in funds from local supporters) from over 900 people, going well beyond the financial target, but most of all lots of enthusiasm, a high level of local participation, and the development of a shared community vision for the area. Backed by the Mayor's funds, on an urban scale this project has the potential to generate new urban governance relationships, where Network Rail (the UK railway line authority) and the London Borough of Southwark will team up with the Peckham Coal Line group in delivering the community vision, and to connect with other green networks, contributing to the transformation of urban spaces on a wider scale. The Peckham Coal Line project in many ways is a successful project: not only has it attracted wide-scale publicity and official support, but it also involved different local organisations and caught the imagination of local residents.

Every crowdfunding project has particular dynamics. There are two notable aspects to the Peckham Coal Line project, and its success is in part a result of these aspects. The first was the way in which the project managed to connect different groups and individuals around what we might call 'a shared vision' of the park. This vision had emerged slowly and was in many ways but open to further development. It nevertheless became a nodal point around which shifting networks of actors, organisations, ideas, and resources clustered. Crucially this vision was communicated through a variety of means – both online and offline – combining social media channels, community meetings, workshops, and face-to-face outreach work. Support was very much grown bottom-up. After the project had garnered support on Spacehive (both financially and through active offers of support received via emails), the organisers invited interested parties to a series of workshops and involvement and participation grew from there. Additionally, they reached out to and gained the support of local groups (e.g. a local nature reserve and a homeless shelter located near the coal line).

The second characteristic, which contributed to the Peckham Coal Line's success, was the fact that, despite the topographical, non-hierarchical organisation of the project, it managed to key into powerful networks that gave the project both real resources and enabled resources and credibility. Local skills played a relevant role. These were not planned for in advance, but were mobilised flexibly around the project and the idea as it developed. Furthermore, a theme of 'connections' stands out as a recurrent feature in this project. The idea of the park took shape through local connections, people discovering and talking about a piece of land and about their ideas for what could be done with it. In this sense, the project itself was about creating not only physical connections between two town centres, but also social and symbolic ones.

Significantly, the sketches and plans produced as part of the development of the project were not intended as definitive ideas, but only to 'add flavour' or 'to help people visualise' what the park might look like. The focal point of the project – of the network of supporters and organisations – combined both the material and the symbolic: a material space, real spatial practices, and a relatively open idea of a park and creating connections. Indeed, at the moment, despite the tangibility of the space this project concerns, there is still a chance that the project might not be realisable.

### *Global Garden, Global Kitchen*

The 'Global Garden, Global Kitchen' project is located in Haringey, North London, an area with multi-cultural communities. It is a community food hub and, as it happened in the case of Peckham, it started with an idea. The originator of this initiative, Dexter, after retraining for a year as an urban gardener, decided to find some local, unused land, start growing organic vegetables, fruit, and herbs, and distribute it at affordable prices. The aim of 'Global Garden, Global Kitchen' was in fact to reconnect and re-educate communities regarding healthy eating by offering alternatives to poor, fast-food habits ('*Lots of obesity . . . You can still keep healthy on a budget*'). As with the other London project, his ideas started growing organically when he spotted vacant land near a local school's grounds in Haringey, which ended up becoming the location of Global Garden. '*It was a walk way, where people walk through, a public walk way*'. After a not very successful approach to the school, he contacted the Selby Trust, a charity located near the school and where he used to volunteer as a youth worker. Selby Trust, which acts as an umbrella for many community organisations, granted him permission to use the land for his project. The management of the charity gave him confidence in his own ideas ('*There is lots of potential ... let's try it*') and employed him as the project manager.

Dexter's vision was that of creating an inclusive space where people with very different cultural backgrounds could volunteer and grow fruit and vegetables using raised beds, learn new skills, and contribute to local healthy lifestyles. Very coherently, the project fitted into the ethos of the charity – 'Many cultures, one community' – which became the major partner in this initiative. Unlike the Peckham project, Global Garden did not reach out to other partners, such as the local council, but rather focused on engaging with the different, diverse local communities and generating a long-lasting impact on people's lifestyles. At the end of 2012, Selby Trust decided to use the platform of Spacehive to raise funds to support this initiative. The project exceeded the target and benefitted from matched funds from Experian Charity Trust. At that time, this charity, which supports small organisations that aim to make a difference, was offering matched funds on Spacehive exactly like the GLA.

As already pointed out, social media like Facebook and Twitter are an important dimension of the crowdfunding campaigns, reaching out to local communities, involving them, and getting their support. But as Dexter admitted: '*I am not a social media person: I am a gardener!*' A great, well-timed help to the fundraising campaign came from the BBC programme 'London Inside Out' (Selby Trust, 2013), which interviewed Dexter and broadcast him on TV promoting his initiative. This helped him to connect offline with local communities. Dexter has a very clear vision for the future of the site. He aims to expand his project even more by creating a rooftop garden with beehives, by setting up a farmers' market, and by using part of the local crop to feed into the Trust's local kitchen where local communities ('*The Turkish, the Caribbeans, the Greeks ...*') can come and share what and how they cook.

Global Garden is not just an allotment. It made use of vacant land and it aimed to generate connections with the local context, its diverse, low-income communities and their needs, and to promote education. Although Dexter raised concerns about the future of the garden in terms of making sure the project will keep running and the council will carry on granting the use of the land, what clearly emerges is the replicability of such a project. To some extent, and without undermining its amazing value, its ordinary dimension, rather than unconventional one like the Peckham project, helps its feasibility.

### *Reflections on the London case studies*

Although both of these projects are very different in terms of scale and aim, they both typify the three aspects of crowdfunding projects we laid out at the beginning: 1) horizontal social organisation; 2) flexibility; and 3) a combination of symbolic and material contexts. Moreover, the difference between the projects can be captured with reference to these three dimensions.

With regard to their social organisation, these projects both plugged into and created a network of individual actors, groups, and organisations; however, while Global Garden mainly connected to local communities, the Peckham Coal Line project combined a more diverse network of local residents, local community groups, and powerful actors (including the local council and an MP). Its network was therefore more far reaching and more powerful when it came to garnering support (although to what extent this will translate into the material success of the project remains to be seen).

With regard to the second dimension, flexibility, neither of these projects started with rigid or formal proposals, but evolved organically, allowing them to be shaped and reshaped over time. In the Global Garden project, the idea of one individual was combined with local needs and the vision of a local charity. The Peckham Coal Line, even more radically, evolved through the ideas of many local individuals (crowds), groups, and organisations. As such both projects were grounded in the local specificity of the area and the community they were based in, and were able to inspire participation (this was particularly the case for the Peckham Coal Line).

In terms of the third dimension, combining the symbolic and the material, both projects were about more than a material intervention in the landscape. The Global Garden aimed to create a space through which communities could connect to each other and their locality, and the Peckham Coal Line, again more radically, became a symbol for participation and local community around which diverse groups and individuals could come together.

## Stories of micro-regeneration from Milan

In this section, we discuss the civic crowdfunding framework programme launched in 2014 by the Municipality of Milano in the broader context of civic crowdfunding initiatives in Italy. These two Milanese projects show significant variations in terms of success and ability to strengthen horizontal ties and to fully exploit the innovative potential of this tool within the same programme. The projects, one located in a residential neighbourhood and the other in the rural fringe of the city, show two different approaches to the use of civic crowdfunding. It is worth noting that both these crowdfunding initiatives were part of larger projects and this presented some challenges in communicating the projects to potential donors/supporters and resulted in a lack of clarity about what exactly each pledge would fund.

### *Itmakesyourlifeeasier (Tifacilitalavita)*

The first initiative is part of WEMI (WElfare MIlano), co-funded by a local grant-making foundation and promoted by the Municipality of Milano with a number of community organisations and cooperatives. The aim of WEMI is to create an online platform, matching citizen needs with the supply of social services, both public and private ones, giving specific attention to the neighbourhood scale. To help achieve this wider objective, WEMI is also piloting two community hubs – one in District 5 and one in District 8 – set up as physical spaces to facilitate offline opportunities for strengthening community ties and brokering needs with potential suppliers.

L'Impronta Onlus, a charity involved in the project, decided to launch a civic crowdfunding initiative using the municipal programme, focused in particular on the opening up of the District 5 Community Hub (created in a former shop), with a lesser involvement in the District 8 Hub. The crowdfunding campaign, which took place in the spring of 2016, put the charity, which was using crowdfunding mechanisms for the very first time, under significant pressure. In order to reach the funding goal, L'Impronta mainly mobilised offline resources (e.g. community events, networking, etc.). As a matter of fact, L'Impronta, as with many other Milanese small charities and community organisations, did not have extensive online networks or the ability to start developing new ones within the very short timeframe (fifty days).

From the interview with L'Impronta, it clearly appeared that the organisation of four offline events – one hosted by the other neighbourhood organisation in District 8 – has been crucial in convincing people to pledge, but also that these same events tended to involve people who already knew L'Impronta and its activities. It thus appears that the use of a potentially innovative tool relied in fact on quite traditional and locally embedded networks, mainly based on personal relations.

### *Put the Hurt on the Mafia (Facciamo la festa alla mafia)*

Another successful project supported by the Municipality of Milano through the Eppela platform is *Put the Hurt on the Mafia* and, more precisely, 'The Welcoming Garden' (*Il Giardino Accogliente*), part of a broader project promoted by a group of social cooperatives. The broader project concerns the reuse of the largest asset confiscated from organised crime in the Milan urban region, Casa Chiaravalle, an abandoned villa with a private garden and 6 hectares of agricultural land, located in a rural area on the southern border of the city. The Welcoming Garden, in particular, aimed at collecting resources, but also ideas and projects, for the reuse of the garden; the villa, originally owned by a family involved in organised crime, had been confiscated by the state and originally was given to the SIS social cooperatives group for social purposes.

While the buildings will be converted to housing for fragile social groups, and the surrounding land will host an innovative social agriculture project, the abandoned garden will be devoted to activities for the local community. In parallel with the crowdfunding campaign, which took place in autumn 2016, the promoters have been running an open consultation on the participatory decision-making platform *Oxway* about ideas for possible functions and actions for the garden. *Oxway* is a crowd-consulting platform, which allows citizens to first develop proposals and solutions to a common issue or problem, and then to vote and rank them. In this case, the project has been able to use online and offline tools and successfully involve both already existing networks and people who did not know the project or the promoters.

### *Reflections on the Milanese cases*

In terms of the ANT perspective, both projects show a relevant socially horizontal organisation, but while, in the first case, it is organised mainly through already existing offline networks, in the second case the promoters have shown the ability to articulate such an organisation both online and offline; moreover, in this case the identification of a group of citizens responsible for the project's implementation is one of the outcomes of the consultation phase. Looking at other initiatives within the framework programme, the predominance of horizontal over vertical relations seems largely diffused, also because the Municipality of Milano never played a central top-down role, apart from the final pledging, leaving the scene to local networks.

In terms of flexibility, the *TiFacilitaLaVita* initiative tried to constrain a potentially innovative tool within its existing networks, mainly due to a capacity gap and a lack of time (and support) to build new, more appropriate skills and networks; this in turn suggests, in line with evidence from other cases, that for established local organisations, already rooted in dense and strong networks, civic crowdfunding may not always be the most appropriate fundraising tool, other, more traditional tools, seem more effective and targeted (Pacchi and Pais, 2017). The Welcoming Garden showed a greater degree of flexibility in the choice, design, and combination of appropriate tools; indeed, since the project was not aimed at functions already decided upon, the promoters decided to accompany the process with the parallel Oxway consultation, aimed at identifying relevant ideas and proposals coming from the community and thereby giving full room to flexibility.

As far as the material and symbolic dimensions are concerned, they are strictly connected and mutually reinforcing in both projects. In the first case, the offline dimension offered the main support to both dimensions: people identified themselves with the project for a future community hub by actually meeting and exchanging material and symbolic resources much as the hub would do in the future. In the second one the evaluation was more articulated: the material dimension can be seen in the importance of the actual space that will offer opportunities for community action, while the symbolic one revolves around the opportunity of giving back to the public an asset originally belonging to organised crime.

## Discussion

All four case studies present similarities and differences. First, all projects have been developed with a strong, inclusive vision and the involvement of local people in developing the project ideas, with the aim of addressing the needs of the local, diverse communities. Second, all projects are rooted locally and show great understanding of the local, both physically and socially.

Unlike the others, the Peckham project proposes a vision for a new infrastructure, which will require time and additional funding to be developed. The current funding is only for a feasibility study. Interestingly though for the organisers, this does not matter as much as it might seem. The value of the project at present lies in the way it has mobilised communities and created local networks. The Haringey and Welcoming Garden projects, albeit with differences, are smaller in scale, discrete, and with a much more immediately measurable impact. The Haringey project shows its high level of replicability elsewhere in London and the Milan Welcoming Garden appears as a discrete, deliverable project set within a much broader and complex programme.

Institutional endorsement can be given to strategically important projects, as in London, or to those projects that appear to raise community support relatively quickly, as in the Milan examples. This institutional backing not only translates into money, but the endorsement itself generates positive feedback loops, leading to more backing from the wider community. But if support is to some extent engineered, can it really be seen as a proxy for a public mandate? Moreover, only a detailed analysis of the amount and distribution of pledges would illustrate if support is really widespread and growing at the community level, or if it is supplied by a small number of pledgers, already connected to the project promoters. This is clearly the main challenge in the first of the two Milanese cases.

The degree of specificity and uniqueness of the circumstances determining projects will affect their replicability. The Peckham Coal Line project is the product of a relatively unusual set of issues – spatial, social, and political – and, while other projects may learn from it, it is not immediately replicable. The kitchen garden, on the other hand, responded to very widespread issues in a relatively common situation and its model could be easily adapted to other sites. Even the Welcoming Garden, offering a contained package within a highly specific context, also could be to some extent replicated. The Welcoming Garden also holds a highly symbolic value, in that it involves the community in the transformation and reappropriation of a confiscated asset, previously owned by organised crime. Since there are many such assets in search of new uses and functions across Italy, replicability is particularly relevant here.

In the WEMI cases it is important to underline that replicability is a central dimension, because the Municipality of Milano is significantly involved in supporting local communities in the opening up of local or urban hubs, not exclusively devoted to welfare and services, but also to cultural production, food and innovation in agriculture, or those characterised by a hybrid nature (hosting and mixing different urban functions). Such hubs tend to reuse abandoned or under-utilised public or private space, and they can play a pivotal role in neighbourhood regeneration strategies.

## Conclusions

In this chapter we have discussed the emerging field of civic crowdfunding as a way of initiating and supporting projects and initiatives that benefit a range of communities and that are able to produce *alternative* urban spaces through *alternative* partnerships, governance, and financial modules. We discussed civic crowdfunding in relation to ANT and diverse economy frameworks and through four case studies in London and Milan. The projects discussed vary substantially in scale and type of financial support received but they share significant experiences. Common to these projects is the significant journey from elaborating initial ideas to reaching the financial target and implementing the project, a journey in which citizens become engaged in discussions/visions/strategies about the future of their cities, through designing innovative projects, mobilising financial resources, and transforming urban spaces. Yet, some projects more than others seem to succeed in establishing wider networks of participation and collaboration with local communities and institutions, creating a multiplier effect. This has the potential to generate shifts in urban governance and to deliver innovative projects that consolidate a culture of citizen-led action. We argue that such projects need to be better understood and shared to support learning across networks and collective strengthening of initiatives that, while being progressive and transformative, would otherwise only have a localised impact.

Building on our case studies, further research paths open up. While there is a need for more accurate quantitative and qualitative analysis of crowdfunding campaigns, there is also a strong need to identify more precisely criteria and indicators for evaluating their impacts and possible shortcomings or externalities, also in the light of the critical remarks highlighted in the preceding sections. Are crowdfunding campaigns really opening up alternative and potentially transformative new spaces of local democracy, or are they contributing to create club goods, thus replicating and not tackling spreading urban inequalities? Under which (cultural, societal, administrative, or political) conditions are they producing one or the other? Furthermore, as public administrations wake up to the potential of civic crowdfunding to support local cultural and economic development and urban regeneration, how are they going to mediate their need to formalise processes to guarantee accountability with the intrinsic flexibility and topological structure of crowdfunding projects?

## Acknowledgments

We are extremely grateful to all the crowdfunding groups that agreed to discuss their projects with us, and to the participants in the workshops we organised at the Design & The City Conference (Amsterdam, 19–22 April 2016) and at the Politecnico di Milano (Milan, 13 May 2016) for all their critical and insightful contributions. We feel particularly indebted to Louise Armstrong from the Peckham Coal Line project and James Parkinson from the

Greater London Authority for the many fruitful conversations we have had with them over the past two years.

## Notes

1 The match funding approach that the GLA is using shows how the process of crowdfunding is changing, at least in London. From a recent interview with the GLA (June 2017), it emerged that there had been an increase in formality in the funding process in order to make it more transparent. As the money invested in supporting such initiatives is public, the GLA is increasingly under pressure to make sure the projects it supports are: deliverable, meeting wider community needs, and talking to a wider audience. The risk, however, is that this increase in formality might come at the expense of losing local spontaneity and creativity.

2 At the time of writing this chapter, the Peckham Coal Line vision was under threat as a planning application for a residential development on a small site along the route of the Coal Line had recently been put forward. Although discussions between local groups, the Council, and the developers were ongoing, this recent turn highlights how fragile and vulnerable this type of project can be.

## References

Bailey, N. and Pill, M. 2015. Can the State Empower Communities through Localism? An Evaluation of Recent Approaches to Neighbourhood Governance in England. *Environment and Planning C: Government and Policy*, 33(2), 289–304.

Belleflamme, P., Lambert, T., and Schwienbacher, A. 2013. Individual Crowdfunding Practices. *Venture Capital*, 15(4), 313–333.

Comune di Milano. 2014. *Indirizzi per la sperimentazione di azioni di crowdfunding dedicate alla promozione di progetti innovativi ad impatto sociale, alla promozione delle reti sociali, dell'aggregazione sociale e della città accessibile* [Towards Experimenting with Civic Crowdfunding Actions to Promote Innovative Projects Aimed at Generating Social Impact, Promoting Social Networks, Social Aggregation and Accessibility]. Milan: Comune di Milano.

Davies, R. 2013. Civic Crowdfunding from the Statue of Liberty to Now. MIT Center for Civic Media (online). Available at: https://civic.mit.edu/blog/rodrigodavies/civic-crowdfunding-from-the-statue-of-liberty-to-now (Accessed: 22 February 2017).

Davies, R. 2014. Civic Crowdfunding as a Marketplace for Participation in Urban Development. In: *The Internet, Policy & Politics Conference 2014*. Oxford: Oxford Internet Institute (online). Available at: http://ipp.oii.ox.ac.uk/sites/ipp/files/documents/IPP2014_Davies.pdf (Accessed: 20 June 2015).

Evans, J. and Jones, P. 2013. *Urban Regeneration in the UK*. London: SAGE.

Gibson-Graham, J.K. 2008. Diverse Economies: Performative Practices for 'Other Worlds'. *Progress in Human Geography*, 32, 613–632.

Greater London Authority (GLA). 2016. *Understanding the Social Impacts of the Mayor's Crowdfunding Programme*. London: GLA.

Hollow, M. 2013. *Crowdfunding and Civic Society in Europe: A Profitable Partnership?* (SSRN Scholarly Paper No. ID 2333635). Rochester, NY: Social Science Research Network.

Imrie, R., Lees, L., and Raco, M. (eds) 2009. *Regenerating London: Governance, Sustainability and Community in a Global City*. London: Routledge.

Langley, P. 2016. Crowdfunding in the United Kingdom: A Cultural Economy. *Economic Geography*, 92, 301–321.

Latour, B. 1993. *We Have Never Been Modern*, Translated by C. Porter. Cambridge, MA: Harvard University Press.

Law, J. 2009. Actor Network Theory and Material Semiotics. In: Turner, B.S. (ed) *The New Blackwell Companion to Social Theory*. Chichester: John Wiley & Sons, 141–158.

NESTA. 2013. *Working the Crowd*. London: NESTA.

Pacchi, C. and Pais, I. 2017. Il crowdfunding civico tra reti, comunità e ruolo del governo locale [Civic Crowdfunding between Networks, Community and Local Government]. In: Lodigiani, R. (ed) *Milano 2017. Una metropoli per innovare, crescere, sognare, Fondazione Ambrosianeum*. Milan: Angeli, 117–134.

Palermo, P.C. (ed) 2002. *Il programma Urban e l'innovazione delle politiche urbane. 1: Il senso dell'esperienza: interpretazioni e proposte* [The Urban Programme and the Innovation of Urban Policies. 1. The Sense of Experience: Interpretations and Proposals]. Milan: Franco Angeli.

Pickerill, J. and Chatterton, P. 2006. Notes towards Autonomous Geographies: Creation, Resistance and Self-Management as Survival Tactics. *Progress in Human Geography*, 30, 730–746.

Presidenza del Consiglio dei Ministri. 2016. Bando per la presentazione di progetti per la predisposizione del Programma straordinario di intervento per la riqualificazione urbana e la sicurezza delle periferie delle città metropolitane e dei comuni capoluogo di provincia [Tender for Urban Projects Aimed at the Regeneration and Safety of Urban Peripheries of Metropolitan Cities and District Centres]. Available at: www.governo.it/sites/governo.it/files/Bando_periferie_urbane.pdf.

Sbetti, F., Rossi, F., Talia, M., and Trillo, C. (eds) 2013. *Il governo della città nella contemporaneità. La città come motore di sviluppo. Tema 1. La rigenerazione urbana come resilienza* [The Government of the Contemporary City. The City as Development Engine. Theme 1. Urban Regeneration as Resiliency]. Urbanistica Dossier (online). Roma: INU Edizioni.

Selby Trust. 2013. *Global Garden, Global Kitchen Appearing on BBC1 on the 14th January*. London: The Selby Trust. Available at: http://www.selbytrust.co.uk/articles/global-garden-global-kitchen-appearing-bbc1-14th-january.

Sheehan, R. 2011. Actor-Network Theory as a Reflexive Tool: (Inter)Personal Relations and Relationships in the Research Process. *Area*, 43, 336–342.

Sheehan, R. and Vadjunec, J. 2012. Placing Community through Actor-Network Theory in Oklahoma's No Man's Land. *Journal for Social and Cultural Geography*, 13(8), 915–936.

Stiver, A., Barroca, L., Minocha, S., Richards, M., and Roberts, D. 2015. Civic Crowdfunding Research: Challenges, Opportunities, and Future Agenda. *New Media & Society*, 17(2), 249–271.

Urban Task Force. 1999. *Towards an Urban Renaissance: The Report of the Urban Task Force Chaired by Lord Rogers of Riverside*. Executive Summary. London: Urban Task Force.

# 13 An international dialogue on the production of alternative urban spaces

*Jens Kaae Fisker and Letizia Chiappini*

## Introduction

Although they proceed from a shared point of departure, the preceding eleven chapters are pregnant with perspectives and insights that go well beyond the loose conceptual framing provided in Chapter 1. The task that remains is to harness the multiplicity of voices thus engendered by staging an international dialogue on the production of alternative urban spaces. More than a summary of chapter findings, this results in a complex mapping of similarities, resonances, differences, tensions, and disagreements. In staging the dialogue we have not confined ourselves to juxtaposing the chapters but also relate their findings to existing literatures, revisiting in particular the debates included in Chapter 1. The dialogue has two main aims: first, it can be read as a contribution to urban studies in which we try to sketch the scholarly orientations necessary for this cross-disciplinary field to retain and reinvigorate its political and practical relevance; and second, it can be read as a resource of inspiration, affirmation, and encouragement for those more directly invested in the production of alternative urban spaces on a practical and political level.

The chapter is organised into two sections. In the first we revisit the three themes that have served to structure the book and, in the second, we identify and reflect on some of the themes, questions, and concepts not anticipated in the introductory chapter. The first section reads as part-by-part conclusions that sum up the insights that can be gleaned from individual chapters in relation to each theme (but drawn from across the book rather than just the part in question). By contrast, the purpose of the second section is to ask how the chapters have broken, if not new, then other grounds than the ones that we set out to dig into. This includes a distinction between tactical and strategic alternatives; the role of urban interstices and urban rhythms, respectively; and finally, the keeping alive, in both urban theory and political practice, of a multiplicity of constitutive outsides of the urban.

## Revisiting the key themes

Three broad themes have served to organise and animate the chapters of this book: (1) alternative spaces of work, exchange, and consumption; (2) alternative spaces of dwelling; and (3) alternative spaces of public life. As mentioned in Chapter 1, this reflects a purely analytical distinction and it follows that no single chapter can be meaningfully confined within the theme formally assigned to it. In summing up, synthesising, and discussing key findings below we therefore draw on insights derived from any chapter that can be brought to bear on the theme in question.

### *Alternative spaces of work, exchange, and consumption*

Conceived in its broadest sense, this theme concerns the production of alternative urban economies. Bracketing the urban for a moment, this is a theme that has been pursued persistently by J.K. Gibson-Graham in their efforts to map out diverse economies populated by an entangled plethora of capitalist, alter-capitalist, and non-capitalist enterprises; wage, alternatively paid, and unpaid labour; and market, alternative market, and non-market exchange (Gibson-Graham, 2006: 59ff). Together, these categories make for a useful heuristic device for mapping elements of diverse urban economies as they are reflected across this book. Such a mapping is presented in Table 13.1. Conventional capitalocentric analysis would undoubtedly find a way to present these heterogeneous elements as somehow all being derivatives of the capital relation from which they can never escape. Such a conclusion, however, would only be reasonable in the sense that everything is somehow connected to everything else. To deny that alter- and non-capitalist practices are imbricated in relations of dependency with their capitalist counterparts would be untenable, but it would be equally unreasonable to suggest that such dependency is a one-way street. The salvagers of scrap metal in Accra (Danso-Wiredu, Fisker, and Pugalis, Chapter 8) may be dependent on global capital for the influx of e-waste from which to salvage, but global capital is also dependent on them for avoiding expensive waste treatment. They are intertwined, but one is not necessarily subordinated to the other in any straightforward way.

However useful this mapping may be, it offers no more than a cross-section of the differential urban becomings that we have seen emerging in their specific relation to the capitalist mode of production. The alternative-to-what question is thus answered only with reference to capitalist urbanism broadly defined (this is not to be conflated with the narrower term neoliberal urbanism to which we return later). Yet even if these are all economic practices, the configurations in relation to which they are posed as alternatives cannot be confined within narrow economistic terms. The sex workers of Chandigarh (Sharma, Chapter 9) are not just producing their spaces of labour as alternatives to conventional wage labour. They are navigating a complex situation in which their gender identity and sexual orientation make them targets for legal persecution and violent harassment. To avoid these threats they seek out urban interstices where an alternative mode of life is possible.

Within Part 1 of the book, the chapters focused on two distinct subthemes: alternative food spaces (Chapters 2 and 3) and alternative work spaces (Chapters 4

*Table 13.1* Mapping of diverse urban economies covered in the book with chapter numbers in parentheses

| *Exchange* | *Labour* | *Enterprise* |
|---|---|---|
| MARKET<br>Supermarkets and malls (2, 3)<br>Mortgage markets (6)<br>Real estate markets (8) | WAGE<br>Regular employment (4, 11) | CAPITALIST<br>Supermarket chains (2)<br>Real estate developers (3, 11)<br>Banks (7) |
| ALTERNATIVE MARKET<br>Direct producer-consumer relations (2, 3, 11)<br>Farmers' markets (2, 3)<br>Guesthouses (3)<br>Canteens (3)<br>Informal rental markets (8) | ALTERNATIVELY PAID<br>Scrap metal salvagers (8)<br>Self-employed coworkers (4)<br>Sex workers (9) | ALTER-CAPITALIST<br>Consumer/producer coops (2)<br>Coworking spaces (4)<br>Makerspaces (5) |
| NON-MARKET<br>Civic crowdfunding (12)<br>Distribution of free food (11)<br>Squatting (8, 11)<br>Resisting eviction (6) | UNPAID<br>Urban gardeners (11)<br>Volunteer community leaders (8) | NON-CAPITALIST<br>Social centres (11)<br>Social movements (6)<br>Crowdfunding platforms (12)<br>State (5) |

Source: adapted from Gibson-Graham (2006)

and 5). The former resulted in remarkably similar experiences emerging from two very different urban contexts. Johansen and Hoff showed how in Copenhagen alternative food provisioning (1) reconfigures the senses in ways that allow urban dwellers to radically reconnect with the practice of obtaining food; (2) reintroduces informal social interaction between consumers and producers of food (e.g. at farmers' markets); and (3) alters the rhythms of food provisioning by reintroducing the seasonal rhythms of food production and by allocating certain weekly time slots for food provisioning. The centrality of social interaction is reaffirmed in Beirut where Mady found that the Souq El Tayeb non-governmental organisation (NGO) has used Lebanese food traditions to frame the creation of reconciliatory spaces of encounter while simultaneously providing alternative sources of food provisioning for urban consumers and livelihood opportunities for small-scale food producers. She also adds to the picture by detailing how local knowledge and discursive framings play pivotal parts in the production of alternative urban space: (1) the NGO organisers facilitate interaction between public, civic, and private actors, offer advice on everything from legal to aesthetic matters, and take care of the discursive framing of projects/activities. But each of the projects are run by locals whose efforts and knowledge are the key driving forces. (2) Souq El Tayeb deliberately frames their activities to avoid sensitive and dividing discourse relating to the civil war, focusing instead on food traditions that unite rather than divide people. In both Beirut and Copenhagen the desire to reconnect with food is emphasised as a key motivational driver. The result is a de-alienation of urban food economies, manifested in the proliferation of direct producer-consumer relations facilitative of both economic exchange, social interaction, and mutual learning.

The other subtheme focused on coworking and maker spaces in Berlin and Milan. Both Chapter 4 by Pacchi and Chapter 5 by Chiappini and Törnberg critically evaluate the transformative potential of new urban workspaces and productive sites that have been promoted widely as nothing less than revolutionising interventions in urban economies. The authors agree that such claims are exaggerations that nevertheless speak to an actual potential for enacting urban change that both coworking spaces and makerspaces carry with them. Coworking spaces, according to Pacchi, seem to be caught in the middle between the defensive strategies of a growing precariat and the transformative potentials that they also harbour. They are certainly alternative urban spaces, but their radical potential may easily 'fizz out', making coworking spaces little more than compliant and defensive responses to labour market changes. The potential is still there but will require a politicisation in which coworking spaces become urban nodes for building new collective identities and for organising precariat forces. While Chiappini and Törnberg are equally hesitant about the transformative potential of maker spaces, they do identify some of the pieces that seem to be missing in the coworking puzzle. Maker spaces thus represent bottom-up initiatives that seem to partially fill some of the gaps in welfare provision left behind by neoliberalised public and private sectors; in the Italian context this gap has been exacerbated by a simultaneous withdrawal of the church. In the wider perspective of alternative urban workspaces the combined findings of the two chapters point to the still latent learning potential that resides in the collective experiences of such spaces taken together. Rather than engaging in a competition about who 'the real revolutionaries' are, proponents of coworking, the maker movement, and similar groupings of urban workers stand to learn much simply by encountering each other.

### *Alternative spaces of dwelling*

Our choice for this theme of the word 'dwelling' instead of the more frequently used 'housing' was motivated by our emphasis on the urban as process and performed reality. As a verb, 'dwelling' alludes to an action, a doing, whereas the noun 'housing' tends to indicate little more than a material amenity, a particular kind of built environment. By choosing the verb instead of the noun, we compel ourselves to 'consider the city as a place that is not just inhabited but which is produced through that inhabiting' (McFarlane, 2011: 651). If housing connotes a fundamental need of urban inhabitants, then dwelling indicates the production of urban spaces of home by the people who inhabit it. More than a lens for analytical attention, this has also been a way of sharpening our critical edge, because it highlights how people are often excluded from playing their due part in this process. Indeed, the critical blade often has been dulled by a scholarly fixation on housing as a consumption good and the associated casting of urban inhabitants as mere consumers (Jacobs & Smith, 2008).

The very reasonable demand for inclusion on the part of urban dwellers is at the heart of the Lefebvrian call for the right to the city, identified precisely as a right 'of all those who *inhabit*' (Lefebvre, 1996: 158). While this right extends to urban life as a whole, it has urban dwelling as its base. It is a right of those who actively inhabit the city, rather than those who passively consume it, or, even worse, those who attempt to control urban space at a distance, such as absentee landlords, real estate speculators, or authoritarian governments. It is in questions of dwelling that the most sharply drawn political frontier towards neoliberal urbanism emerges; and it is the right to the city that opposes it. Mark Purcell has made the political stakes exceedingly clear:

> Neoliberalism ... constructs the city as a strategic node in a network designed to maximize capital accumulation. Urban space is imagined to be owned property and its role is to contribute to economic productivity. The right to the city destabilizes that neoliberal answer and offers a distinctly new vision for what the city is for. The right to the city demands that we see the city first and foremost as *inhabited*. The city is a collective creative work by and for inhabitants.
>
> (Purcell, 2008: 105)

This notion of a frontier between the city-as-property and the city-as-inhabited permeates the present volume, even if it is not often directly articulated. Moreover, in real urban worlds it co-exists with other cross-cutting frontiers, all of which are mutually constitutive of one another. Direct articulations of the right to the city are found in Peiteado's analysis in Chapter 7 of discursive and extra-discursive repertoires of contention in the Spanish housing movement People Affected by Mortgages (PAH). Its relative success in securing rights for urban dwellers resulted from a counter-hegemonic redefinition of 'housing' in which the term has been discursively dissociated from private property and reattached to social needs and human rights. Furthermore, it has challenged private property regimes by articulating housing as an urban commons. PAH thus has been able to effect a broader discursive change whereby the right to housing comes before the right to private property. If this change can be sustained, then it aides struggles for the right to the city, because it puts the social needs of urban dwellers before the economic needs of capital. While discursively centred on 'housing' the extra-discursive struggles of PAH also include broader engagements more aptly captured by 'dwelling'.

As hinted above, extra-discursive struggles also play key roles in asserting the right of inhabitants to actively produce their own urban spaces of dwelling. Chapters 6 (Shalabi and Pugalis) and 8 (Danso-Wiredu, Fisker, and Pugalis) in particular bear witness to this. That dwelling is an active verb is underscored emphatically by the practices of slum-dwellers in Old Fadama, Accra, explored in Chapter 8. They have produced an alternative space of urban dwelling in which solutions are developed in ways that may be makeshift and informal but that are also highly creative, well coordinated, and organised. Inhabitants have organised an informal real estate and rental market that continues to respect customary land claims. In this sense, residents do not squat (as claimed by the Ghanaian state) but have bought and rented their land directly from its previous inhabitants by following informally organised and regulated procedures. They have managed to integrate heterogeneous systems of authority to engender complex governance arrangements where organised grassroots with translocal connectivity cooperate with ethnic and religious leaders representing the various groups that make up the community. Similar achievements can be attributed to the Syrian refugees of Beyt al-‘Ayla on the outskirts of Cairo (Chapter 6). Faced with the unfavourable combination of exclusion from the formal Egyptian labour market and dwelling in a neighbourhood neglected in terms of basic urban services such as medical facilities, education institutions, and adequate sources of food provisioning, inhabitants have developed informal solutions to gain access to employment and services. These include miniature shops on balconies, bread ovens in the street, urban agriculture, and day-care facilities.

The presence of cross-cutting frontiers, taking us beyond the property-habitation opposition, is most clearly exemplified in Chapters 6 (Shalabi and Pugalis), 9 (Sharma), and 11 (Tanulku and Fisker). The situation facing the Syrian refugees in Chapter 6 is the combined result of legislation discriminating against refugees and the neoliberalised policy regime of Cairo in which both private and public investment in urban development is predicated on the profitability of providing services and infrastructure. The neglect of the neighbourhood has to be seen, furthermore, in the light of a historic succession of spatial fixes in the Egyptian economy. Similarly, the daily lives of *kothi* men in Chapter 9 are multiply interstitial. Apart from the interstitiality of their neighbourhood as induced by urban planning practices, *kothi* men also live interstitial lives due to their gender identity and sexual orientation that fall between formally recognised categories in Indian society. Like their neighbourhood, they exist outside of well-established categories and their associated regulatory frameworks. Finally, in Chapter 11, Istanbul inhabitants are faced with a peculiar variation of neoliberal urbanism that has been coupled with national and religious conservatism as well as an increasingly authoritarian and oppressive regime at both national and urban levels of government. This results in a contradictory situation where liberal-minded middle-class inhabitants become urban activists struggling against neoliberal urbanism.

### *Alternative spaces of public life*

For the third and last structuring theme we chose to focus on the spaces of public life, thus eschewing the more confining term ‘public space’. The motives behind this choice are related to those animating our previous choice of dwelling over housing. Just as dwelling connotes something more than an amenity and parcelling of urban space, 'spaces of public life' hints at something much broader than sites formally designated as 'public spaces'. We were interested in any space playing host to public urban life, no matter what its formal designation might be, without thereby wishing to deny that such designations can have repercussions for the kinds of public life actually lived there. With Andy Merrifield (2012: 278) we could say, then, that alternative urban spaces of public life 'are public not because they are simply there, in the open, in a city center, but because these spaces are made public by people encountering one another, there'. They engender, in other words, a politics of the urban encounter, as 'spaces in which social absence and social presence attain a *visible* structuration, a political coherence' (Merrifield, 2012: 278).

Ostensibly, the most emblematic and straightforward case presented in the book is the Viaduto Santa Tereza in Belo Horizonte (Chapter 10), a public space with interstitial characteristics appropriated by urban grassroots for politically charged cultural events and emerging as a breeding place for new political subjectivities claiming their right to the city in general, and this space in particular, as an urban commons. It is also a dwelling place for homeless people and has for many years been a priority target of redevelopment for urban authorities. As such it has also become a hotly contested space due to the diverging visions of counter-hegemonic grassroots organisations and authorities regarding its future. There are sharp contrasts between these contentious interventions of urban grassroots organisations and the collaborational projects that emerge out of the civic crowdfunding platforms investigated in Chapter 12. Both arguably reflect bottom-up interventions to reappropriate urban spaces of public life, but they operate in different registers. Whereas the struggle for Viaduto Santa Tereza produced confrontation and conflict, civic crowdfunding initiatives have been embraced by urban authorities in London and Milan that have willingly added the new platforms to their urban governance toolbox. In a collaborational register, civic crowdfunding offers transformative potential in the pursuit of cities produced by and for inhabitants rather than for the interests of capital and small urban elites. Yet, it is far from certain to what extent this potential will be realised as it comes with pitfalls of its own. The fact that urban authorities have so quickly turned to civic crowdfunding is at the same time encouraging and concerning. Gullino, Cerulli, Seetzen, and Pacchi thus raise their banner of hope alongside a warning sign, pointing to the very real danger that civic crowdfunding will replicate rather than disrupt urban inequalities. A critical question that will have to be dealt with is whether counter-hegemonic grassroots actors can use the platforms in ways that enable them to benefit from cooperation without falling victim to cooptation by neoliberal or other hegemonic forces.

The past decade has seen a proliferation of spectacular urban protest movements utilising sustained occupation of public spaces such as squares and parks rather than isolated demonstrations. In other words, protesters have actively appropriated these urban spaces instead of merely using them as passive backdrops for contention. What many of these instances have in common is their efforts to transform their spaces of protest into microscopic alternative urban worlds of their own. Yet, in spite of their sustained nature, these microcosms are nevertheless ephemeral constructions, leaving open questions about what happens afterwards. Chapters 7 (Peiteado) and 11 (Tanulku and Fisker) provide important glimpses into the radical afterlives of such protests. The eventual discontinuation of the Gezi Park occupation in Istanbul did not spell the end of the protests that found an afterlife in the production of a number of alternative urban spaces in various neighbourhoods around the city. The two cases analysed by Tanulku and Fisker show all the difficulties associated with the transition from protests against a common enemy and the production of ephemeral commons in Gezi Park to the initiation, development, and continuation of alternative urban spaces of a more permanent nature. Both turned out to have only a limited lifespan, but both also undoubtedly produced lasting effects in their neighbourhoods: the Don Quixote Social Centre produced spin-offs of its own, sustaining the ripple effect of Gezi Park, and the Imrahor Garden has been formalised as a municipal green space. Peiteado's investigation of the Spanish PAH exemplifies another way in which urban social movements can exploit major protest events such as those associated with the 15M demonstrations by absorbing the discharge of defiant energies through recruitment among protesters. Rather than a spin-off from the protest this is a practice of creating channels towards already existing urban movements for people to sustain their activism in purposeful and organised struggle. Both examples indicate that the impact of spectacular protests should not only be evaluated on the basis of their immediate outcomes but also through consideration of their multiple activistic afterlives.

## Breaking other grounds

In addition to the three key themes that served to organise the book, authors have grappled with a range of other questions and issues that also speak to the ways in which alternative urban spaces are produced. In this second half of the conclusion we turn attention to what we have found to be the most pertinent 'other grounds' thus broken into. We start by making an important distinction between strategic and tactical pursuits of alternative urban spaces that may prove useful in working out the precise nature of the transformative potentials embodied by urban alternatives. The next two subsections deal with the *wheres* and the *whens* of alternative urban spaces, by considering the role of interstitial spaces and urban rhythms, respectively. Finally, we return to the key notion of constitutive outsides, forwarded in the introduction as indispensable to the continued relevance of urban studies and to the political pursuit of alternative urban futures.

### *Strategic and tactical alternatives*

The production of alternative urban space may come about on the back of deliberate attempts to disrupt prevailing urban trajectories, but it also may be initiated as the unintended side effects of such trajectories. Examples of both are represented in the chapters of this book. Thus, the alternative spaces emerging as spin-offs from the Gezi Park protests in Istanbul (Tanulku and Fisker, Chapter 11) are clearly the results of a deliberate political decision to show that other urban realities are possible. This can be referred to as the *strategic* production of alternative urban space. By contrast, the informal urban settlement of Old Fadama in Accra (Danso-Wiredu, Fisker, and Pugalis, Chapter 8) has emerged and evolved over many years of rural-urban migration during which time the provision of affordable housing in the city has been completely insufficient to house the many newcomers. Here, alternative modes of dwelling and informal governance arrangements arose not on the basis of a collective strategic decision but out of the need of urban dwellers to get by on a daily basis. This can be referred to as the *tactical* production of alternative urban space.

To be sure, we do not make this distinction in order to suggest that particular instances can always be clearly identified as one or the other, nor to imply that a tactical alternative can never become strategic or the other way around. We do so rather because it proves useful in making broader sense of the complexities involved in the production of alternative urban space. Other chapters thus represent examples of a more hybrid character in which the distinction can be used to identify tactical and strategic *moments* in the production of alternative urban space. The farmers' markets in Beirut (Mady, Chapter 3), for instance, emerged tactically from the unstable context of a war-torn city in which the daily activity of obtaining food had become a challenge, while the possibilities for public encounter between urban dwellers had diminished. The initiative, however, evolved to become a strategic alternative aimed at producing diverse urban economies capable of providing a lasting alternative to the encroachment of neoliberal urbanism after the civil war.

Whereas a transition from a tactical to a strategic moment is clearly observable in Beirut, other cases illustrate the indeterminate nature of such a trajectory. Coworking spaces in Berlin and Milan (Pacchi, Chapter 4) have emerged as tactical responses to changing urban labour markets in which highly skilled workers are increasingly precarianised and flexibilised. Although their arrival has produced new spaces in which these 'privileged' precariat classes meet, it is less than clear whether those new workspaces will transition into politicised spaces to become bases of new precarian politics. It seems just as likely that they are en route to become one of the latest components in what Negri (1989) dubbed 'the social factory' (see also Gill & Pratt, 2008), where capitalist relations of exploitation are diffused throughout social space and everyday life. Here, the tactical moment is decidedly defensive, a situation mirrored in Chandigarh (Sharma, Chapter 9) where *kothi* men have been able to carve out an alternative space of relative safety for their marginalised way of life without thereby pointing towards any radical recasting of wider urban trajectories. The distinction between tactical and strategic moments of differential socio-spatial production can then usefully be complemented by a cross-cutting distinction between defensive and offensive moments, indicating that any combination of these designations is possible in explicating the nature of urban alternatives.

### *Interstitial spaces as cradles of differential becoming*

To the extent that the present volume can be seen as a mapping of present possibilities towards alternative urban futures, a key question is *where* in particular conditions seem to be ripe for enacting moments of differential urbanisation. A recurring theme – sometimes explicitly addressed, sometimes a silent presence – that provides important hints to answer this is the notion of urban interstices (see also Chapter 9). These have made appearances, first, in the narrow sense of the *terrain vague* that Ignasi de Sola-Morales (2014: 26) describes as 'strange places' that 'exist outside the city's effective circuits and productive structures' and hence places that are 'foreign to the urban system, mentally exterior to the physical interior of the city, its negative image, as much a critique as a possible alternative'. Such spaces are both pregnant with residual histories and inviting of reactivations and reappropriations. But the urban interstice also has appeared in the broader definition promoted by Brighenti (2013: xvi), who conceives of it as '*minoritarian* vis á vis other spaces that surround or encircle it'; 'other spaces that are either more institutionalized, and therefore economically and legally powerful, or endowed with a stronger identity, and therefore more recognized or typical'.

Urban interstitiality thus becomes more visible where majoritarian spaces are particularly strong and monolithic, because the urban interstice in such settings appears in an exceptionally contrasting light. This is most emphatically the case in planned cities such as Chandigarh (Chapter 9) and Belo Horizonte (Chapter 10). These urban places share a similar history: both were founded as state capitals and minutely planned at the height of modernist beliefs in the ability of urban form to shape and 'improve' urban life in the sense of imposing order, rationality, linearity, and functional segregation. In such a context it is not surprising that urban alternatives spring forth precisely from the spaces that escape the grid and the gaze of such modernist planning follies. In Chandigarh, and other Indian cities, it was the *lal doras* – themselves products of the planning regime – that slipped between the cracks, whereas in Belo Horizonte it was the very infrastructure designed to achieve a rational city of uninterrupted circulation that produced residual spaces whose identity as urban interstices gradually matured. In both cases, urban interstitiality has functioned as a magnet for marginalised groups of urban inhabitants seeking them out either for safety – *kothi* men in the Kajheri village in Chandigarh and the homeless under the Viaduto Santa Tereza in Belo Horizonte – or as a breeding ground for new political subjectivities and urban expressions.

A radical ambiguity is at play here: on the one hand, urban interstices do provide fertile grounds for the production of alternative urban spaces, while on the other hand, they also carry with them a precariousness that sticks to anyone who dares to appropriate them. Furthermore, the widespread adoption of temporary urbanism as a tool in urban governance repertoires threatens – or promises, according to one's perspective – to institutionalise urban interstices by integrating them into the cycles of urban change and renewal. This creates a trap in which radical urban projects are given tempting opportunities for unopposed appropriation of a building or a small tract of land on the condition of ephemerality. Such projects often turn out to become gentrification drivers, doing the hard legwork of driving up real estate values before the bulldozers and the real estate developers eventually move in. While this dilemma becomes glaringly obvious where urban interstices and temporary urbanisms are concerned, it also has broader significance as exemplified by post-Gezi alternative spaces in Istanbul (Chapter 11). These too appear to have played an unintended role in the acceleration of gentrification processes. Cautioning against the perils of cooptation is hardly an original finding, but that should not diminish its perceived importance and continued relevance. Fortunately, cooptation is not the inevitable fate of all attempts to produce the urban differently. But its persisting presence serves as a reminder to be on watch and consider carefully what unintended consequences radical interventions may also engender, especially in terms of playing into the hands of whatever hegemonic power may be in play in the present conjuncture.

### *Disrupting and changing urban rhythms*

If interstitiality indicates *where* alternative urban spaces may be produced, everyday rhythms of urban life may hold the key to figuring out the *whens* of such alternatives. Spatiality and temporality cannot be meaningfully separated and any approach that eschews the latter is likely to produce only static accounts that have little to say about processual aspects. Since we see the urban as process that would be unfortunate. Rhythm comprises a particularly beneficial entry point for this purpose, because a rhythmic perspective 'avoids the conception of place as static, for rhythms are essentially dynamic, part of the multiplicity of flows that emanate from, pass through and centre upon place, and contribute to its situated dynamics' (Edensor, 2010: 3). Towards the end of his work and life, Henri Lefebvre grappled with urban rhythms to produce a crucial addition – presented in *Rhythmanalysis* (Lefebvre, 2004) – that inflects in substantial ways upon his previous body of work on everyday life, the production of space, and the urban revolution. While the concept of rhythmanalysis originates with Santos (1931) and has been developed by Bachelard (2000), it was Lefebvre who turned it into an analytic device for urban studies.

Rhythms are brought to the fore in Chapter 10 where Di Quarto shows how musical rhythms are activated to produce borderless and transgressing soundscapes that mess with the rigid order of a planned city designed to control socio-spatial behaviour and enclose activities in preordained and carefully segregated parcels. Police and city authorities accept this to the extent that activities do not overflow their assigned spatial and temporal parcels too much, but they are always ready to strike down hard if transgressions threaten to either redefine spaces or seriously disrupt the linear rhythms that the urban infrastructure is meant to facilitate. With Lefebvre, a critical edge is added by juxtaposing rhythms dominated by either cyclic or linear notions of time. Modernity and capitalism have brought with them the prevalence of the latter, marginalising cyclical time and its associated rhythms in the process. This tension between different kinds of rhythm is a key theme in Chapter 2 where Johansen and Hoff observe how the decision to pursue alternative practices in one aspect of everyday life, however minute and ostensibly isolated, can have repercussions across the board because it requires one to disrupt rhythms that have become routinised patterns of urban life. Seen in the light of Lefebvre's thoughts about the linear rhythms of capitalist modernity, it is interesting to observe that what the rhythmic disruption associated with the production of alternative urban food spaces (re)introduces is precisely the cyclical rhythms of nature embodied here through local small-scale organic agriculture drawn into the heart of urban life by food cooperatives and farmers' markets.

### *The role of constitutive outsides*

At the beginning of this book we suggested that in order for urban studies to stay politically relevant it needs to embrace multiple constitutive outsides of the urban. Since such outsides are the conditions, or limits, that make urban insides possible, they need to be invited in rather than be excluded by the disciplinary policing of more-or-less arbitrary boundaries defining what gets to count as important urban knowledge. On the abstract-simple level at which these thoughts were presented in the introduction they may be at risk of confusing more than they clarify. Their pertinence only becomes clear in the concrete-complex analyses conducted in various chapters.

The most obvious and explicit treatment of constitutive outsides takes place in Chapter 2, where Johansen and Hoff demonstrate how alternative spaces of food provisioning in Copenhagen are produced in creative interplay with the constitutive outside of the rural, resulting in what they call a *rurbal* space. They identify three arenas in which the urban inside is altered by drawing on a real-and-imagined rural outside: (1) the sensorium, where the senses are reconfigured in a process of reterritorialisation on a received territory of sensuous sterility and visual dominance; (2) sociability, where food provisioning is used as an occasion for generating new spaces of encounter that draw together urban consumers and rural producers; and (3) everyday rhythms, where daily life in the city is reconnected with, and thus subjected to, the limits engendered by rural rhythms of agricultural production and thereby with the natural rhythm of the seasons. This latter arena also exemplifies how the constitutive outside is not limited to the rural, but draws at the same time on a natural outside conditioning a cultural inside.

These findings are corroborated in Chapters 3 and 8, respectively. In Chapter 3, Mady similarly highlights how farmers' markets and other food-related activities in Beirut create spaces of encounter between urban consumers and rural producers. Here, however, such spaces are not just posed as alternatives to supermarkets but also, and perhaps more importantly, as alternatives to the encroaching commercialised public spaces that engulf and constrain public urban life in Beirut in its post-conflict conjuncture. In Chapter 8, Danso-Wiredu, Fisker, and Pugalis substantiate furthermore that these findings are not confined to the theme of food provisioning. They present a similar example of how seeds for urban alternatives are found in rural outsides by analysing how traditional practices of rural compound-dwelling in Ghana are transposed to urban settings in Accra, informally in the Old Fadama slum and on a more formal basis in the Amui Djor Housing Cooperative. In all of these examples it is furthermore worth noting the close kinship between constitutive outsides and urban interstitiality, especially if one considers interstices according to the definition offered by Sola-Morales that we quoted earlier; therein the *terrain vague* is conceived of precisely as constitutive outsides by being 'mentally exterior to the physical interior of the city' (2014: 26).

On a more subtle note, several chapters also provide hints that allude to the constructive and creative uses of constitutive outsides. The designation of various counter-hegemonic movements as urban struggles affords the possibility of connecting, for instance, labour-based and neighbourhood-based struggles in cross-cutting alliances that centre on their specifically urban dimension. Such a potential is clearly present in Chapter 4, where Pacchi shows how the transformative potential of coworking spaces depends in part on the extent to which precarian coworkers are able to connect their labour struggle with the neighbourhoods that play host to them. In partially filling the gap left by a retreating church, a crumbling welfare state, and superseded Fordist industries, the makerspaces in Chapter 5 (Chiappini and Törnberg) may have highlighted one of the ways in which such a connection can be enacted. While they are hardly en route to fulfilling their transformative potentials for urban economies, their connection to neighbourhood issues and their role in welfare provision for the urban poor may prove to be the opening that allows for the maker movement to recast itself as an urban movement connecting post-Fordist labour struggle with the right to the city, focusing on the enactment of bottom-up organising with a point of departure in the daily lives of the urban poor.

What is at stake here is not so much the relation between the urban and its constitutive outside per se, but more the relations among these multiple outsides. The fact that an urban condition is shared so widely means, in other words, that the urban dimension is ideally placed to act as a glue that brings together heterogeneous struggles for alternative futures, however contingent and ephemeral such alliances may be. In the coworking spaces investigated by Pacchi this potential is still latent and may never come to fruition. If it did, however, we could see precariat classes coming together with neighbourhood residents in a combined struggle for the right to inhabit in a mode of self-determination, where 'inhabiting' is conceived of both in terms of housing, labour, and urban commons. A sensitivity to constitutive outsides thus can generate ways of forging intersectional forms of urban struggle similar to those called for by Harvey (2012: 128ff) in *Rebel Cities* where he encourages radical urban movements to link up with their class-based siblings.

## Conclusions

From the outset, this book has been a politically motivated work of scholarship aimed at digging out of the present urban conjuncture ways and means that point towards alternative urban futures. Inspired by the Lefebvrian notion of the differential production of space, we have focused our academic gaze on the production of alternative urban spaces. Despite the Marxian tinge that marks our entry point, however, we have not confined ourselves to a search for alternatives to capitalism. Instead we have engendered a less restricted point of view in which conjunctural urban moments take precedence as the conditions from which alternatives will have to spring forth, conditions that may include any number of cross-cutting political frontiers and always have to be understood as the outcomes of differentiated geohistories. Urban alternatives, then, are contingent and always incomplete becomings produced in complex relational interaction with their specific urban contexts. Specific, however, cannot be equated simply to the local setting, although this is certainly a key component. The specificity of any urban context, on the contrary, is defined through relational processes with a spatial reach that is easily planetary in scope. For these final concluding remarks we have opted to hone in on the political stakes that we see emerging from our heterogeneous engagements with the production of alternative urban spaces, focusing in turn on each of the three key themes and the four 'other grounds broken'.

Taken together, alternative urban spaces of work, exchange, and consumption are key ingredients in the development of diverse urban economies. Posed as alternatives to capitalist urbanism they are nevertheless intertwined with the latter, both in terms of their evolutionary history and their day-to-day functioning. They are not, however, part of a simple binary in which resisting alternatives emerge to counteract already dominating capitalist forces. The economic practices embodied today by urban alternatives are direct descendants of variegated urban economies with long histories; what is new is their designation as alternative, a label that only makes sense in a situation where one kind of urban economy seems to prevail monolithically. Capitalism evidently appears today as such a monolith, but as an increasing number of economic geographers have made clear in recent decades, capitalist dominance is invariably made to appear more complete than it is. While the degree to which the capital relation conditions and constrains urban lives should not be underestimated, it is also important that its prevalence is not used as an excuse not to pursue alternatives on the grounds that any such attempt is bound to be futile and inconsequential.

Alternative urban spaces of dwelling embody the resurgence of claims for a radical right to the city conceived as the right to *inhabit* urban space in the fullest possible sense of the word. As such the notion of dwelling overflows the related notion of housing by speaking to something more than mere domesticity; the home may be a key site, but it is not the only site that makes urban co-habitation possible. Still, affordable housing and liveable neighbourhoods should continue to headline the struggles of urban dwellers for their right to the city, but not without the accompanying insistence that urban processes ought to be controlled by inhabitants rather than real estate speculators, absentee landlords, and oppressive governments who decide the fates of urban dwellers at a distance. The slogan 'cities for people, not for profit' continues to ring true, but it is important to remember that there are other things than profit that cities should not be for. Thus, beyond the slogan we see a need to develop political subjectivities that emphasise its first half by exploring what cities for people may look like, rather than getting stuck on its second half that leads no further than uniting urban dwellers against a common enemy.

With dwelling overflowing mere housing issues, the above already indicates a necessary engagement with alternative urban spaces of public life. These attenuate a politics of the encounter that goes against and beyond the individualisation of urban life, the compartmentalisation, segregation, and homogenisation of urban space, and the encroaching commodification, sanitisation, and gentrification of public spaces. The right to the city, then, may proceed from dwelling in the sense of domestic spaces but exceeds their limits and spills into the streets, parks, and squares, in other words, into the spaces of public life. This aspect is indispensable for dwelling to become urban in the sense of co-habitation beyond the family group and similar close-knit domestic units. Likewise, the relations of exchange that allow urban economies to hang together depend for their production and sustenance upon the presence of public spaces attuned to their needs. The production of alternative spaces of public life, then, is also instrumental in generating conditions favourable to the proliferation of diverse urban economies. If urban dwellers can only meet in commodified, tightly controlled, and heavily policed pseudo-public spaces then their possibilities for engendering novel relations of work, exchange, and consumption are detrimentally constrained.

It should be clear that we see diverse urban economies, the differential production of urban dwelling spaces, and alternative urban spaces of public life as radically intertwined to the extent that they rely upon each other for their realisation and perseverance. Rather than simply concluding that everything depends on everything else, thereby confirming that our urban worlds evolve through overdetermined and ultimately indeterminate processes, we wish to end by placing a few markers that indicate what political action in the pursuit of alternative urban futures may look like. They also indicate what kinds of scholarly engagements may be useful in supporting and informing such efforts.

First, we attach exceeding importance to *shifts between tactical and strategic modes of socio-spatial production*. This is meant to suggest only that knowing what kind of political action one is currently committing to is crucial in ensuring its effectiveness. A strategic mode is not always preferable to a tactical mode, but knowing how to distinguish the two is the first step in being able to effect deliberate and timely shifts between different moments of struggle. Second, we find that substantial transformative potentials stand to be unleashed through the *(re)activation of the terrain vague and the appropriation of urban interstices.* While the production of alternative urban spaces theoretically can proceed from anywhere, understanding and mapping urban interstitiality helps to locate sites where conditions are particularly favourable. The challenge is to eschew the unintended production of new enclaves and instead activate these sites in ways that overflow their boundaries by tapping into urban processes in ways that alter prevailing trajectories. Third, the *disruption of urban rhythms* appears to us as a moment of alternative becoming that should not be overlooked by overemphasising the spatial in a spatio-temporality that cannot be divided into separate components of time and space. Urban rhythms are decidedly spatio-temporal phenomena pointing towards actually lived urban spaces: changing rhythms amounts to changing the way urban lives are lived. Finally, and permeating the previous points, the successful pursuit of alternative urban futures depends on the extent to which we can enact *reconnections with the constitutive outsides of the urban.* This point speaks, on the one hand, to critical urban studies whose continued political relevance we find depends on retaining a multiplicity of urban outsides that allow for the positive assertion of an urban inside, and, on the other hand, to urban political practice where the same urban outsides stand out as vital sources of inspiration for an urgently needed redirection of urban processes.

## References

Bachelard, G. (2000) *The Dialectic of Duration.* Translated by M. McAllester Jones. Manchester: Clinamen Press.

Brighenti, A.M. (2013) *Urban Interstices. The Aesthetics and the Politics of the In-Between.* Farnham: Ashgate.

Edensor, T. (ed) (2010) *Geographies of Rhythm.* Farnham: Ashgate.

Gibson-Graham, J.K. (2006) *A Postcapitalist Politics.* Minneapolis: University of Minnesota Press.

Gill, R., Pratt, A. (2008) In the Social Factory? Immaterial Labour, Precariousness and Cultural Work. *Theory, Culture & Society.* 25(7–8). 1–30.

Harvey, D. (2012) *Rebel Cities. From the Right to the City to the Urban Revolution.* London: Verso.

Jacobs, J.M., Smith, S.J. (2008) Living Room: Rematerialising Home. *Environment & Planning A.* 40. 515–519.

Lefebvre, H. (1996) *Writings on Cities.* Translated by E. Kofman & E. Lebas (eds). Oxford: Blackwell.

Lefebvre, H. (2004) *Rhythmanalysis. Space, Time and Everyday Life.* London: Continuum.

McFarlane, C. (2011) The City as Assemblage: Dwelling and Urban Space. *Environment & Planning D.* 29. 649–671.

Merrifield, A. (2012) The Politics of the Encounter and the Urbanization of the World. *City*. 16(3). 269–283.
Negri, A. (1989) *The Politics of Subversion. A Manifesto for the Twenty-First Century*. Cambridge: Polity Press.
Purcell, M. (2008) *Recapturing Democracy. Neoliberalization and the Struggle for Alternative Urban Futures*. New York: Routledge.
Santos, L.A.P. (1931) *La Rhytmanalyse* [*Rhythmanalysis*]. Rio de Janeiro: Societé de Psychologie et de Philosophie.
Sola-Morales, I. (2014) Terrain Vague. In: Mariani, M. & Barron, P. (eds) *Terrain Vague. Interstices at the Edge of the Pale*. London: Routledge.

# Index

For Product Safety Concerns and Information please contact our EU representative GPSR@taylorandfrancis.com Taylor & Francis Verlag GmbH, Kaufingerstraße 24, 80331 München, Germany